JESUS FROM OUTER SPACE

T0340971

JESUS FROM OUTER SPACE

What the Earliest Christians
Really Believed about Christ

RICHARD CARRIER, PhD

Pitchstone Publishing
Durham, North Carolina

Pitchstone Publishing
Durham, North Carolina
www.pitchstonebooks.com

10 9 8 7 6 5 4 3 2

Library of Congress Cataloging-in-Publication Data

Names: Carrier, Richard, 1969- author.
Title: Jesus from outer space : what the earliest Christians really
    believed about Christ / Richard Carrier, PhD.
Description: Durham, North Carolina : Pitchstone Publishing, 2020. |
    Includes bibliographical references and index. | Summary: "Summarizes
    for a popular audience the scholarly research on the earliest Christian
    beliefs about Jesus and argues that modern attempts to conceal,
    misrepresent, or avoid the actual evidence about these original
    Christian beliefs call into question the entire field of Jesus
    studies"— Provided by publisher.
Identifiers: LCCN 2020026081 (print) | LCCN 2020026082 (ebook) | ISBN
    9781634311946 (hardcover) | ISBN 9781634312080 (ebook)
Subjects: LCSH: Jesus Christ—History of doctrines—Early church, ca.
    30-600. | Jesus Christ—Historicity.
Classification: LCC BT198 .C325 2020 (print) | LCC BT198 (ebook) | DDC
    232.9—dc23
LC record available at https://lccn.loc.gov/2020026081
LC ebook record available at https://lccn.loc.gov/2020026082

Original cover art by Rena Davonne

Contents

Preface

Did Jesus even exist? The idea that he didn't has often been dismissed as something defended only by hacks, cranks, and conspiracy theorists. But it turns out no conspiracy theories are needed. And some evidence for this conclusion really does hold up. Indeed, many experts are now starting to question the historicity of Jesus. Because when you clear away all that's ridiculous about this claim (and much indeed has been ridiculous), there remains enough evidence to genuinely suspect that maybe, just maybe, Jesus didn't exist after all.

Of course, all mainstream experts agree the Gospel Jesus is mythical. Only fanatics and fundamentalists think otherwise. But the mainstream consensus still holds that there must have been some real man buried underneath all that legend and mythology. Yet, the consensus ends there: these same experts promote countless contradictory theories about who Jesus was and what he taught or did. But in 2014, for the first time in nearly a century, an alternative theory that proposed Jesus likely never existed at all passed peer review at a mainstream biblical studies press, Sheffield-Phoenix. That book, written by the very author of the book you are now reading, was titled *On the Historicity of Jesus*, and was written after I received my Ph.D. in ancient history from Columbia University and then completed my own grant-funded postdoc research study. Though that book was met with irrational hostility by many experts who fear the consequences of its thesis, others are entertaining the possibility that that thesis, or something like it, might be right.

Key to all this is a fact not often known to the public: that the earliest Christians taught Jesus came from outer space. Not in a fully modern sense, but in an ancient sense. By the time of Christianity, Judaism had long incorporated what was then "modern science," which taught that multiple spheres of heaven physically surrounded the earth, with a spherical earth at the center, and that those heavenly realms were held up not by pillars as in more ancient teachings, but by gaseous or ether-filled spaces, extending all the way to the moon and beyond. All of that encompassed what we today mean by outer space. So the most accurate English translation of words that meant "the heavens" in antiquity is quite simply "outer space."

Of course, the ancient people of Judea didn't believe in an extraterrestrial vacuum (some then did, just not Jewish theologians). But that's not what even we mean by "outer space." We mean everything above Earth's atmosphere, all the space "out there." And that's what they believed too. Many imagined a thinner kind of material occupied the remainder of the universe, whether some kind of invisible fire or ether, notions we wouldn't even abandon ourselves until the end of the nineteenth century. And they imagined creatures of various kinds lived in every level thereof—which we would call space aliens today. Which only means they had different beliefs than we do about what exactly was *in* outer space. But they certainly had the same conception we do of what *was* outer space. So we ought to refer to their ideas just as they would have understood them, and not obscure their beliefs behind inaccuracies. The modern idea of "heaven" is of an other-dimensional space that has no physical location inside our universe—and that idea bears no resemblance at all to what they believed back then. So "heaven" is an inaccurate and indeed misleading translation today. "Outer space" is much closer to what their real beliefs were. And this is exactly the point of this book's title: when we translate the words of the earliest Christians to better reflect what they were *actually saying*, things look very different than you might have assumed.

What does this all mean? The most accurate description of earliest Christian thought is that Jesus was an angelic extraterrestrial, who descended from outer space to become a man, teach the gospel, suffer an atoning death, and rise again to return to his throne among the stars, even more powerful than before. On these facts most leading scholars agree. But what if, in fact, Jesus was originally thought to have resided *only* in outer space? To never have visited Earth *at all?* What if even his incarnation and death were celestial events? We all agree the Christians originally believed Jesus was from outer space. So the only question is, in the original creed, how far did they think he actually descended from there to effect his cosmic sacrifice? A good case can be made that Christians originally thought Jesus descended only as far as Satan's realms in the sublunar sky, and the notion that Jesus went all the way down to Earth to live and preach there was invented a lifetime later.

The complete, sober, academic case for this conclusion, with all the requisite evidence, cited scholarship, footnotes, and apparatus, you will find in the near seven-hundred pages of *On the Historicity of Jesus*. Here in your hands is a much briefer, more colloquial, but still informative summary of that more serious academic monograph, a concordance to which you'll find at the end of this book. I've also written on the problems of methodology plaguing Jesus studies in my other peer-reviewed book *Proving History*. I also reproduced all my peer-reviewed research articles on the subject in my book *Hitler Homer Bible Christ*, up to the year 2014. And I continue to write on this subject and respond to critics through my website at richardcarrier.info. But in the book you are now reading you'll get a look at all the actual evidence that exists for a historical Jesus, as well as all the evidence that astonishingly doesn't. You'll also see the best reasons why his existence is indeed worth doubting, and all the surviving clues pointing to there having been Christians who once thought the earthbound Jesus was a useful myth, and to the conclusion that theirs may have been the original view. But their writings, almost entirely, and certainly as originally written, are all lost. All we have now are what much later Christians chose to preserve or fabricate.

To make all this clear, I have pared down what needs to be said to the bare essentials. In chapter one I survey some of the looming problems with identifying a historical Jesus you might not have heard about. In chapter two I survey the overall case for why his existence is doubtable. And in chapter three I show why attempts to get around this rely on invalid methods and approaches. Then in chapter four I reveal that, contrary to what you might have heard, we actually have no evidence Jesus existed other than the Bible. Then in chapter five I compare Jesus to other historical figures of antiquity, revealing that in every possible case we trust they existed because of evidence we simply don't have for Jesus. I then show in chapter six that Jesus has far more in common with other nonexistent, mythical figures of the ancient world, than with any actual historical person. I then pause in chapter seven to survey what we can surmise about how Christianity evolved from a celestial, revelatory cult to one claiming its extraterrestrial Lord was a historical man from Galilee. And in the last two chapters I address the only real evidence there is for a historical Jesus: a few vague, ambiguous references in the letters of Paul, the earliest Christian writings we have, that could indicate he believed Jesus had human parents and brothers. I show that that's not really the most credible interpretation of what Paul actually meant, or at least, we can't know whether that's what Paul meant or not.

By the end of this book, you'll understand why it's reasonable to suspect Christianity began in dreams and visions of a celestial man facing a celestial fate, and that stories of his being a Galilean preacher evolved far later. We can't know that for certain. But as everything surveyed in this book makes clear, we do not actually have the evidence we'd normally need to rule out this alternative explanation of the origin of Christianity. It's a thesis remarkably consistent with all the evidence we have. Which does seem improbable . . . unless it's true.

1

Which Jesus Are We Talking about Exactly?

The Talmud tells us this about Jesus the Nazarene, son of Mary:

> On the eve of the Sabbath, which happened also to be the eve of
> the Passover, Jesus the Nazarene was hanged. A herald had already
> gone forth before him forty days declaring, "Jesus the Nazarene
> is going forth to be stoned because he practiced sorcery and
> instigated and seduced Israel to idolatry. Whoever knows anything
> in his defense may come and state it." But since they did not find
> anything in his defense, they hanged him on that Sabbath eve, the
> eve of Passover.

This is the earliest real mention of Christianity in any surviving
Jewish text. Only one slight problem. The Talmud says this occurred
somewhere around 75 B.C. That's almost a hundred years before the
Romans even took control of Judea, and a full hundred years before
Pontius Pilate was put in charge of it, the guy our Gospels claim
executed Jesus sometime in the thirties A.D. How could the Jews be

so mistaken about when Jesus lived that they put his life a full century earlier than our Gospels do?

Inventing a History for Jesus

This Talmud was written as a commentary on Jewish law by Rabbis in the fifth century or so, the early Middle Ages. It was composed outside the Roman Empire, eastward in the region of Babylonia. And its contents are often very sketchy. It's hard to ascertain where its authors were getting any of their information, or how old it really was.

We can only be certain of one thing: though surely putting their own spin on it, these Rabbis were getting the gist of this from actual Christians of their time. Not only should that be obvious—they were after all writing in a time and place surrounded by Christians who had been preaching their gospel among them for centuries—but we've also confirmed it from a Christian author of the same time, Epiphanius, who tells us about a still-Torah-observant sect of Christians in the East who were still calling themselves the Nazorians. This looks a lot like the original Christian sect, which taught Torah observance and called itself "the Nazorians" (Acts 24:5). Epiphanius includes in his discussion of these same Christians a teaching that Jesus lived during the reign of what was reputedly the last Davidic king, Alexander Jannaeus—who died in 76 B.C. This teaching held that it was upon the death of Jannaeus that Jesus came into his kingdom and began preaching the gospel, ensuring an uninterrupted line of Davidic kings as prophecy foretold.

This saddles us with a rather big problem. Since this puts Jesus in completely the wrong historical period, we can't use the Talmud as evidence our Jesus existed. It's either wholly unreliable—or it's not our Jesus. Unless *the Gospels* are the ones who fabricate a history for Jesus, relocating the real Jesus, who died shortly after Jannaeus, to a time a hundred years later under Pilate, so they could "modernize" the story to their present circumstances under Roman rule. The Christians in the East would have had no need to do that, as they were not in the Roman Empire. Notably, the Apostle Paul never actually says anything in his letters that clearly places his life in the first century A.D. Those letters could actually have been written a century earlier. All the first apostles, like Peter and the brothers James and John, may have also lived a century earlier. The Gospels we have might be a total fiction.

On the other hand, it could be that *neither* of these accounts is true. Maybe the Eastern gospel that placed Jesus under Jannaeus is just as fabricated as the Western gospel placing him under Pilate.

But there's another problem here. There was another Talmud, called the Jerusalem Talmud, which was composed a little earlier, in Judea and thus within the Roman Empire. But it never mentions Jesus in any clear fashion. It has some vague remarks about Christians as heretics, but not much else. It hasn't survived complete, so maybe it once did say more about Jesus, but we can't know what. All we know is that the Rabbis who wrote the Babylonian Talmud knew only of a Christianity that preached a gospel of Jesus set a hundred years earlier in history. They *also* only knew of a Christian gospel that had Jesus being stoned and then hung in accordance with Jewish law. That means the Christians outside the Roman Empire were not preaching a Christ crucified . . . at least, not a Christ crucified *by Romans*.

Because it just so happens that the ancient words for "hanged" and for "crucified" meant the same thing. They vaguely referred to *any* nailing or lashing up of a convict for public display, dead or alive. And Jewish law mandated, indeed the very Bible itself commands, that when someone was executed by stoning, their body was then to be lashed to a tree or post for public display. This is commanded in Deuteronomy 21:22–23, which in Galatians 3:13 Paul even says was carried out for Jesus. So Paul actually is never clear on whether Jesus was crucified in *our* sense of the term. And he's our earliest source for Christianity. Since the words he uses are identical to the words used for the Jewish method of displaying executed bodies, Jesus may well have been stoned, not "crucified," much less by Pontius Pilate.

This poses a problem for answering the question, "Did Jesus exist?" *Which Jesus do we mean?*

Of course, there were thousands of men named Jesus in every generation of Jews. It was one of the most common Jewish names (it's actually, in fact, the name Joshua). And there were surely many men so named who were executed by Pontius Pilate or any Jewish court in any decade you choose. So we aren't asking about whether some Jesus got himself executed. We are asking specifically about the Jesus whose execution launched the Christian religion. And in that role, Jesus might not even have been his original name, but a name assigned him after his death. The name means, after all, "God's Savior." Most scholars already conclude he was not called Christ, from the Greek for Messiah (literally, "an anointed one," hence "chosen one"), until after his death. The same may be true of "Jesus." If after his martyrdom his closest followers, reassured by dreams and visions of his spiritual victory, started calling him "God's Savior and Messiah," they would be calling him "Jesus Christ." So he might not have even originally been called Jesus!

So really, what we need to ask is, was there at least a Jewish man (by whatever name) who gathered a following and then was executed (whether by a Jewish court or Roman) and who had some followers, led by Peter (or "Cephas" in Aramaic), who became convinced God had resurrected and exalted him to be their Lord and Savior, the true and final Messiah for all time? If we can be certain of only just *that*, that would be enough to settle that there was a historical "Jesus" who started the Christian religion. Even if it turned out this all happened in the 70s B.C. Or any time and place.

But there has to have been at least that. Otherwise, no such man, no such Jesus. If Peter and gang were not claiming an *earthly* predecessor was killed and resurrected and now the exalted Savior, then there is no meaningful sense in saying there was a historical Jesus. *They* might have believed him real; but we wouldn't.

How Could That Be?

How else then could Christianity have begun? Don't all religions have founders? Of course they do. And if there was no Jesus, the founder of Christianity would be Peter.

Indeed, most religions *also* have *fictional* founders: the gods, angels, or demigods who introduce the new system to the earthlings below. In history, Joseph Smith was the founder of Mormonism, and Muhammad the founder of Islam. But in their own mythologies, that's not the case.

The Mormons claim their actual founder to be the angel Moroni, and Smith merely his messenger. The Muslims claim their actual founder to be the angel Gabriel—as the instrument of Allah, who revealed the words of the Quran to Muhammad. Those words are not Muhammad's words, you see. He just wrote them down. In Islamic mythology, those are the words of Allah, spoken through Gabriel. And Gabriel is not a historical person. Neither is Moroni. *Though both were believed to be—* just only as celestials. And it may well be the same for Jesus. Originally he may have been just like them: the heavenly archangel who *revealed* the gospel on which the religion was founded; not the actual man communicating those revelations to the public. The guy first receiving those spirit communications would be Peter—and subsequent apostles whom Peter's report then inspired to experience or claim the same.

On this view, Jesus exists in mythical parallel to his nemesis Satan. Satan was an archangel, believed to be a historical person, yet of course we know he was only imagined to exist. But back then, in the imagination of many a Jew, Satan had existed from near the dawn of time and lived in outer space. From which he fell to regions below, but still above the earth—contrary to much later Medieval legend that encamped him in Hell. Before then, it was popularly believed he resided in the far reaches of the sky. Just like (as we'll see) his Egyptian counterpart Set (associated in Greek with the monster Typhon).

And Satan has a history. In fact, a historical event happened to him that changed the nature of the universe. The tale was that at some point in history he and a legion of angels under his command rebelled against God in heaven, and for that crime God expelled them from the upper reaches of outer space. Trapped in the lowest sphere of space to dwell in, the one below the orbit of the moon, they still reigned from above, bringing death, decay, sin, and corruption to the lower cosmos. By the time Christianity began it was well known the moon was hundreds of thousands of miles distant from Earth. Most people of that time believed the atmosphere, in some form, extended all that way. We now know it doesn't, so where Satan lived was still what we now call outer space; it's just that back then they thought this area of space was still full of breathable air. So Satan was stuck in outer space, his punishment being that he could only occupy the lowest level of it. There he found or built castles and gardens in the air, far up in the vast sky, where he and his demons and angels battled each other, and meddled in earthly affairs from above, far beyond the sight of anyone on Earth.

God then plotted Satan's defeat. The Jews of the time hoping for the end of the world were hoping for God's plan to come to fruition, for Satan to be defeated, and for the world to be remade into a new paradise.

Enter Jesus. He becomes the anti-Satan in this saga. He, like Satan, was an archangel who existed from the dawn of time. In his case literally: even from the start, Christians preached that he was the first thing God ever created and that it was *Jesus* who was then tasked by God with creating everything else (just read 1 Corinthians 8:6; see also: 10:1–4; Philippians 2:6–9; Romans 8.3). Jesus thus existed before Adam and Eve, and lived through the whole of their lives, and through the entirety of biblical history—also, like Satan, usually residing in the far reaches of outer space, in his case in the celestial temple of God where Jesus served as God's supernal high priest, in charge of that divine structure of which the earthly temple in Jerusalem was but a crude copy (just read Hebrews 4 and 9). And also like Satan, this other archangel, Jesus, acquired a history. A historical event happened to *him* that changed the nature of the universe. In parallel to Satan, who descended to the lower realm of outer space to bring evil and death, Jesus descended to the lower realm of outer space to *defeat* evil and death—to defeat, in fact, Satan. And all of this is not conjecture. It's a well-known fact of what the first Christians taught. So, just as Satan was believed to be a historical person—yet of course we know he was just imagined to exist—it could well be that Jesus was *also* believed to be a historical person. Yet really, he was only imagined to exist.

On this account, Jesus is to the apostles just like Gabriel is to Muhammad, and Moroni to Joseph Smith. His Satan-reversing drama, of arranging for his incarnation and death, was not witnessed on Earth. It was revealed to the apostles by Jesus after his resurrection. In either dreams or visions, the apostles, beginning with Peter whose original claim inspired the rest, came to *believe* that this all had happened, but in Satan's realm—"outside the walls" of the *celestial* Jerusalem, meaning the upper heavens Satan was locked out of—and not outside the walls of its merely crude copy, the Jerusalem on Earth. And they were told of in those dreams or visions (or intuitively found on their own) secret hidden messages from God in the ancient Jewish Scriptures that not only confirmed all this but also filled out for them many of the details of what actually happened, and why.

That's the theory. And it does fit all the evidence we have.

As the Apostle Paul later said (we believe in the 50s A.D.), because of these celestial communications from the archangel Jesus, it was "now" possible to tell everyone what happened, because "the gospel and the preaching of Jesus Christ" was only *recently* made available to the public "according to the revelation of the mystery that had been kept a secret since times eternal" through "the scriptures of the prophets, according to the commandment of the eternal God." And so this gospel and preaching can "now" be "made known unto all the nations" so all may be obedient to the faith (Romans 16:25–26). What was thus revealed to them Paul summarizes in snippets in various places, such as 1 Corinthians 15, 2 Corinthians 12, Philippians 2, and Galatians 1. Paul never says anything about anyone having been a historical witness to any of it, of having heard any of it from an actual earthly Jesus. He knows only two ways anyone ever learned what happened to Jesus and anything Jesus taught: revelations and hidden messages in scripture. This seems evident already from 1 Corinthians 15:3–8, where in Paul's account of the origin of the religion, no one ever saw or met Jesus until *after he had died*. Just as with Paul himself—as he describes in Galatians 1.

The Timeline of Evidence

Understanding all this is helped by knowing the timeline of the evidence that survives. Detectives, after all, must gather their evidence onto a clue board, and put it in order.

Though Jesus and his first apostles would have spoken Hebrew or Aramaic, no original sources for Christianity exist in those languages (except the much later Talmud, which we just saw is no use as a source). Everything that survives was written in Greek, the language not of ancient Palestine, but of pagans, and of the Jews among them.

The earliest documents we have from Christians are the authentic letters of Paul (only seven; the rest are now known to be later forgeries), and perhaps a few other letters in the New Testament, like 1 Peter, James, Jude, and Hebrews, and possibly the first letter from Clement of Rome. Though some scholars date these later, a reasonable case can be made that they all likely date to the 50s and 60s A.D., two to three decades after Jesus is supposed to have died in the 30s A.D. Yet they curiously lack any references to Jesus having ever ministered on Earth, or communicating with anyone in any other way than by mystical revelation from on high— whether to the apostles or the Prophets of old.

Then the Jewish War utterly upheaved the Judean world. Begun in 66 and concluded in 70 A.D., it left the region devastated, much of the populace enslaved, dead, or shipped abroad, and the city of Jerusalem in rubble, not to be inhabited again for nearly a hundred years. The great temple of the Jewish God and its cult was destroyed forever. This was cataclysmic for the Jews. And yet the world did not end. This was perplexing for the apocalyptic Christians who had been certain the end of the world was very nigh (just see Romans 8, 1 Corinthians 10:11 and 15.23–26, and 1 Thessalonians 4:14–17). But four decades having passed, and the heathens now having destroyed God's temple and holy city, how is it still the world goes on? That was starting to become confounding. It appears only *then* that Gospels started to be written. Though some Gospels are speculated to date earlier, we have no actual evidence any were. The earliest Gospels we have, in fact, appear to have been written in an attempt to explain this strange state of affairs and to rehabilitate the Christian religion with new and improved teachings, and a new apocalyptic timetable.

The earliest Gospel we are sure was written is that of Mark, which was most likely composed in the late 70s A.D., forty years after Jesus would have died. This is because this Gospel is fully aware that God allowed his temple to be destroyed and strives to explain that tragedy (as we'll see later), and because it borrows ideas from the tale of Jesus ben Ananias published by Josephus around 76 A.D. as part of his account of the war (as we'll also see later).

It's not commonly known, but the way all the Gospels are labeled in the New Testament is with a Greek idiom that identifies a source, not an author. Thus, the Gospel of Mark is actually "the Gospel according to Mark," meaning Mark didn't write it. Its actual author, wholly anonymous, was claiming Mark *as his source*. Or possibly not even they were claiming that—there's reason to believe this attribution was added by a later editor. But either way, we actually don't know who that Mark was. Or who the author was that was claiming to have gotten his tales from him. Late legends about these authors don't agree with the facts and have no sources themselves, so we can't trust any of that. Even so, I'll just call the author "Mark" for convenience. Beyond that mysterious name, he makes no other reference to having any sources. Even though historians of antiquity often told us who their sources were and why they trusted them, especially if they themselves were witness to the events they record, Mark names no one. He says nothing about how he learned any of his stories. He never even says he did learn them—as opposed to having manufactured them entirely on his own. Which for all we honestly know is what he did.

All mainstream scholars—meaning those who aren't conservative or fundamentalist Christians—agree none of the Gospels were written by any disciples or eyewitnesses, or by anyone we know at all. They are effectively anonymous. Even what the surviving manuscripts claim was their named "source" (from which they earn their titles now mistakenly identified as "authors") is wholly unknown. The Gospel according to Matthew, for example, never says it was written by a disciple of that name, or had a disciple as its source at all. It simply doesn't identify who the Matthew is in its title, nor calls them a disciple. Like Mark, the name appears to have been added by later editors. Even so, again, I'll call the author of this Gospel "Matthew" simply for convenience. One thing we know for sure is that Matthew, whether we mean the author or their claimed source, was *not* a disciple, or any kind of eyewitness. Because Matthew writes in Greek, using Greek scriptures as his base text, something only foreigners, not witnesses, would do. And then he simply copies verbatim most of Mark; and then embellishes Mark by adding five long speeches and some additional lines and mythical scenes. That also isn't how witnesses write down their own recollections. It's how someone redacts and expands someone else's text.

It has long been believed that Matthew got some of his additions from another, now lost source commonly called Q (for Quelle, the

German word for "Source"). In fact, there is no actual evidence this is true. And even if it were, the content of Q can also be dated after the Jewish War. It was also written in Greek, also using Greek translations of the Jewish scriptures, so it did not originate with early Christians in Palestine. And some of its contents reflect knowledge of the Jewish War. Which means we still can find even in this totally hypothetical Q no reliable evidence of any Gospel earlier than Mark. And since Matthew copied Mark, Matthew dates later. Scholars think maybe he wrote in the 80s A.D., although it could well have been decades later than that. We don't know.

The next Gospel to be written was Luke. Again, "according to Luke." But we don't really know who this Luke is. Or who the author claiming him as his source was. Again, much later legends about that can't be verified. I'll again just call the author "Luke" for convenience. Luke also copies most of Mark. He also copies most of Matthew, and rewrites some material from Matthew. (Or "Q," if you still believe in that, though I cannot explain why anyone still does; Luke is obviously just redacting Matthew and Mark, combining pieces of them into a single text.) And then he adds some material of his own. Luke is the first author among the Gospels to pretend to be writing history, with attempts at dating events, and a preface that resembles other history books of the time in declaring the use of sources—although it's conspicuously vague about that, not naming any of those sources or identifying their merits or why he trusts them. Yet we can tell now who those sources were: Mark and Matthew. There is no evidence he had any others. So really, he's just rewriting and embellishing previous Gospels.

Since Luke, who is also the author of Acts, used Mark and Matthew, he dates after them. And since he is also known to have relied for some of his background material on *The Antiquities of the Jews* published by Josephus in 93 A.D., it's increasingly agreed that Luke wrote his two books after that year. So, that means, at the earliest, in the late 90s A.D., sixty years after Jesus would have died. But Luke's Gospel is also missing from the account of the Gospels known to Papias, the earliest known Christian story-collector. Luke may even be responding to Papias. So it's also believed by many now that Luke and Acts were written *after Papias*. Papias wrote a collection of hearsay and speculations about Christian history, now lost, but from which a few quotes survive. And he might have written almost anytime in the second century, though scholars often "guess" it was somewhere around 130 A.D. But that means Luke and Acts may well date later still. We don't know. Though a date around 115 is now commonly proposed. We can only confirm that Luke wrote before the 160s A.D., when the Christian apologist Justin Martyr becomes the first to allude to either Luke or later Gospels dependent on Luke.

The next Gospel to be written was John. Again, "according to John." But once again we don't know who this John is. Or who the authors claiming him as his source were (and yes, *authors*, plural: John 21:24). I'll again just call its author "John" for convenience. Several leading experts on this Gospel agree John wrote in response to Luke, and occasionally draws material (sometimes nearly verbatim) from Mark. That means John dates later than Luke, and is thus the last of the Gospels in the Bible to be written. John does not use the method the others did, of simply copying and making adjustments and additions to previous material. He mostly uses sources the way most other authors in antiquity did: he rewrites their stories in his own words. And he does Luke one turn better: he claims to have an (unnamed) eyewitness source, and that what he recorded is proof that those things actually happened (and not merely were taught), and that the reader should thereby be persuaded to believe! And yet John is the most unreliable, distrusted, and fabricated Gospel in the canon. His "witness" is now deemed by mainstream experts to be a fiction. Even the Catholic scholar Candida Moss recently outright admitted in an article for *The Daily Beast*, "Everyone's Favorite Gospel is a Forgery," that John falsely claims to have an eyewitness source.

John's Gospel is also unknown to Papias. And since John must date after Luke, as well as (probably) Papias, most experts today place John in the early to mid-second century. Hardly anyone dates John earlier than 100 A.D. anymore. And 100 to 140 A.D. is a common estimate, which puts John seventy to a hundred years after the fact.

Around the same time all these Gospels were being written (between 75 and 140 A.D.), others were being written, too. But we know almost nothing about them. Insofar as we have any information at all, they mostly appear to have been dependent on these Gospels and so are later compositions. The few exceptions are too bizarre to date more precisely.

But even the so-called Gospel of Thomas has been shown to rely on what experts call the "Synoptic" Gospels (meaning the ones that share a lot of identical material in common: Mark, Matthew, and Luke). It therefore dates later than them, and may even have been written in response to John. Likewise the fragmentary Gospel of Peter. And so on, to the tune of over forty Gospels we know by their fragments or titles. There's no evidence any of these Gospels contain any reliable information in them. They, like probably all Gospels, are just made up.

As we can see from all of the above, Mark appears to be the only real Gospel. None precede Mark. And every subsequent Gospel is just, in one way or another, a rewrite of Mark, naming no sources for anything they add or change.

The next Christian sources we have all date after 110 A.D., eighty years after Jesus would have died; and really none can be reliably dated earlier than *a century* after the fact, around 130 A.D. We'll survey the only ones worth looking at later; likewise the only *non*-Christian sources we have before then as well, which are but a scant few. Nothing written after that date has any evident content that comes from any other sources but these—and the Gospels. So no later sources are of any use to us in this quest. In fact, as we'll see in the later chapters, there *are no sources at all* that are independent of the Gospel of Mark. Which means Jesus only appears as a historical character *in the Gospel of Mark*; and all subsequent redactions, rewrites, and retellings of it. For no one after that had any other source for a historical Jesus but Mark—and people whose knowledge derived from Mark. That's a serious problem.

It's even more seriously a problem when you realize the average life expectancy back then, for anyone who survived childhood, was just 48 years. Which means on average, anyone who was a teenager when Jesus died, would likely have been dead by the conclusion of the Jewish War. And anyone *older* in his day would most likely have been dead well before then. It's thus very curious that the first time anyone tries anything resembling the representing of Jesus as a figure in human history, it's precisely when everyone *who could know he wasn't* was dead or dying. By ancient standards, Mark waited a whole human lifetime before putting pen to paper. That's suspicious.

And Mark, remember, does not represent his tale as history any more than a parable. He, and anyone who used his Gospel for anything, had plausible deniability. They could just pass it off as allegory. Matthew only barely pushes his content as history, but he's again writing even later than Mark—and really, just rewriting Mark. The first author to actually assert that he's writing a historical account of Jesus is Luke. Who wrote *sixty to ninety years later*. Or even later still. Anyone who was a teenager when Jesus would have lived, would have to be in their seventies in the earliest decade Luke could have written. Fewer than one in twenty people then lived so long. Fewer than one in two hundred lived even so much as another ten years. So Jesus was only passed off as a *definitely* historical person long after pretty much everyone of his alleged time was dead, by an author writing in a foreign land and language, whose text was probably never seen by anyone in Palestine.

Also realize, that this is it. That's all we have. All the other correspondence among Christians and Christian churches and leaders in the very period the Gospels were being written has been erased from history. No other writings from then exist. We have some of the letters written before the Gospels. And we have some Christian writings in the decades after the Gospels. But in the intervening period, we have nothing. So we actually can't tell what anyone was saying *about* those Gospels and their claims, for a whole half-century—from about the year 70 to the year 120. That's also suspicious. Precisely where we need to look to see if people were challenging the Gospels' newly invented history for Jesus, is precisely where we have been forbidden to look. Everything any challenger might have said or wrote was destroyed. All we have are the Gospels. And silence.

Pick Your Mythical Jesus

Already it's the consensus of mainstream scholars—those, again, who aren't Christian conservatives or fundamentalists—that the Gospel Jesus is a myth. They all agree that most of what the Gospels say of him was made up later for the convenience of infighting sects. They each created a fictional Jesus who said and did all the things they wanted or needed him to. But still the usual view is that there was *some* historical Jesus, an ordinary Rabbi, whose real story is hidden somewhere beneath those mountains of myth and legend. Though one should be tempted to ask . . . if we already admit *most* of it is myth and legend, why not all of it?

Today the most ardent defender of a historical Jesus behind the heavy layers of mythology in the Gospels is Bart Ehrman. As he declares it:

> Despite the enormous range of opinion, there are several points on which virtually all scholars of antiquity agree. Jesus was a Jewish man, known to be a preacher and teacher, who was crucified (a Roman form of execution) in Jerusalem during the reign of the Roman emperor Tiberius, when Pontius Pilate was the governor of Judea. (*Did Jesus Exist?* 12)

That's the minimal guy who could have existed. But I've already shown you some problematic assumptions here. Crucifixion, by the words then used, was not an exclusively Roman form of execution; it also referred to the Jewish form. It could also be carried out by demonic beings in supernatural realms. His preaching and teaching was also explicitly said in our earliest sources to come from visions and ancient scriptures, not an itinerant Rabbi anyone claimed to have met in person. And Christian sects eventually disagreed on whether Jesus died under Pilate or *a hundred years earlier*, depending on whether they preached inside or outside the Roman Empire. And before Mark published after the Jewish War, no Christian text even says he was crucified on Earth at all. That's nowhere in Paul, Hebrews, 1 Clement, 1 Peter, James, or Jude.

So the consensus Ehrman describes seems to be resting on a lot of questionable assumptions rather than evidence, assumptions that can't explain how Christians could come to differ so greatly on the historical period Jesus lived under, or how in their earliest writings they could speak of only knowing his gospel and teachings through visions and scriptures. Baseless assumptions, too. Like that being "staked" on a "post" (the actual words Paul consistently uses for crucifixion) must mean Roman crucifixion, when, in fact, it can mean many other things (as in Esther 7:9). As you go through this book you'll see again and again how the historians who insist Jesus in some sense existed rely on all kinds of unwarranted claims and assumptions like this as if they were established facts. This "consensus" is made on a bed of sand. Or, indeed, air—just like Satan's castles. And that's the most suspicious thing of all.

The best and earliest evidence we have only securely establishes that the religion we know as Christianity was founded by its first apostle, Peter. His revelation of the Christ Lord's tribulation and victory is what appears to have actually sparked the religion, inspiring Peter's followers (such as "the twelve") to have or claim similar revelations, and then inspiring others to as well. This is the sequence of events Paul describes in 1 Corinthians 15:3–8. If Jesus was originally taught to have been an angelic being who tricked the Devil into crucifying him in a distant sky kingdom, and this was claimed to have been known only through dreams and visions and hidden messages in the scriptures (as outright declared in Romans 16:25–26), then there wasn't even a man whose death launched the religion. His worshipers still of course believed he existed, just as they believed Satan existed, or any angels, like Gabriel or Michael. But we today well know that's not really sufficient to believe Satan or Gabriel or Michael ever really existed. And so, too, Jesus. He was just another member of the host of angels with names and histories like them.

There are therefore many mythical Jesuses to choose from. The Gospel Jesus is already agreed to be mythical, in the sense that the real historical Jesus won't have been much like him. Or it may well be that Jesus is fully mythical, that there was never a real historical man to pile those legends onto in the first place. And if that's the case, then there would be yet another layer of myth to all this. The "real" Jesus in early Christian belief would then be their imagined cosmic superbeing, but we now would deem that mythical as well. There would thus be the myth of the celestial Jesus. And then there would be the myth of the terrestrial Jesus that placed his drama in Earth history, surrounding him with appropriate historical characters. And that's what I think happened. I think it's myth all the way down. The rest of this book will explain why.

The idea that Jesus was *entirely* mythical, and not just mostly, has often been dismissed. Usually rightly, as something defended only by cranks and conspiracy theorists, who employ a massive edifice of dubious facts and fallacies, confidently asserting really elaborate theories with no real evidence. Indeed, the enthusiasm of such amateurs has clouded the debate, hiding under their elaborate nonsense some real evidence that, at a more fundamental level, they might be right. I and others within the field have been revealing this fact, by clearing away all the indefensible claims and lousy arguments, and leaving behind what actually holds up to valid expert scrutiny.

Many genuine experts are starting to agree there is at least cause to doubt whether Jesus ever existed. This includes Arthur Droge, a professor of early Christianity at the University of Toronto; Kurt Noll, a professor of religion at Brandon University; Hector Avalos, a professor of biblical religions at Iowa State University; two retired professors of some renown: Thomas Brodie, professor emeritus of biblical studies in Ireland, and Thomas L. Thompson, a professor emeritus of Old Testament studies in Denmark; and three independent scholars: Robert Price, Raphael Lataster, and Richard Carrier (your present author), all with relevant PhD's—mine in ancient history; Lataster's in religious studies; and Price with two, in theology and New Testament studies. This is not something that's only coming from amateurs outside the field. There is a real challenge being made to the consensus. Already that's three sitting professors, two retired professors, and three independent scholars with full credentials, with at least two mainstream peer-reviewed monographs arguing the case (mine and Lataster's, who in 2019 published *Questioning the Historicity of Jesus* through Brill). And there are no doubt many others who simply haven't gone on the record for fear of consequence to their careers or social standing.

We also have sympathizers among mainstream experts who might still endorse historicity but acknowledge we have a respectable point, that the nonexistence of Jesus is at least plausible, like Philip Davies, a late professor emeritus of biblical studies at Sheffield University; Zeba Crook, professor of religious studies at Carleton University; Francesca Stavrakopolou, professor of Hebrew bible and ancient religion at the University of Exeter; and independent scholar Tom Dykstra, who has a PhD in Renaissance Christianity and is published in the field of New Testament studies. (For all these experts and what they've said on this point see my summary in Item 22 in my continually updated blog article "Ehrman on Historicity Recap" at richardcarrier.info.)

So the historical community needs to set aside the previous claims of cranks and amateurs pushing this thesis, and look at the more careful, well-vetted, peer-reviewed arguments now published—and then mount an honest response, one that addresses what we are actually saying, and one that isn't rooted in dogma and specious rationalization. So far the community has responded only with ad hominem, dishonesty, contradictory claims, and unsubstantiated assertions. That suggests the consensus is not based on anything real. It's based on a need to maintain funding and reputations. Or it's based on an ideological inertia that despairs of admitting they've been wrong all this time, that all their past work has been folly. Or so it is for any secular and non-Christian experts. The rest of the consensus usually cited is based on faith, not history. Many Christian scholars are even *forbidden* from admitting Jesus didn't exist. Their very jobs, the respect of their friends and family, their hopes and dreams, all depend on there having been a Jesus. They can never admit he didn't exist.

The Scandal of Confusion

The scandal in the field today is that historians all promote wildly contradictory conclusions about Jesus, yet never properly establish that he even existed in the first place. They simply start with that as an unquestionable assumption. But the fact that they all reach different conclusions about Jesus suggests they have no method capable of reaching reliable conclusions about Jesus. The "consensus" that Jesus existed is thus actually not founded on any coherent or reliable argument. It's instead a mere axiom that, when challenged, historians will merely attempt to rationalize. It's a presumption, one maintained mostly by threats of excommunication from the academy through the instrument of ridicule or attacks on one's livelihood, by implying any who dare challenge this consensus will never be hired again, maybe lose grants or tenure, and certainly respect, status, and prestige.

They have to resort to such tactics. Because when you clear away all the dubious facts and arguments, there remains enough at least to suspect that maybe Jesus didn't exist after all. And that's a scary realization for someone who has based their entire career on there being a Jesus. In fact, far more so than the *last* time we went through all this, when the historical existence of Moses began to be challenged from within the academy. In the 1970s this was a view that was not to be tolerated, and some who argued it were punished or interfered with in every way that could be managed. Yet now it's the mainstream consensus. Now nearly everyone who aren't Christian or Jewish conservatives, or fundamentalists sworn to believe the Bible is the inerrant Word of God, agree that Moses is a mythical character, invented, along with his equally mythical family relations and life story, to create an authority for a system of laws and theology a later Jewish priesthood wished their people to adopt.

The experts likewise have concluded all the Patriarchs of the Old Testament are likely myths, from Abraham to Joseph. And probably the prophet Daniel as well; and quite possibly the legendary Jewish sorcerers Elijah and Elisha. The invention of historical persons and their biographies was simply not uncommon back then. The Jews did it as often as the pagans. They all had their mythical heroes. And yet, no religion depended on these people existing, so much as Christianity now depends on Jesus existing. So opposition to this proposal is even stronger now than it was against the same conclusion for Moses and the Patriarchs. Yet there was mainstream opposition even to that. Secular scholars now fear shocking and alienating their Christian peers and patrons with so radical an admission about Jesus. But the evidence looks to be trending toward no other conclusion.

As we'll see, all the evidence we actually have evolves over time from discussing Jesus as a revelatory being undergoing a mystical ordeal (such as in the letters of Paul), to a sacred allegory hiding the real intended meaning behind extended parables about Jesus as a symbolic character (in the Gospel of Mark and possibly Matthew), to attempts to make this look like real history with presumed sources (in the later Gospels of Luke and John). The trend is not from a more mundane, historical Jesus to a more mythical and fantastic one, as is often assumed. The trend went the other way around. Mark's Jesus is no less fantastical than Luke's or John's, except precisely where Luke and John fabricate more overt uses of the Lord's wonders as historical evidence designed to convince you. The difference is that Mark never pretends to be writing history. He never talks about anything he writes as evidence that should persuade you. That only starts to happen many decades *after* Mark, when people came to compose the Gospels of Luke and John. Matthew's Gospel sits in between these two stages, adding wonders, but only mildly historicizing them with references to prophecy. And what he adds, is more obviously mythic fabrication than anything that could claim to be historical memory. In other words, the Gospels only become increasingly fabulous precisely in respect to becoming more *un*historical, while at the same time making increasingly assertive claims to *be* historical. This looks like the evolution of the myth from intended parable to purported history. Not from history to parable. The Gospel Jesus was a man whose history was being created, not recorded.

In *On the Historicity of Jesus* I wrote on how the Jewish invention of Moses served much the same goal as the British invention of King Arthur and early technophobes' invention of Ned Ludd, the mythical founder of the machine-smashing Luddites; and likewise the Melanesian invention of the various mythical founders of the Cargo Cults, from Tom Navy to John Frum. Turning Jesus into a historical character served the same function as all of these: to promote unity within the movement, and hopefully society, by promoting a popular myth to rally behind and believe in. The Cargo Cults, for example, began with visions from diverse prophets, but that proved too disorganized to succeed. Later leaders turned to amalgamating those various sources and visions into a singular figure who spoke in person, rather than through spirit mediums. And once you've done that, continuing success increasingly depends on selling the myth you've created *as true*.

As with Moses, Frum, Arthur, or Ludd, so with Jesus:

> To deny the historicity of these men or their stories would quickly become tantamount to denying the unifying message their stories were crafted and employed to sell. Promoting their historicity also made it easier to effect moral reform, by attaching the authority for that reform to a historical person. Because a "made-up man" was not generally considered capable of having any moral authority at all. (*On the Historicity of Jesus* 10)

But more even than that, the previous model of apostleship, though more democratic and grassroots, was not sustainable for a growing institutional hierarchy. If Jesus was only known through visions and secret Bible codes, *anyone* could claim apostolic authority. Shutting that down *required* fabricating a legend of a real earthly Jesus passing teachings down through personally appointed historical "tradents," an anthropological term for relayers of a tradition.

The latter is especially important. Originally, in Christianity as for the Cargo Cults millennia later, everyone learned of their Savior's will through secret revelations to anyone who could successfully convince people they were chosen for the task—creating a kind of arms race to prove one's election to apostleship by the celestial Lord through oratorical battles, charitable deeds, feats of suffering, and magic acts. This left no consistent centralized control. It ultimately led to chaos and factionalism. But if you could sell the claim instead that your Savior was a historical person, who handed his teachings on to a select few he chose in life, thus closing all subsequent claims to apostolic election—if you can claim that your church's preferred Gospel was based on the teachings of actual historical successors of those first apostles—then you can start to organize a stable hierarchical control of the operation. Upstarts will then have a much harder time breaking into leadership from outside the church's oligarchy. And you will have a much more tangible basis for declaring dissent a heresy. This is how a historical Jesus began. Just as Moses did. Or King Arthur. Ned Ludd. John Frum. Tom Navy. It's all the same process, serving the same purpose.

Where the Clues Begin

The biggest clue to this being the case is that one fact I already noted is not often known to the public: that the earliest Christians taught that Jesus came from outer space; and he was only known as "the Lord" when he was seen in dreams and visions after his purported death.

On these two facts most leading scholars now agree in substance, even if they would nervously eschew my more accurate vocabulary. Even the renowned Bart Ehrman concedes this, arguing that there remains no valid case left to deny it (see, for example, his 2014 book *How Jesus*

Became God). Ehrman thinks the first Christians taught these things of a historical man, that they believed he had descended from outer space *all the way to Earth* to preach his ministry in Galilee and Jerusalem, and *then* reascended into outer space to communicate by revelation from there. But what if Jesus was originally thought to have resided *only* in outer space? To never have visited Earth at all? That crucial step of "being on Earth" is absent from the letters of Paul. So had Paul ever heard of the preacher from Galilee? Or was that a later fiction?

It's certainly strange that the Gospels hide the original Christian teachings of an eternal celestial being. Christians certainly had not changed in that belief—the belief that Jesus was an eternal starlord who descended, incarnated, and ascended back to his home above remained a constant for centuries. So why was it kept out of the Gospels? (Except by the authors of John, who at long last reincluded it, but only in a single introductory line.) This is a definite clue that the Gospels are allegories, that they *intended* to hide the true celestial doctrine—behind a veneer of earthly storytelling. The *real* truth, that Jesus was an archangel all along, whose actual ordeal took place in the sky, would be told only to initiates of sufficient rank. Everyone else would be told the "front story" instead. Just as we know was the case in every other savior cult of the era. The average Joe would be shown the stage act, a tale like that told of Moses. The truth behind it would remain behind the curtain, to be revealed only to the elect—just as Jesus was made to recommend (Mark 4:11–12).

We can be certain of this. Because in what Christians wrote decades *before* the Gospels, and in every wave of writing *after*, Jesus is always an extraterrestrial who has lived among the stars since the dawn of time. He was imagined to have descended from the farthest reaches of outer space to assume a human body and submit to the forces of darkness so as to defeat them, joining in result a well-known class of mythical supermen who underwent similar ordeals.

For example, in his letter to the Philippians, Paul says Jesus was a preexistent superbeing, who eventually had a body of flesh manufactured for him so he could die (2:5–6). In his first letter to the Corinthians, Paul says Jesus was alive in the time of Moses (10:4). In his letter to the Romans, Paul confirms that Jesus was sent from outer space by God and given a mortal body to wear for the mission (8:3). In his letter to the

Galatians, Paul reveals that Jesus was indeed an angel (4:14). And again in his first letter to the Corinthians, Paul says Jesus was God's agent of creation at the dawn of time (8:6), a belief confirmed by the authors of Hebrews (1:2, 2:9-10, 2:17) and Colossians, who wrote that Jesus was indeed "the firstborn of all creation" (1:15). The author of Hebrews 9 also confirms that Jesus was the high priest of God's celestial temple in the farthest reaches of outer space—a role we know ancient Jews always reserved for an archangel, usually Michael, or an ambiguous "archangel of many names" (as the Jewish theologian Philo describes it in *On the Confusion of Tongues* §146–47, which predates all Christian writing).

The evidence is amply secure that the original story the Christians taught was that Jesus was God's supreme archangel, eternal high priest of God's celestial temple, his firstborn creation and adopted son, viceroy of the universe, and the original superbeing who carried out all of God's other acts of creation and that he ruled the resulting cosmos on God's behalf. A being whom Philo reveals Jews *already believed in*. Which means we already have a mythical "Jesus" at the very dawn of the religion. The first Christians simply added the belief that recently this starlord descended from his extraterrestrial seat of power to wear a body of royal Jewish flesh just to sacrificially die and thereby effect God's secret plan (and maybe was then named "Jesus," thus being called "God's Savior," if this archangel hadn't already shared that moniker before). But it appears only *then* did this Jesus begin sending anyone messages and communicating his teachings, by revelation—not in a prior ministry, which we'll see later is never mentioned in the earliest Christian documents.

If Jesus was never really a historical person, then what the original Christians were teaching was that this ancient archangel descended from the superior heavens, not to Earth, but into the sky, below the lower ring of outer space, then known as a vast and terrifying region between the earth and moon, the realm of all flesh, where death and decay, and Satan and his demons, were known to hold sway. And there is where Jesus was originally believed to have died, crucified not by the Romans on Earth, or by the Jews, but by Satan or his agents, far above the clouds. And there is where Jesus's mortal bodysuit was buried, perhaps in some garden among the demonic sky castles. And three days later he rose from the dead and revealed his glory to all the heavenly creatures, Satan among them. And thus he defeated sin and death, and with that, all of Satan's power. Then, and only then, this archangelic Jesus appeared in dreams and visions to the first apostles, first of all to Peter, whose report then inspired others to have similar experiences (or claim to). It is in these dreams and visions that Jesus told them all this had happened, and that it was all secretly foretold in the sacred scriptures of old, where they would find confirmation of it.

If this is true, then tales that Jesus was a miracle-working preacher touring the hillsides of Galilee were invented decades later, originally as symbolic allegories, useful myths for promulgating the values of the gospel. But all along, the religion had really begun by teaching something quite different, a story then continued in secrecy only among ranking initiates.

Fragments of that original Gospel might still survive. Some of its text may lie in what scholars today call *The Ascension of Isaiah*. It may even be more accurate to call the earliest form of that we can reconstruct the "Gospel of Isaiah." Medieval Christians tried to hide that by meddling with its text, but we have enough evidence now to confirm most of what the original said—though key portions remain forever lost, destroyed by those later meddlers. We'll look at that later. Other clues have survived as well, of a lost Christian sect that believed the Gospels were just "cleverly devised myths" (2 Peter 1:16), perhaps intended to market a new savior god and a new package of social values. But virtually all their writings were destroyed. Even their existence was almost erased from history.

In fact, nearly the only writings allowed to be preserved to us by the later Roman-controlled Church were those that met the approval of its upper ranks. And yet this was a Church that had pinned its authority on claims that the historical Jesus was a real historical figure, so that they alone could claim to have inherited his teachings from his original hand-picked disciples. Thus no longer could one be chosen as an apostle for the Lord by dream or vision, as Paul had been (Galatians 1), or indeed as it seems all the apostles originally were (1 Corinthians 9:1, 15:5–8). And so the Roman Church could shut out all competing claims for authority and control, declaring all others heretics, suppressing them and their writings for over a thousand years. As indeed we see they did—not by any organized conspiracy, but simply by every agent in charge of preserving documents working independently for the glory of their Church to further its claims.

So how likely is this scenario, of an evolution in ideology from a celestial atonement drama to an earthly one? From a spaceman tangling only with Satan, to a spaceman touring Galilee? Let's look at the evidence and see.

2

There Is a Good Chance Jesus Never Existed

Near the end of the first century, around the same time the Gospels were being written, the Greek scholar Plutarch honored Clea, a priestess of the mysteries of Isis, with a treatise about her religion entitled *On Isis and Osiris*. In this he explains why her cult had adopted a certain belief about the life and resurrection of Osiris, in the "true" account reserved for those who, like her, were initiated into its secrets. He said the *real* truth was that Osiris was never really a historical person whose activity took place on Earth, as public accounts portrayed him to be. Osiris was, rather, a celestial being, whose trials and sufferings took place in outer space just below the moon, where death and turmoil reign. Thence Osiris descends every year, becomes incarnate by assuming a mortal body of flesh, and is killed by Set (in Greek, Typhon, the Egyptian analog to Satan). Then he is resurrected—literally undergoing, Plutarch says, an *anabiôsis*, a "return to life," and a *palingenesia*, a "regeneration" (the same word used of the resurrection in Matthew 19:28). From there Osiris ascends back to heaven in glory.

That means there were public stories that portrayed the death and resurrection of Osiris as taking place on Earth, in human history; these also imagined him descending to rule the underworld. But, Plutarch explains, those stories disguised the true teachings reserved for those of sufficient rank. "You must not think," he says, "that any of these tales actually happened." No, we "must not treat legend as if it were history at all." Gods like Osiris were never really "generals, admirals, or kings, who lived in very ancient times" only to become gods after death; to the contrary, they were always celestial deities in some form, whether living as gods far above, or as demigods invisibly "in the space about us," carrying "the prayers and petitions of men" up from Earth into outer space, and transporting divine "oracles and gifts" back from those same stellar reaches to the earth below. Accordingly, Plutarch reminds Clea, "the holy and sacred Osiris" does not rule "beneath the earth" as the ignorant public thinks, but "is far removed from the earth, uncontaminated and unpolluted and pure from all matter that is subject to destruction and death."

As Plutarch further explains in that same treatise, "that part of the world" subject to "destruction is contained underneath the orb of the moon," whereas all the real "relations and forms and effluxes of the god abide in the heavens and in the stars" above. That's how Osiris can become incarnate, die, and rise back from the dead *every year.* This wasn't happening down here in Earth history; it was happening in the distant skies above. So those public myths were all a disguise. Osiris did not rule the dead from the underworld, but from the celestial realms above; and to maintain that reign he dies and rises cosmically every year, not once upon a time on Earth. Which means he was never really a historical pharaoh. And Egyptian records are continuous enough that we can confirm there indeed never was a historical Osiris. So we know the "gospels" of his deeds on Earth were mythical. Only his *cosmic* death and resurrection were "real" to his priesthood. Just as Plutarch said.

Could this be the same sort of thing originally believed of Jesus?

Egypt borders Judea, and housed a large community of Jews who often observed, combated, or studied the religions of their surrounding and ruling Gentiles, and a lot of pilgrimages took place yearly, with countless Egyptian Jews visiting Jerusalem, and trade with all quarters of Judea was common. And Osiris cult was not only in Egypt, but everywhere. And pilgrims and traders from every province crisscrossed Judea on a regular basis. Even Galilee had within and around it several Gentile cities and regular commerce with the outside world. And Osiris cult was not the only savior cult experiencing popularity among Gentiles at the time. The cults of Hercules-Melqart and Adonis-Tammuz were thriving at Tyre and beyond. The cult of Bacchus-Dionysus and the Eleusinian mysteries were in every province. And other savior cults are known, and though less data on them survives, for most we know enough to see a common pattern, a pattern then unseen in any other part of the world. There were no such savior cults in ancient China or India or Persia. They were a unique feature of Mediterranean religious culture at the very time Christianity arose. So it cannot be a coincidence that Christianity looks exactly like them—or to be more precise, exactly like *a Jewish one.*

Christianity as Jewish Savior Cult

What did most of those other popular savior cults have in common?

- They were personal salvation cults, often evolved from prior communal agricultural cults. Just like Christianity from its parent cult of Judaism. Judaism's communal salvation scheme, also originally based around agriculture, became a personal salvation cult instead. Christianity carried that feature to its now-fashionable conclusion.

- They guaranteed the individual a good place in the afterlife, a concern not present in most prior forms of Western religion, including early Judaism. Although again that notion had already been picked up by Judaism before Christianity evolved from it, so Christianity merely developed that theme into further conformity to popular fashion.

- They were cults you joined membership with, as opposed to just being open communal religions. Judaism was mostly a racial and national religion like every other, though to a small extent it had already been exploiting the prospect of "joining" through conversion through circumcision (Exodus 12:48). Christianity would soon do away with even that requirement, and replace it with baptism, the same "joining" ritual found in other mystery cults.

- These cults also enacted a fictive kin group: members were now all *brothers* and *sisters*, *fathers* and *mothers*—just as we see Christianity did, more concertedly than its native Judaism ever had.

- They were joined through baptism: the use of water-contact rituals to effect an initiation, often through a "remission of sins" (as described, for example, in Plato's *Republic*, and beyond). Several sects of Judaism already had adapted various water rituals; the Christians likely adapted one of them into a cult initiation ceremony so similar to that of Gentile savior cults as to even retain the pagan concept of "baptism for the dead" (as Paul mentions in 1 Corinthians 15:29), allowing initiation even of the deceased into salvation *after the fact*, by baptizing a living proxy, which had long been a feature of the Bacchic mysteries.

- They were maintained through communion: regular sacred meals enacting the presence of the god. Christianity adapted for this what Judaism already had like it, which was its Passover ritual, celebrating a past (and also quite mythical) rescue from death. But the savior cults employed such meals as a security for one's *future* rescue from death, in the form of a blessed afterlife—and so now did Christianity.

- They involved secret teachings reserved only to members; and some only to members of rank. Paul speaks often of such secret teachings and his inability to fully express them in his letters.

- They used a common vocabulary to identify these ideas, such as talk of "children" (as the lesser initiated) and "adults" (as the fully initiated), "milk" (the outward stories for lower initiates) and "meat" (the inner mysteries reserved for higher initiates); descriptions of our mortal, aging bodies as mere cloaks, tents, or tombs; referring to hidden secrets available to the more informed as "mysteries"; and so on. Such vocabulary is found throughout the letters of Paul, our earliest Christian source.

- They were syncretistic—which means, they modified this common package of ideas with concepts distinctive of the adopting culture. Thus *every* savior cult was different from every other; the differences reflected the adopting native religion: Osiris cult was distinctively Egyptian, Adonis cult was distinctively Mesopotamian, Bacchus cult was distinctively Greek, and Christianity was distinctively Jewish.

- They were all mono- or henotheistic, just like Judaism: they preached a supreme god by whom all other divinities are created or to whom all are subordinate or otherwise mere facets (whether these other beings were called gods or not).

- They were individualistic: they relate primarily to salvation of the individual, not the community. Just like Christianity.

- And they were cosmopolitan: they intentionally crossed social borders of race, culture, nation, wealth, and sometimes even gender. Just like Christianity.

Already you might wonder how Christianity could be so similar. But it goes beyond even that. Just consider what the central savior-figures of these cults *also* mostly had in common:

- They are "savior gods," literally so-named and so-called, always sent in service to the supreme god as their agent or representative. Hence it's already peculiar that even "Jesus" means, literally, "God's Savior."

- They are the "son" (sometimes daughter) of the supreme God. Just like Jesus.

- They undergo a "passion," which means a "suffering" or "struggle," literally the same word in Greek: *patheôn*.

- That passion is often (though not always) a death, followed by a resurrection and usually an ascension to heaven in triumph.

- By which "passion" (of whatever kind) they obtain victory over death.

- Which victory they then share with their followers; typically, again, through baptism and communion.

- They all have stories about them set in human history on Earth.

- Yet so far as we can tell, none of them ever actually existed.

Just mix in the culturally distinct features of Judaism that this fashionable package was syncretized with—such as messianism, apocalypticism, scripturalism; the particularly Jewish ideas about resurrection; Jewish soteriology, cosmology, and rituals; and other things peculiar to Judaism, such as an abhorrence of sexuality and an obsession with blood atonement and substitutionary sacrifice—and you would literally have Christianity fully spelled out . . . before it even existed.

That we could have fully described Christianity *before it even existed*, by merely combining Judaism with the cultural package common to all other savior cults of the time, *surely* cannot be a coincidence. Christianity is unmistakably a Jewish version of this same Western cultural trend— and was such from its very founding. This already-popular savior-cult model was simply Judaized—and very quickly (under Paul) made even more alike, rendering it even more popular. Thence the Christianity we know was born. The "differences" from all those other cults are the Jewish element. The similarities are the Western cultural influences that brought forth something new.

This is just as happened the last time the Jews were subject to a great empire, when under Persian rule they adopted Persian Zoroastrian ideas of an apocalypse, a messiah, a linear view of history, resurrection of the dead, and Satan as enemy of God and creator of death. All converted into a Jewish form, surrounded and altered by Jewish ideas of course. Judaism is not, after all, Zoroastrianism. But it was forever transformed by it. And so under Greco-Roman dominion, it was transformed again, by the equally popular construct of the mystery religions, into what we know as Christianity.

That none of those other savior gods were really historical, yet all were portrayed as such, lends sufficient grounds to at least *suspect* Jesus is not the lone, strange exception. That the Gospels are rife with other markers typical of mythical persons only further secures that suspicion (a point we'll explore in chapter six).

Where Is the Evidence?

From there we have to ask, is there any evidence that secures Jesus as being indeed that exception? Can we rescue Jesus from our justified suspicions?

When we look at evidence outside the New Testament, we end up with nothing usable to that end. The earliest mentions we have, sixty to ninety years later, are found in the *Annals* of Tacitus and the *Antiquities* of Josephus. Even if authentic (and there are good reasons to doubt they are), these would be the only mentions of Jesus as a historical character (outside the New Testament) until a hundred years after the religion began. Yet they give no indication of having any other source of information but the Gospels or informants relying on the Gospels. They are, therefore, incapable of corroborating the Gospels; because we cannot establish they are anything other than echoes of them. And after that, there is nothing else. Just more echoes of the Gospels, direct or indirect. There is no independent corroboration of anything in them about Jesus. Which means none existed that could be cited; or it was all somehow lost or ignored. Either way, no evidence exists for us to consider.

So all we have is the New Testament. But what in that collection of Christian propaganda even attests to there being a real historical Jesus? The Gospels are the earliest texts clearly placing Jesus in human Earth history. But we can find no external evidence that anything in them comes from any source at all. Even when John, the last of those Gospels, alone claims to be using some lost written text by an unnamed disciple for some few details, we can tell he is fabricating, both that source and that disciple. In truth, John is just a freestyle rewrite of the previous three Gospels, portraying what its author *wanted* Jesus to have said or done. We have no evidence this author had any evidence any of those things were true. And its patently mythical structure, explicitly stated propagandistic aims, evident deceptions, and dependence on prior Gospels don't lend it any weight as evidence for historicity.

When we look at the earlier Gospels, meanwhile, they name no sources at all, and are really just expanded, reimagined redactions of each other. Luke is hardly more than a creative rewrite of what's in

Matthew and Mark, and Matthew is hardly more than a creative rewrite of Mark. Which means really, we cannot establish any source for the historicity of Jesus other than the "Gospel according to Mark," a text written in a foreign language, in a foreign land, an average lifetime after the fact, by someone who wasn't there and who doesn't identify anyone as his source for any detail. So as far as we really know, all other Gospels are just expanded, redacted rewrites of this one text. We can "assume" they had other sources; but we cannot justify any of those assumptions. We have no evidence of it. And what we have no evidence of, we cannot affirm.

Even when Acts makes allusions to the historicity of Jesus (which is actually more rarely than most scholars think, indeed more rarely than should be the case), we cannot establish those as anything more than rewritten echoes of these same Gospels. Because, again, for none is any source cited. And Acts is demonstrably a work of revisionist fiction in the guise of history, not a source anyone can trust. And yet it peculiarly erases a historical Jesus from most of its account: at no point do the Jewish and Roman authorities reacting to the Christians even seem aware a man named Jesus had recently been active, outside visions and revelations; and once its public account of the church begins (in Acts 2), it suddenly has no knowledge of any of the family of Jesus, and Pontius Pilate (and his role in suppressing the Christians) has vanished. In other words, even what Acts might possibly have derived from sources independent of the Gospels, appears not to have included a historical Jesus, but merely an angelic figure known only by revelation (Acts 23:9). Everything else may well just be a redaction or elaboration of the content of Mark. Once again, we have no evidence otherwise.

So the entire historicity of Jesus rests on a single, extremely dubious text: the Gospel of Mark. Which is not plausibly a historical text; it is composed neither like anyone's personal memoir or a researched historical account, but is an overtly mythical text intended to illustrate the teachings of Mark's sect through parables and tales. It has no identifiable sources. And any "assumption" that any of its content derives from sources is unjustifiable by any evidence. At best one can argue that Mark knew of Paul's Epistles and composed his stories to mythically reify their teachings. And by further inference we could say that Mark (like other Gospel authors) might have had similar sources now lost, of Pauline or other Apostolic teachings about what the Jesus they worshiped "revealed" to them in visions or scriptures, or what parables and stories they themselves wove to illustrate them. But that still does not get us back to a real Jesus; only an imaginary one. There is nothing in Mark that can secure us anything more substantive than that. Assumptions, such as that Mark had access to some sort of memorized tradition dating back to witnesses, are not evidence, nor can produce evidence. They are just assumptions. And knowledge does not follow therefrom.

That leaves us with only one source of evidence to consider: the Epistles.

Do the Epistles Attest a Real or Only an Imaginary Jesus?

The letters forged in the second century we must disregard; fake evidence is not evidence. So the Pastorals are out. As is Revelation, as bizarre as it is, which implausibly describes itself as an extended prophetic hallucination and says nothing independent of Gospels already written. Likewise, letters we cannot establish are authentic, like the Johannine Epistles, or early enough to be independent of the Gospels, like those, and Colossians, 2 Thessalonians, and Ephesians. And most of what remains never clearly places anything Jesus said or did on Earth, like 1 Peter, James, Jude, or Hebrews.

That only leaves us with what are still considered the seven authentic Epistles of Paul. Of which only four say anything that could plausibly be construed as referring to a real historical man named Jesus: Romans, Galatians, 1 Thessalonians, and 1 Corinthians. Passages elsewhere, read in context and in the original Greek, make no such reference. Like 2 Corinthians 5:16 declaring that all Christians, particularly the distant Corinthians, once "knew Christ according to the flesh," which is not about witnessing the ministry of Jesus but the present spiritual condition of the believer, who is the one "in the flesh" meant, not Jesus. The Corinthians never met Jesus. Likewise, 2 Corinthians 8:9 declaring, "though he was rich, for you he became poor, so that through poverty you may become rich," does not mean Jesus was wealthy and gave all his money away, or that Christians will become wealthy, but rather is referring to the Lord's abandonment of supernatural power to enter a mortal state (Philippians 2:6–8), in order to secure *spiritual* riches, as all faithful Christians thereby will too. And so on. All such passages can simply be referring to their theological belief that Jesus assumed a mortal body that was tempted, abused, killed, and buried in an aerial realm, not on Earth, just as for Osiris. We can't tell one way or the other. Consequently, we can't use such passages as evidence one way or the other.

So we are left with those other four Epistles of Paul. But even they do not contain any clear reference to Jesus being on Earth.

1 Thessalonians only mentions revelations of Jesus (such as Paul's knowledge of the apocalypse in 1 Thessalonians 4:15–18). But such revelations did not come from a historical Jesus even had there been one. They therefore cannot be evidence of one. Likewise all other passages in other letters where Paul cites teachings of Jesus: Paul himself says those all came by revelation, or hidden messages planted in ancient scriptures (Romans 16:25–26). So we cannot establish from Paul that any of those teachings came to the apostles in any other way. Indeed, in Romans 10:14–16, Paul appears to say those teachings were preached to no one *but* apostles, that the only way any Jews can ever have heard Jesus is by apostles communicating what has been mystically revealed to them. Which rules out a real ministry. Just as Philippians 2:7 says Jesus abandoned all supernatural powers in his incarnation, becoming a "slave" to the natural world order, which rules out his ever having performed miracles or exorcisms. By comparison, the one passage damning the Jews for killing Jesus (1 Thessalonians 2:15–16), which would be the only clear reference to a genuinely historical Jesus in all the letters of Paul, is not credibly authentic. Few scholars believe Paul wrote it, and the evidence is pretty heavily against his having done so. One can "speculate" as to *how much* of that passage is forged or original, but we have no knowledge in the matter. It is tainted evidence and thus inadmissible.

1 Corinthians also never clearly references a real historical Jesus. Indeed, when we look at the creed Paul declares original to the faith, in 1 Corinthians 15:1–8, we very peculiarly find a description of the origins of the religion that lacks any reference to anyone ever seeing Jesus before

he died. It is only *from scripture* that his death and burial was known. The first time he is ever said to appear to anyone is after his resurrection. Which we know to be imaginary. As in all of Paul's Epistles, there is never any evident knowledge of Jesus having had a ministry, performing miracles, being an exorcist, teaching in parables, or doing anything at all while alive, other than act out a cosmic drama. For instance, the ritual Jesus established "on the night before" his death, speaking to all future Christians, Paul ascribes to a revelation in 1 Corinthians 11:23–26 ("from the Lord" always meaning in Paul "by revelation," per Galatians 1:11–12, 2 Corinthians 12:1), much like Peter's vision of a meal in Acts 8:10–17. Paul mentions no one being present, and never places the event on Earth. He does not even call it a "last" supper, and thus does not attest to Jesus ever having had another.

The Epistle to the Romans likewise never references any facts or events of Jesus's life on Earth, only his cosmic role and importance; theological beliefs, not genuinely historical ones. Indeed, here Paul outright says the preaching and gospel of Jesus is known *only* by revelation and scripture (Romans 16:25–26). No mention of human witnesses, disciples, or faithful tradents. So when Romans opens with the credal declaration that Jesus "came from" the "seed of David," note that Paul does not say Jesus *descended* from David. Peculiarly, he not only avoids such terms, but even deliberately avoids the only word he elsewhere employs for human birth (which is elsewhere *genaô*, "beget"), and uses instead the word he employs for direct manufacture of bodies by God (*ginomai*, "come to be"), such as the creation of Adam (1 Corinthians 15:45–49) and our future resurrection bodies waiting for us in heaven (15:37; cf. 2 Corinthians 5:1–5), neither of which are "born" to human parents. That Jesus, a preexistent archangel, had a mortal body manufactured for him (as the pre-Pauline creed in Philippians 2:5–11 says), just like Osiris, is not evidence of a belief this happened on Earth, just as it was not for Osiris. Thus that Paul frequently refers to Jesus as becoming a "man," and his murder and burial as real, still does not tell us *where* he thought any of this happened.

We already know Jewish prophecies mandated the messiah's body had to be Jewish, indeed Davidic; so we already could have predicted Christians would construct the theological belief that God manufactured said body out of such seed. In fact, the prophecy most clearly stating this (2 Samuel 7:12–14) was demonstrably *false* . . . unless the seed indeed came directly from David, and not by descent. For the prophet Nathan had said the seed of David would *sit upon his throne* forever; which throne had ceased to exist for decades by the time Christianity arose, so only a direct begetting of Jesus by David could now fulfill that promise (as only Jesus would rule eternally). Thus such a belief would actually have rescued a falsified prophecy, which is a more than adequate reason for Christians to construct it. Consequently, given Paul's peculiar grammar and vocabulary and extraordinary obscurity and the ready availability of multiple interpretations, this passage cannot be used to confirm anyone of that time believed Jesus had been on Earth. It's ambiguous—indeed peculiarly so—and therefore useless. We'll look more closely at this in chapter eight.

We similarly can infer nothing useful from Paul's equally vague and theological declaration that Jesus "came from a mother" in Galatians 4:4. Which is uttered only in an extended argument that is allegorical from beginning to end (starting at Galatians 3:23), and explicitly declared to be in its conclusion (Galatians 4:24). Paul clearly intended no other meaning here. It's possible Paul *also* thought Jesus had a real earthly mother. But we cannot conclude he did from this passage, as here he is not referring to that. He is referring instead to how Jesus was given a mortal body subject to the corrupt world order in order to defeat it; which event could have taken place on Earth or, as for Osiris, above it. We cannot tell from what Paul says. He again peculiarly avoids using his preferred word for "born" (despite readily using it in the very same argument of human births just a few lines later), and uses instead his preferred word for direct manufacture by God, just as with Romans 1:3. Which so disturbed later historicizing Christians that an attempt was made to alter this word in *both* these verses, in Romans 1 and Galatians 4, replacing it with Paul's preferred word for human births. So they understood the problem. Which means even at best, this verse is again simply too ambiguous to evince a historical Jesus was meant by it. So we can't use this evidence either. We'll also look more closely at this in chapter eight.

That leaves us with only one more item of evidence to rescue historicity with: Paul's two references to "brothers of the Lord," generically as a group in 1 Corinthians 9:5, and specifically as an appellation of a certain "James" in Galatians 1:19. But these are equally ambiguous. Paul actually believed all baptized Christians were Brothers of the Lord (e.g., Romans 8:29; in context: Romans 6:3–5, 8:15–29; cf. Galatians 3:26–29). And the only time Paul ever uses this full, pleonastic phrase is when he needs to contrast ordinary Christians with Christians of Apostolic rank. All were brothers of the Lord, but that was already known of apostles, so it never had to be said of them. Just as saying, "I met the Pope and a Christian named James," in no way implies the Pope is not also a Christian. But if Paul also knew there are *biological* brothers of the Lord, he would need to make that distinction if ever referring to them; so that he never does, implies he knew of no such distinction needing to be made. And since the only Brothers of the Lord Paul explicitly attests knowing of are baptized Christians, we actually cannot take these two passages as evidence he knew of biological brothers. They are, again, too ambiguous to draw such a conclusion from. Maybe it's what he means. Maybe not. We cannot know. So this evidence is also useless. Still, we'll look more closely at this, too, in chapter nine.

All these evidences from the Epistles are hopelessly vague and theological, not plain references to an earthly life of Jesus at all. Which is already by itself extremely strange. Why is *this* all we have, and not numerous debates and discussions and questions about Jesus' ministry and trial and death or his miracles or parables or how he chose or affected or instructed the people who knew him? How has Paul never heard of the word "disciple" or that anyone was Jesus' hand-picked representative in life? Why is he always weirdly vague; for instance, ascribing the death of Jesus to "archons of this eon" (1 Corinthians 2:6–10), which he characterizes as spiritual rather than terrestrial forces (as he there says they would understand esoteric details of God's planned magical formulae), rather than to "Pontius Pilate" or "the Romans" or "the Jews"? Why does he never say Jesus' death occurred "in Jerusalem"? How can Paul avoid in some 20,000 words ever making *any* clear reference to Jesus being on Earth? How can every question, argument, or opposition he ever faced have avoided referencing things Jesus said or did in life? He never referenced them. He never had them cited against him. He is never asked about them. That's weird. And weird is just another word for improbable. Unless the only Jesus any Christians yet knew, was a revealed being, not an earthly minister.

It's additionally revealing, therefore, that modern translators will "presumptuously" add implications not in the text. For instance, almost all Bible translations imagine Paul as referring to the "betrayal" of Judas in his account of his Eucharist vision, when in fact Paul says no such thing. He instead uses the same language he does elsewhere, of God (not Judas) "handing over" Jesus to those who would effect his atoning sacrifice (Romans 8:32). Few Bibles get this right, but those include the Darby Bible and Young's Literal Translation. Similarly, some translations will render Hebrews 5:7 as saying that "during the days of Jesus' life on Earth" he cried and prayed for his deliverance (such as in the supposedly more accurate NIV Bible). No such words are in the Greek. The text, in fact, says that "during the days of his flesh" Jesus did this (as many Bibles will more honestly read, from the King James to the modern NASB). No reference to *where*—at all, much less "on Earth." And so on. Anytime you find a verse in the Epistles that seems to say or imply Jesus was ever on Earth, you'll find the actual Greek does not say that. We are never told a location for any of this. Vague terms are always used as to what was happening, where, or by whom. And that's just weird.

Conclusion

The silences of the Epistles are thus the strongest evidence against historicity. And this includes Hebrews, 1 Peter, and even 1 Clement, which are also weirdly silent about Jesus being discovered anywhere outside scripture and revelation. Coupled with our suspicion already established, there remains no strong reason to believe Jesus existed. It appears just as likely, if not more so, that he began his existence as an imagined figure experienced in revelations and "discovered" in ancient scriptures, just as Paul says in Romans 16:25–26, 1 Corinthians 15:1–8, Galatians 1:11–16 and 3:1–2, and beyond. And only when Mark, a lifetime later, in a foreign land and language, "invented" a historical version of this figure, as was done for all other mythical savior gods, did any notion of a real historical Jesus arise. Subsequent authors embellished his invention. And subsequent observers echoed that invention. And that's it.

Hence the fact remains that no evidence exists before Mark that Jesus was ever really a historical person. Indeed a definite belief that he was might not even appear in the record until the second century, depending on how one dates certain disputed texts. His conversion into an earthly figure is the same as every other savior's. And since centuries later a historicizing sect took control of all document transmission for a thousand years, we have not been allowed to see any evidence otherwise. So why should we conclude he *wasn't* as invented as every other savior?

We know there were Christians who thought the Gospel stories were "cleverly devised myths" and not witnessed events (as attested in the forgery of 2 Peter 1:16–2:3); but we are not allowed to hear anything from or about them. We know there were Christians composing stories around the same time as the New Testament Gospels, in which Jesus appears to be killed by Satan and his demons in the sky, and not on Earth (in the original edition of the *Ascension of Isaiah* 6–11); but as that text was subsequently doctored to erase this, we are not allowed to verify it. We know there were Christians teaching that events of Jesus' life took place in the heavens (as Irenaeus would later polemicize against); but we don't get to see what they actually said (at all, much less their earliest texts). We only get hints through the late, distorted polemics of their enemies. Indeed, modern scholars have dubiously lumped into their invented notion of "Docetism" (the idea that Jesus only "seemed" to be killed) too many diverse perspectives in the earliest suppressed Christian sects. In actual fact, some claims or sects we now call Docetic appear to have been saying the stories of Jesus on Earth were fully mythical. But we aren't allowed to check—because all their writings were destroyed.

There is, in fact, no more evidence for a living Jesus than there is for a resurrected Jesus. And this is the most telling fact of all. All mainstream scholars agree the resurrection of Jesus was really only imagined in revelations; it was not verifiably historical. Yet the normative belief quickly became that the Disciples hung out and dined with a risen, walking, flying corpse, indeed even for a whole month (Acts 1:1–11). The original belief, of mere "visions" of a risen Christ, does not appear in the Gospels. And it was never adopted in any subsequent sect of Christianity that survived to control what texts we are allowed to see. They historicized the risen Christ. Which means they could just as easily have historicized Christ altogether. What, after all, is the difference between these two versions of Jesus? If they could reify one Jesus, the risen Jesus, who *in reality* was only known in visions, without any surviving record of anyone noticing or complaining—and they did—why could they not similarly reify the *other* Jesus too? Do we honestly have any evidence they didn't?

3

A Plausible Jesus Is Not Necessarily a Probable Jesus

To make the point, let's consider the proposal of another minority group in academia, the defenders of the view that Jesus was a violent revolutionary, a member of the Judean "zealot party," who was later whitewashed by his followers into a pacifist spiritual leader. Advocates of this view include Fernando Bermejo-Rubio and Reza Aslan, and though it's not accepted by the mainstream consensus, it is widely regarded as a plausible position worth a place at the table of debate. And yet it's even less defensible than Jesus not existing at all. So if even *that* view is respectable, so should ours be.

Making the Comparison

How *does* doubting historicity altogether compare with that? It's certainly *possible* Jesus was historical, even a violent revolutionary. But the question is not whether we can make this (or any) hypothesis fit the evidence. The question is whether it's the most probable explanation of the evidence—when compared with competing hypotheses, both historicist and ahistoricist. And can we really be so sure? I've concluded the odds favor the answer being no, though only by a margin. In my peer-reviewed work I found at best a 1 in 3 chance some historical Jesus theory will be correct after all. Respectable odds. But still not high enough to say "more probably than not." Historicity doesn't really have a better case behind it than that.

The fundamental problem with the method of "reinterpreting" the evidence that is used to defend historicity to try and "force" a conclusion like the zealot hypothesis, or any other, is that it doesn't actually work logically. It relies on stacking assumptions on top of assumptions without evidence for those assumptions even being probable much less certain, and then doesn't compare that stack of assumptions with competing stacks, which may be just as likely, or more so. For example, the best competing assumption to theirs is: the Gospels are deliberate fiction, and not incoherent collections of random oral lore as the zealot hypothesis requires. The Gospels do not look like the latter. They look like the former. So even at best these competing assumptions are equally likely; but quite frankly, that's being far too generous to the assumption of "the Gospels are incoherent collections of random oral lore." I don't find that at all plausible. Nor should any scholar. The Synoptic Gospels possess far too coherent a structure and messaging for such a thing to be at all likely (I'll survey some examples of that in chapter six).

Authors don't compile contradictory collections of data and present it as coherent; authors only put in what they want to put in. Therefore every single thing is there for a reason. And that reason is unlikely to be "the author didn't notice it contradicts other things the author wanted said" or "the author didn't care." Authors tend to write coherently, with everything installed for a purpose. What doesn't fit their desired story, they leave out. What they need said, they make up. That this is what *these* authors did is therefore the most likely assumption to adopt.

When we do that, we get completely different results. For example, advocates of the insurrectionist thesis argue that the inclusion of details about John the Baptist, who is depicted as being executed just like Jesus, "can be explained" by their thesis. But it can also be explained without their thesis. On the "deliberate fiction" assumption, each Gospel author is deliberately portraying Jesus as a parallel to John, as both his superior and successor. Each is within his own document completely consistent in doing this: John the Baptist is exalted, then Jesus is made just like him, and then Jesus is shown to be even more amazing. John then conveniently endorses this interpretation in the story, declaring Jesus his successor and superior, thus completing the whole package of propaganda these authors wanted to sell. So here we have the evidence equally likely on this competing theory, and this theory already starts out more likely than the other one. This is why we can't get "Jesus was a whitewashed insurrectionist" to be the most probable explanation of this evidence, or any other. At best it's merely possible. At worst other explanations are more likely.

What happens when we apply this switch in starting assumptions to other examples the "zealot hypothesis" leans on? References in the Gospels to Jesus being targeted as an insurrectionist are all scripturally constructed fiction to position Jesus as the falsely accused and abused righteous man, identified by George Nickelsburg as a common trope in Jewish fiction of the time; to emulate Christian martyrs and missionaries generally; and to repudiate an entire system of violent thinking the Gospels were consistently written to oppose. This fiction all has an obvious theological and mythical basis. Indeed, the narrative incorporates implausible details, like a nonexistent releasing ceremony that frees Barabbas, as in Bar-Abbas, "Son of the Father" (who was even named "Jesus" in some manuscripts), hence Jesus's conceptual twin (the real "Son of the Father"), which makes this all just an obvious mythical emulation of a Levitical Yom Kippur, when two identical goats would be selected—one released bearing the sins of Israel, the other sacrificed to atone for those sins. And the sins being condemned with this fable are specifically being a violent insurrectionist. There is no history here. This is symbolic fiction top to bottom, built out of the Torah, Psalms, Isaiah, and Wisdom literature. If it used any real history at all, we cannot tell. Every element is present to serve the biblical and theological symbolism of the story, with nothing left over that we need "real history" to explain.

Jesus' use of war imagery is likewise all symbolic fiction, teaching by parable and using physical warfare as allegory for spiritual warfare, just as with the two thousand pigs named "Legion" that drown from their own folly. That's no more history than any of these other details are. So there's no way this is a "remembered" event in a militant Jesus' life. It's made up. So who made it up? And why is this made up story being included by writers selling pacifism? If you can't answer those questions, you don't have a plausible theory. Mark and Matthew consistently write with the message that violence is sinful disobedience that only brings ruin. They would not include details to the contrary unless they meant them to support that theme, not contradict it. So already we know other interpretations than "Jesus was a militant" are more likely. These are not "accidental" mentions of Jesus and his entourage being "violent zealots." Authors don't include things by accident. The message is exactly the contrary: the fate of the pigs illustrates the doomed mission of militarism. It does not come from someone who supported militarism.

Likewise, the tale of Jesus disrupting the temple is even less plausible historically and thus even more obviously a scripturally constructed fiction. It all comes out of the old Jewish Bible, not history. Jesus' actions in the temple are a parable conveying a message, not something remembered so badly as to make absolutely no sense militarily. The temple square was a heavily populated space over ten acres in size and guarded by an armed battalion authorized to kill troublemakers on sight. None of the Gospels' tales of Jesus disrupting commerce there make any sense of this fact. The triumphal entry they depict is likewise so brazen and ridiculous a story it can't have happened without Josephus, for example, having mentioned it, and the Romans taking public action against it; whereas every single component of it is easily adapted from Zechariah, 1 Maccabees, and other scriptures, leaving no need of any historical event to explain its presence in the story.

The secrecy element in Mark, too, is fundamentally theological, a reification into fictional narrative the message of Romans 16:25–26 and 1 Corinthians 2:7–10, that God hid his plans from the "rulers of this eon" and only revealed them to the elect. This encodes mystical, not historical events. Why should we think a historical reading is more likely than a mythical one, when we know for a fact these authors write myth (thousands of pigs drowned by spirits, remember?), but we have no comparable evidence that anything they write about Jesus is historical?

At best it's 50/50. At worst the historical reading is always going to be less likely. The whole theme of a messianic secret *is made up*. It's allegory for God's plan, exactly as explained by Paul.

References to establishing a kingdom are likewise allegory. The Kingdom, to which the baptized "are heirs" according to Paul, was *never* a military one. We know that already from Paul decades before any Gospel tale was constructed. The thrones that ranking believers would sit on to judge "even angels" would be in heaven (1 Corinthians 6:3), not in the temporal realm of earthly nations. *None* of their promised rewards are "this" worldly. The Gospels reify the real message of a spiritual kingdom into an allegorical narrative, and consistently target the literal interpretation of it as the false one leading to ruin, not the other way around. That's the whole point of the Barabbas narrative, for example: the mob chooses the sins of the military insurrectionist (their elected scapegoat) over the meek, atoning sacrifice of their spiritual savior—to their doom, not their glory. So none of this can support any reliable belief that the kingdom meant was ever literal. That misses these authors' whole point—and Paul's. Which leaves no evidence Jesus ever taught seeking a kingdom by insurrection.

And so on down the line. In every case, there are already equally if not more likely purposes of the material singled out by zealot advocates today that is instead allegorical, ironical, or scriptural, not literal, militaristic, or historical. And all these explanations are supported by ample evidence and established precedents, and thus in fact demonstrably probable in ways the "zealot hypothesis" is not. Even without that support, they are just as plausible and thus just as likely as any alternative explanation of the same data. Therefore the zealot hypothesis cannot be made more probable by this evidence. If the exact same evidence is just as likely on two competing theories, neither is made more likely than the other by it. And if one of those theories starts out already more probable than the other, it ends that way too. This is an inescapable fact of logic. There is no way around it.

Nevertheless, to try and get around it, methods are introduced that are actually illogical. For example, historicists will argue for "the coherence of the convergent patterns," but that's just another way to phrase a well-known fallacy called "circular argument." If you assume in advance which passages are fake and which authentic, you can construct any coherent pattern you want. And that is how we know this method has no chance at all of finding any real pattern. It presumes its conclusion ("which" passages signify and which do not) in its premises ("which" passages to credit and which to discredit), and does so by abandoning a fairly well established principle of literary analysis—that authors write everything they do on purpose—by imagining these authors just randomly collected stuff for no reason, any coherent message be damned.

If you subtract everything you have decided in advance is implausible, you've already guaranteed what will be left over is plausible—even if it's totally fictional. That's the folly of circular argument. We could historify any myth with this tactic, from the Torah to Homer. Which is why this tactic can never discover history. All it can do is invent better fiction—a fiction never intended by the original author and thus of no use to us as historians. And if you need to "find" more evidence by "reinterpreting" implausible things suited to your hypothesis (like thousands of pigs being drowned by magical spirits called "Legion") so you can "get more evidence in" for your hypothesis (like, say, some secret message about going to war with Rome, rather than a more straightforward message about militarism leading to damnation), then you're doing the same exact thing: arguing in a circle, by presuming your conclusion in the constructing of your premises. When you have to assume your conclusion is true to get the interpretation you want to then use as evidence that your conclusion is true, you're engaging the evidence illogically.

The same or similar flaws attend all the "criteria" used by advocates of *every* version of a historical Jesus, not just the zealot hypothesis. As I demonstrated in my peer-reviewed book *Proving History*, and as many other scholars I cite there have found as well, in every single case, these criteria are either applied illogically, or when applied logically, don't actually apply.

This loopy methodology is nowhere more evident than in the bizarre attempt by zealot-hypothesis advocates to interpret a parable Mark explicitly designed to *promote* paying taxes as being somehow evidence that Jesus taught exactly the opposite. This is Mark 12:13–17, reifying the teaching of Paul in Romans 13, which notably never references Jesus having ever taught anything at all on the subject, so already the zealot hypothesis is dead in the water: that Jesus even taught *anything* about taxes was a later invention! But even if we "assume" Paul somehow "didn't know" Jesus taught any position on taxes, there is simply no evidence that Jesus supported a tax *rebellion*. Instead, that conclusion is being assumed true, in order to change the entire obvious meaning of a story in Mark, and then using that result to "prove the conclusion true." You can't get more fallaciously circular than that. It's all the worse, because this trick is pulled by citing Luke 23:2 as evidence, where Jesus is said to have been "falsely" accused of preaching a tax rebellion, as if Luke didn't also write 20:20–26, which replicates Mark depicting Jesus explicitly *promoting* the paying of taxes, and his accusers "failing" to get the evidence against him they wanted. So what Luke later portrays as a *false* accusation by the accusers of Jesus, is now being treated as "what Luke actually meant to be true," rather than as simply a recurring theme of common Jewish hero tales: the falsely accused righteous man.

This is not a logically valid way to read an author. Luke included that false accusation to depict Jesus' accusers as liars and Jesus as falsely accused. Not because he dug up some obscure lost oral lore about this accusation actually having been made (or indeed made because it *was true!*) and decided for no sound reason to include it in a story that he wanted to convey exactly the opposite message. That's simply not how authors work. It's not how texts ever came to be composed in the ancient world. Luke is, rather, just embellishing the theme already given him by his source, Mark, that "Many testified falsely against him, but their statements did not agree" (Mark 14:58–59). Luke needed these characters in his story to make false accusations. So he gave them some false accusations to make. That does not gain us any evidence this actually happened—much less that those "false accusations" must have been true! If historicity can be defended with such bad logic as this, why are we so reluctant to accept the contrary conclusion when it requires no such fallacies of reasoning?

Another example is the claim that it's weird "that the four Gospels agree that Jesus was crucified along with other men," therefore that must also be true. This takes facts out of context, falsely declares there is no other meaning that kept this detail resonant across four Gospels, and then, the conclusion thus inserted back into the premise, the premise thus established is used to prove the conclusion! In fact, all scholars know this whole narrative is constructed out of scriptures, especially Isaiah 52–53 and Psalm 22. It's not history. It's pesher, a Jewish practice of inventing new scriptures out of disparate passages of old scriptures. And this detail more obviously reifies Psalm 22:16 (as much else in Mark's crucifixion narrative does) by having Jesus "surrounded" by dogs and "encircled" by "criminals"; and Isaiah 53:9, that the chosen one will be, though innocent, "condemned to the grave with criminals."

This is also why it matters that the Gospels do not say Jesus was crucified merely "with other men." They very specifically say, "They crucified two criminals with him, one on his right and one on his left" (Mark 15:27; Matthew 27:38; John 19:18, 32), who both mock Jesus. Luke changes this story into an even more implausible parable but keeps the peculiar detail of there being only two such men (Luke 23:32–43). Why specifically two men? Why specifically "at his right and his left"? Why bother mentioning any men at all? The author would not do that *unless it served some purpose the author had*. We therefore cannot claim to know the actual reason this detail is here if we do not even contemplate what the author's reason for putting it there is. The zealot proponents have no credible answer for this. That's how we know their theory is implausible.

Why do you think Mark—the inventor of this tale, all the others merely his redactors—would say Jesus was crucified "with one on his right and one on his left"? Because Jesus was really a zealot and these were his soldiers and by coincidence there were only two of them, and Mark just mentions all this for no reason but simply because it was what the lore said and so he just lazily put it in? No such details are in the story. Nor does Mark ever write that way. Do you know how Mark *does* write? Do you know what *is* in Mark's storyline? That the brothers James and John, Jesus' number two and number three, had argued over who would sit at Jesus' right and left in his glory, at which Jesus cryptically says, "You do not know what you are asking," and just as cryptically says those positions have already been reserved for some other pair (Mark 10:35–45). I wonder why Mark would have Jesus say that? Could it be because Mark knew he was going to switch James and John out for common criminals in accordance with scripture when it actually came time to sit "at the right and left" of Jesus? Because Mark loves irony. Because irony captured the meaning of the gospel: "the least shall be first," every expectation upended, precisely the message with which Jesus concludes Mark 10:35–45!

Indeed this is exactly the kind of irony Mark repeatedly uses. Mark had even just done the same with Peter. In another argument about joining Jesus in his glory, which thus really meant suffering and martyrdom, Jesus tells his number *one*, Simon Peter, that "whoever wants to be my disciple must deny themselves and take up their cross and follow me," because "whoever wants to save their life will lose it, but whoever loses their life for me and for the gospel will save it" (Mark 8:34–35). And then . . . guess what? Mark switches Simon Peter out for a different Simon, a stranger from Cyrene, as the one who actually "takes up his cross and follows" (Mark 15:21). Everyone is getting switched out here, exactly conveying the gospel message itself. This is symbolic myth. Parable. Not history. That Luke gets this as the point of the "two criminals" at the cross is revealed by how he changed that story: by having that very message understood by one of the two criminals, to whom Jesus thereby promises salvation. Clearly those criminals are not included in the story "for no reason." They are put there to teach a lesson about the gospel. We therefore cannot conclude there is any history behind this. We have no evidence *that's* the reason. Whereas we have plenty of evidence the reason was literary. And even at worst, again, either interpretation is *equally likely*, making this evidence *for neither*.

Contrary to the zealot hypothesis, the Gospel authors were taking the whole phenomenon of violent messianic pretenders and inventing a Jesus as their opposite, to teach that only those who "get it" shall thus find salvation, the rest damnation. The violent model's folly was particularly acute when the Evangelists wrote, as it had just led to the total destruction of Jerusalem, Judea, and God's own temple and temple cult in the year 70—the very temple cult the Christians had always sought to replace with their own atoning celestial sacrifice (as explained in Hebrews 9). We cannot take everything they wrote to convey this message *out of its context*, the very context they chose to give it, and then proclaim we know better why they included it. That's the exact opposite of how to understand an author. If you want to know why an author put some particular scene or saying or detail where he did, you need to look at what function it serves in the context its author chose for it: the immediate context of the story or scene it's in (or in between or surrounds), and the overall context of the repeated themes of the whole narrative, even the context of the story it is redacting and thus changing (and thus what the author intends to mean differently than his source). And whatever *that* is, it will be entirely, intentionally coherent within each author, though not necessarily *between* authors; the whole point of redacting Mark into what we call Matthew and Luke and John was to change the messaging. But each writes what they do with their own coherent aims, leaving nothing to random chance, nothing to undermine them. If you ignore that fact, you will surely fail to understand what they wrote and why they wrote it.

So when we come to compare the zealot hypothesis not with competing hypotheses of historicity but with the competing hypothesis I've laid out here, the futility of the enterprise becomes even more clear. The Gospels unmistakably are writing myth and fiction, parables to convey moral teachings and messages about the gist of the "gospel" and God's plan. That's true even if there was a real Jesus. It's true even if they used some real things about Jesus in their fictions—though we have no logically valid way to discern if they did. But if this all started as Paul appears to say, in revelations of a hidden cosmic atoning death and resurrection (1 Corinthians 2:6 and 15:3–5, Galatians 1:11–17, Romans 16:25–26; even, soon after Paul, Hebrews 9), then contrary to advocates of the zealot hypothesis, or any other hypothesis, we don't need a "political" reason for the teaching that Jesus was "hung as a curse" to atone for the world's sins (Galatians 3:13). We already have a fully plausible mystical, scriptural, and cultural reason for that. Just as we don't need a "political" reason to explain the murders of Osiris or Romulus or Inanna or Bacchus or any other slain-but-exalted personal savior. Paul himself tells us the reason for the crucifixion was cosmic and mystical—to trick the "archons of this aeon" who, as 1 Corinthians 2:6–10 says, would understand the esoteric magic at work and thus would *not* have killed Jesus if they knew what would happen. So it was *not* political—as every earthly authority, Paul tells us in Romans 13, does not but do God's will. We have no evidence it was ever really otherwise.

This same error of circular reasoning appears throughout the writings of zealot-hypothesis defenders. For example, their argument from the Testimonium Flavianum—a paragraph about Jesus in the manuscripts of Josephus that Christians clearly installed there to glorify Jesus. Defenders of the zealot thesis ask why someone today can edit that paragraph to get "a negative evaluation of Jesus," unless Josephus had originally written a hostile account of Jesus that Christians later "fixed." But this is self-fulfilling prophecy: you can do that with any text. If you decide in advance all the clearly positive things are false, and everything that remains is to be *interpreted* negatively, what remains will always be negative. The conclusion is being used as the premise to get the conclusion. Invalid.

When we look at that passage as the coherent text that it is, it exactly matches Christian propaganda; in fact, it derives from the Emmaus narrative in the Gospel of Luke, and not a single sentence in it matches Josephan style or practice as a historian. The conclusion should be obvious: Josephus didn't write any of this. By contrast, even the "negative" passage we can "invent" by deciding to remove everything positive from it doesn't explain its location in Josephus's narrative, which is a list of events that drove the Jews to war. Even edited to strip everything triumphal out of it, the Testimonium that's left over still makes no sense in such a context. There is simply no basis to believe any of this came from Josephus. Whereas we can fully account for every word and sentence of that paragraph, and their completed arrangement, with the hypothesis of Christian forgery. *And we don't have to edit one word of the text to get that result.* We therefore need no other explanation of it. Occam's Razor truly prevails here.

The zealot advocates do this again when they say something like, for instance, "Once stripped of all the legendary stuff, the Gospels contain material which is not plausibly reducible to mere invention." Of course. Because you just arbitrarily removed its literary context. If you circularly assume that "context doesn't matter," and then remove it, and then act surprised that what remains doesn't fit the author's intentions, you are eating your own tail. Your conclusion is being used as a premise to prove the conclusion. This is not how historians should be reading stories. They should not be arbitrarily removing material and acting like what remains would have been familiar to the author. No. The author wrote the whole thing on purpose; all the parts serve a function, together. You cannot understand what they wrote by removing pieces. Nor, indeed, should you even be reading the Gospels as if they were intended literally, when their original author specifically warned us not to do that (Mark 4:10–13). The more so when no literal reading makes realistic sense, but it all makes perfect sense as allegory, a known and popular mode of story composition in antiquity. Even more so when the intention of the Gospels is to portray Jesus as the ideal missionary—self-sacrificial, miracle-working, gospel-teaching, a model to follow in every scene. This is what they are inventing. It is an ahistorical ideal; but there is nothing implausible about it being so. All myth operated like that.

Zealot-hypothesis advocates then do the reverse when they criticize several scholars who have noted Mark's adaptation of a later legend of Jesus ben Ananias to structure the trial and death of Jesus. Because their theory needs those elements to be real details about Jesus, not borrowed details from a completely unrelated person—who was also no zealot or militarist. They will do this, for example, by merely mentioning a couple details in common between those two men's stories and concluding that can happen "by chance." But the scholars who originally noted the parallels between these two Jesuses do *not* proceed to that conclusion from a mere couple of details. The zealot advocates are ignoring the actual argument: the parallels number *over twenty* and, moreover, make a peculiar construct *together*, and *that* is how we know Mark is using that legend to build his narrative on. He simply builds on that story using scripture like the Psalms and Isaiah and other "pesherized" texts, and the specific needs of his narrative. In fact, once we add all those up, *there is nothing left in the text.* That's why we doubt there is anything historical in it. Critics of these kinds of conclusions simply aren't addressing the arguments for them. Which is a common failure among defenders of historicity—one of the clearest reasons we know they are wrong.

And this is true of all historicists, including those who propose Jesus was really a magician, that he was a faith-healer, that he was an exorcist, that he was a Cynic sage, that he was a counter-cultural Rabbi, that he was an apocalyptic prophet, that he was a crazed schizophrenic, or any other theory. They all get each conclusion by taking everything out of context, using their thesis as a premise to decide which evidence is authentic and which fake, and then circularly using that outcome to prove their thesis.

This is neither valid nor credible historical reasoning. Worse, they do this by ignoring the evidence in Paul that contradicts every single one of those theories. Paul says, for example, that Jesus relinquished all powers in the incarnation (in Philippians 2:6–11), and thus cannot have performed any miracles or exorcisms—and accordingly, Paul never mentions Jesus ever doing so, not even as examples for Christians to follow in performing them themselves. Likewise, Paul never cites parables; evincing that Jesus never taught with them. That was an invention of the authors of the Gospels. Nor is there any Cynic moralizing from Jesus in Paul. Nor is Jesus ever called a Rabbi in Paul. Nor is Jesus ever called a living prophet in Paul. And so on.

Even when historicists try to defend a "biological kin" reading of Paul's calling a certain James a "Brother of the Lord" in Galatians, for example, they simply import their own assumptions, treating implausible, unsourced legends spun off by Christians a century and a half later as reliable history, and ignoring all arguments to the contrary and all the evidence from the first century which does not support their reading. We should be looking at the evidence nearer in time, and in Paul himself—his actual words and grammar and rhetoric—not at centuries-late legends; we should not be importing assumptions, but asking *why* we are preferring one set of assumptions to another—and then preferring neither when we have no good answer. We should be asking: how likely is it that *Paul* would say this, given what we know *from Paul*? We should not be "assuming" Paul knew or meant things he never says he knew or meant. That would be arguing the wrong way around, using conclusions as premises again to prove the conclusions.

Similarly, critics of doubting historicity argue that it's "possible" for these immense patterns and layers of mythology in the Gospels to be added onto the stories of historical people (like Alexander the Great, Julius Caesar, Caesar Augustus, or Apollonius of Tyana), ignoring that the doubters of Jesus' historicity *have already said that*. So once again they are ignoring our actual argument, which is not that this is impossible, but that it's not common, and is therefore *improbable*, unless we have evidence to reverse that conclusion, precisely as we do in the case of the men they name—none of the evidence we have for whose historicity we have for Jesus. (Of those just named, Apollonius alone may be close in paucity of credible evidence—but his historicity is also likewise doubtable.) As I'll show in chapter six I have demonstrated this by counting up examples of comparably mythologized persons and finding that they so rarely turn out to be historical that we have every reason to doubt any are *except* those we have independent evidence of. If historians wish to argue it's instead *common* for this to happen, that in fact most comparably mythologized persons *existed*, they need to argue this, with data. Otherwise they simply aren't responding to the facts. In chapter five I'll show the contrary point, that persons whose historicity we are confident of always have evidence for their existence that we lack for Jesus. Again, if you wish to argue against this, too, then present the evidence for Jesus that's comparable to the evidence for these others. But alas, there is none. And that's the problem. Ignoring the problem does not make it go away.

Similarly, historicists will falsely claim that our conclusion depends on the passages in Josephus or Tacitus being wholly forgeries—when in fact that has no effect on our conclusion either way. They thus ignore our actual argument: these authors give no indication of having any other source of information but the Gospels or informants relying on the Gospels, and therefore cannot corroborate them, which is a basic principle of all historical reasoning. Someone just repeating what someone else said is simply *not* evidence that what the first person said is true. And if you can't establish that what someone is saying is independent of those other sources you already have, *you can't use it as if it were.*

This failure to grasp the correct logic of our arguments is a common theme among defenders of historicity. You might want to ask why. For example, historicists think we *depend* on auxiliary hypotheses, like that the name 'Alexander' and 'Rufus' in Mark 15:21 are a symbolic reference to the conquerer Alexander the Great and the philosopher Musonius Rufus (a mere possibility I suggested in *Historicity*), when in fact this is no more auxiliary than supposing what is *equally* not in evidence, that Mark mentioned them because these were historical Christian witnesses—or whatever theory you propose to explain why Mark mentioned them. In other words, *both* historicity and mythicism depend on auxiliary hypotheses. And when we measure the arguments for both, it's a wash: neither comes out any more likely than the other. Consequently, we cannot use evidence such as Mark's naming the sons of Simon of

Cyrene to argue *for either theory*. Take careful note here. We do not argue that this detail is evidence against historicity. We've only argued it is *not* evidence *for* historicity. Defenders of historicity frequently confuse these two arguments, and consequently rarely respond to what we are saying. This error describes a lot of what they think they are rebutting, from our position on whether Paul or the Evangelists had any reliable information about Jesus to our positions regarding the redaction history of *The Ascension of Isaiah*, or pretty much anything else.

This blindness to their own auxiliary hypotheses, and mischaracterization of our contrary arguments, and thus their erroneous supposition that historicity is the simpler hypothesis, is thus yet another repeated error. The defenders of historicity accuse us of leaning on auxiliary hypotheses, and then invent a bunch of auxiliary hypotheses of their own, for example, (1) to explain away the very bizarre silences in Paul and the rest of the historical record; (2) to invent a new version-history for the Testimonium Flavianum; (3) to decide which passages of the Gospels to regard as fossils and which fabrications; and so on. All so as to conveniently match their predetermined conclusion that Jesus was a Zealot (a conclusion almost as unpopular in the field as our own), or an Apocalyptic Prophet, or a Cynic Sage, or whatever thesis they are defending, which are all only achievable, just as I've noted, by circular reasoning. Their theory is not simple. It's wildly complex. It requires dozens of hidden assumptions. No fewer than ours. To be fair, all theories must in cases like this—because the evidence regarding Jesus is scanty, deeply contradictory, compromised, and mysterious, and filled with unreliable, unverifiable, and implausible material. So we have to come up with whole bodies of explanation no matter what theory we propose. Which doesn't help their position any more than ours.

We must crucially distinguish between what we have evidence *for*—which we call facts—and what we are proposing to *explain* the evidence we have—which we call theories. Those are not the same things. And any fair comparison of alternative explanations requires addressing that, without circular arguments or assumptions without evidence. When we go back through the texts *logically*, we simply don't get the results historicists claim. Which leads us to a crucial revelation: the fact that historicists depend on illogical arguments should cause us to doubt their judgment—and thus, too, their conclusions.

And indeed that's just what happens. When we undertake *the correct* method for the Gospels, the method of comparing *the best* hypotheses with each other to assess their *relative* explanatory merit, we find nothing in them can be confidently ascribed to history rather than intentional symbolic fiction, just as for all other mythical heroes who were given historicizing biographies, whether in Jewish history (such as Moses or Joseph or Daniel or Tobit) or Gentile (such as Aesop or Romulus or Inanna or Osiris). This has been demonstrated in the literature time and again, from Randel Helms' *Gospel Fictions* and Thomas Brodie's *Birthing of the New Testament* to John D. Crossan's *Power of Parable* and M. David Litwa's *How the Gospels Became History*; even in Dennis MacDonald's *Mythologizing Jesus* and *Two Shipwrecked Gospels*; and in countless more research articles and monographs, by hundreds of experts, over dozens of years. I summarize the evidence fairly conclusively in the tenth chapter of my book *On the Historicity of Jesus*.

There just isn't any way to confidently get history out of the Gospels. Even if any is in there, we can't tell what.

Arriving at the Conclusion

We can already see in the pre-Gospel texts of Paul and Hebrews that no political reason was needed to imagine a Christ crucified: they had fully understandable theological, mystical, and scriptural reasons to have imagined that. It explains their entire ability to reject the temple cult and claim the end was truly nigh. Likewise, no historical reason was needed to make Jesus come from Nazareth. The Gospels themselves *tell* us a Nazareth origin for Jesus was contrived out of scripture (from a passage we know is now lost, cited in Matthew 2:23, and another we still have, cited in 4:12–16; cf. Isaiah 9:1–7). We also know his original title of "Nazorian" originally meant something other than Nazarene, so the latter interpretation must have been invented later. Both facts combine to entail we *can't* say his hailing from Nazareth must have been historical. The betrayal by Judas (whose name essentially, and rather conveniently, means "Jew") is likewise clearly a later invention; it was unknown to Paul, who says Jesus was "handed over" *by God*, not any backstabbing "Jew" (Romans 8.32). In Paul's time it was even a credal fact that "the twelve" were intact at the first revelation of Jesus (1 Corinthians 15:5). That one of them turned coat and hung himself beforehand appears to be a later contrivance. *We have no evidence it wasn't.* And so on, for every detail one might try to pin as historical. We always end up with the same results.

As I wrote in *Proving History*:

> That Jesus had enemies who slandered him, that Jesus went to parties with sinners to save them, that Jesus' family rejected him, and so on, all face the same problems of self-contradiction (had they been a problem, they would have been removed or altered long before Mark even wrote), ignorance (we don't really know whether these stories were embarrassing to the communities who told them at the time they were first told), and self-defeat (any reason to preserve them if true can be just as much reason to fabricate them, and in every case we can easily construct plausible motives for their invention, which often make even more sense than the stories being true).

In fact, all such stories had obvious symbolic reasons to invent them, to teach lessons about the gospel. So there is no logically valid way to confirm their historicity.

I likewise show in my book *Proving History* that every peer-reviewed study of *every* method nevertheless used to try and "extract" history from the Gospels found that they don't work for anything particular to Jesus, and I there illustrate why that finding is quite correct. You simply *can't* get to history by hypothesizing some underlying Aramaic, or by thinking no one ever invented embarrassing stories on purpose, or even assuming you know what these authors thought was an embarrassing story—or that anything novel or deviant must come from Jesus, or that shorter stories are truer, or that vivid details never appear in fiction (or real places and personages or other local color), or that a story so liked it gets retold many times is thereby "multiply corroborated." None of these methods are logically valid; or when valid, never apply to anything in the Gospels. Those leaning on these suspect methods always rely on improbable assumptions, such as regarding how ancient authors even composed stories, or ignore the best alternative explanations of why something is being said by any given author, alternatives that are as likely or even more likely than that "they included it because it was true."

Only a proper comparative method can logically work: you have to compare your hypothesis as to why an author wrote some particular thing, with the *best* competing explanations of that same outcome—not straw men of your own or anyone else's contrivance. You cannot ignore those explanations, or simply dismiss them, or assume without evidence that the explanation you prefer must be any more likely. And yet, that historicity is only ever defended by *ignoring* the most plausible alternative accounts of what the Gospel authors were doing is one of the strongest arguments against it. No legitimate conclusion would depend on such a fallacious approach to the evidence.

4

All the Historians on a Single Postcard

In 75 A.D. a general in the Jewish war against Rome, a man named Joseph (now more known by the Latinized form of his name, Josephus), wrote a history of that war and the century of events leading up to it, aptly titled *History of the Jewish War against the Romans*, but more commonly known today as simply *The Jewish War*. In this he tells us about a man named Jesus, who came to the feast of tabernacles in Jerusalem in the 60s A.D., "when the city was enjoying profound peace and prosperity." And there this Jesus would pester crowds day and night with his warnings of impending doom. "A voice from the east," he would say, "a voice from the west, a voice from the four winds, a voice against Jerusalem and the temple, a voice against the bridegroom and the bride, a voice against all the people!"

The Jewish leaders were outraged and had this Jesus arrested and told him to stop. He would not answer them, so they beat him. But they could not convict him of anything and let him go. Still he continued his preaching. So they accused him of being possessed by demons. And then hauled him into the court of the Roman prefect. The Roman soldiers "flayed him to the bone with scourges." And yet he "neither begged for mercy nor shed a tear" but merely kept repeating, "Woe to Jerusalem!" When the Roman prefect asked him "who he was and where he came from and why he uttered these cries," Jesus "answered him never a word." He just kept repeating his declarations of woe against Jerusalem. The prefect concluded he was insane and let him go. And Jesus continued to preach his woes to the city, until war did come. Then, with the city under siege by Roman forces, "he went round the walls shouting" his dirge, "Woe once more to the city and to the people and to the temple," and then he added one final line, "and woe to me also." At which moment "a stone hurled from a catapult struck and killed him on the spot."

Notice how Josephus tells the story of this Jesus. The narrative, the details, the quotations, the careful description of each step. It is intelligible. It draws us in. It explains itself. It fits its context. And it illuminates something Josephus was trying to communicate about the madness of the times leading to the war he was trying to explain. As I mentioned in the last chapter, we know the author of the Gospel according to Mark patterned his passion of the Christ in part after Joseph's story of this other, wholly unrelated Jesus, Jesus ben Ananias, who lived decades after Christianity even began. But of course this Jesus had nothing to do with originating that religion. He was never even a part of it. The author of Mark simply saw utility in his story, and used the outline of it to structure a story for his own tale of an apocalyptic martyr, his own Jesus Christ.

This tells us two things. One, Mark was making his story up, and using other people's stories as models to do it. And two, if Josephus had ever written about our Jesus, his account of that Jesus would look more like his account of this Jesus: it would have a narrative, it would have details and quotations, there would be a careful description of each causal step. It would be intelligible. It would draw us in. It would explain itself. It would fit its context. And it would illuminate something Josephus was trying to communicate about the madness of the times leading to the war he was trying to explain.

Instead, we get this, in Josephus's later work on the *Antiquities of the Jews*:

> And there was about this time Jesus, a wise man, if we really
> must call him a man, for he was a doer of incredible deeds,

a teacher of men who receive the truth gladly, and he won over many Jews, and also many of the Greeks. This man was the Christ. And when, on the accusation of the leading men among us, Pilate had condemned him to a cross, those who had first loved him did not cease to. For he appeared to them on the third day, alive again, after the divine prophets had spoken these and countless other marvels about him. And even until now the tribe of the Christians, so named from this man, has not failed.

Of course, even at a glance anyone can see this would be an absurd paragraph from the hand of a devout Jew and sophisticated author who otherwise writes far more elegant prose, and usually responsibly explains to his readers anything strange. This passage is self-evidently a fawning and gullible Christian fabrication, in fact matching the same sequence of assertions found in Luke's Emmaus narrative. It also does not significantly match the style of Josephus. It deviates enough even from his preferred vocabulary, but even more so his grammatical preferences, idiom, and discourse features. It also does not match how Josephus writes about any other Jewish sects—where he always describes their doctrines and how they differ from each other, and their role in Jewish society. It also fails to match how he writes about other holy men—like John the Baptist, or Eleazar the Exorcist, or any of the several charismatic figures he describes as messianic hopefuls (thus, "Christs") attempting to emulate the role of the biblical Joshua (thus, "Jesus," that being just a modern respelling of the name Joshua).

So there is no way Josephus wrote this passage. It's also inserted into the text of Josephus at a point where it does not even make any narrative sense. Before and after this he is relating events that led to the Jewish war. This has nothing to do with that. Josephus gives no reason for any digression to occur here either. And immediately after this passage, he begins, "About the same time also another sad calamity put the Jews into disorder." Which clearly refers to the previous passage about Pontius Pilate's violent suppression of Jewish agitators—not this fawning, happy passage about the amazing wonderful Jesus. Moreover, that very next passage is a lengthy narrative about a religious scandal, exemplifying exactly how Josephus would have written up an account of Jesus, had he ever done so—in greater length, detail, and causal clarity. So he probably never did. And just as we'd thus expect, no other author discovered this passage in Josephus until hundreds of years later. The ancient Christian scholar Origen, for example, writing in the early third century, scoured the text of Josephus for passages to cite or respond to about Jesus, yet evidently didn't find this one, or anything at all. So we can be quite certain this wasn't there.

This is actually a common consensus now of mainstream experts. Nearly everyone pretty much agrees Josephus did not write this passage. Many still want to believe that maybe he wrote *something* about Jesus here, something that was meddled with and totally transformed by later Christian forgers, but there is actually no evidence of that. And what we have no evidence for, we ought not assert. There is, rather, a great deal of evidence against *anything* in this passage coming from the hand of Josephus, most of which I already summarize in *On the Historicity of Jesus*, and after that on my blog (at richardcarrier.info), where I also survey the most recent scholarship in "Josephus on Jesus? Why You Can't Cite Opinions Before 2014." I won't belabor the point here. You can check the evidence and the scholarship backing it in my book and ensuing article. The so-called Testimonium Flavianum is a forgery. And there is no honest reason to doubt that.

Even the other passage in Josephus, where he supposedly described the execution of James "the brother of Jesus, the one called Christ," is of doubtful authenticity. I list half a dozen reasons to doubt Josephus ever wrote "the one called Christ" in *On the Historicity of Jesus*, reasons anyone who wants to challenge this must contend with. But that doesn't even matter. We know for a fact all baptized Christians considered themselves Brothers of the Lord (a fact we'll look more closely at in chapter nine), and thus as brothers of Jesus. We have no evidence Josephus understood the difference. So that he relates the death of a "Brother of Jesus" doesn't help us verify this meant an actual *biological* brother of Jesus. Similarly, no matter what "might" have been in the text where that other, fawning homage to the Gospel Jesus appears now instead, we have no evidence it would have derived from any other source than the Gospels, or Christian informants quoting the Gospels. It therefore cannot corroborate them.

Josephus is therefore useless to us as evidence. No matter which way you shake it, all we have in Josephus is, at best, the repetition of claims first recorded by the author of Mark; probably even through the embellishments of Mark's second redactor, Luke. But that doesn't help us determine whether Mark invented those claims or they really happened, or whether Luke's embellishments came from any source outside his own creative imagination. So again all we have as evidence is the Gospel of Mark. *Everything else just repeats or elaborates on that*—even Josephus, if Josephus even wrote anything at all on the matter.

And this is the case, alas, *for all other references to Jesus outside the Bible.* Hence in the words of Bart Ehrman, "Whether or not Jesus lived has to be decided on other kinds of evidence from this" (*Did Jesus Exist*, p. 65). In *The Lost Gospel of Judas* Ehrman said something similar regarding Paul:

> For Paul, what mattered about Jesus is that he was crucified and that God raised him from the dead. What happened before then seems to have had relatively little importance. My undergraduate students sometimes don't believe this, and so I assign a little exercise. I have them read through the letters written by Paul and make a list of everything that he tells us concerning Jesus' life—that is, the things Jesus said, did, and experienced from the time he was born until the time he died. What students are often surprised to learn is that to make a complete list, they don't need even a four-by-six index card.

This is, of course, startlingly bizarre. It's almost as if Jesus had no life to record before his death, that the events of his incarnation, suffering, and death were just cosmic theological events known only, as Paul himself says, through private revelations and hidden messages in scripture (Romans 16:25–26), not the historical culmination of a great man's life. More on that later. But for now, take note: what's almost as weird is that much the same can be said of *all subsequent historians.* If you tried to make a list of all the historians outside the Bible who mention a historical Jesus in the ensuing two hundred years—not merely mentioning that some people worshiped a deity named Jesus, but also that he was an actual man in human history—you "don't need even a four-by-six index card." Worse, not a single entry on that card will be usable as evidence. Every one of them is just a later author repeating what the Gospels said or what Christians relying on those Gospels said; there's not a single instance of any detail being corroborated through any other source.

By itself we can accept this. As I've said before, maybe Jesus was a total nobody, and that's why no one in his time ever mentioned him, and no one after that ever really researched anything about him. Before the Gospels, we only get Epistles that are vague on where Jesus lived and died. After the Gospels, the only written source anyone could get ahold of was simply the Gospels, which all trace back to just one Gospel, the Gospel "according to Mark." And that's it. That could be true and still Jesus could have existed. But we would then have to admit: Jesus can't have been as famous as the Gospels portray. Still, a lot of people don't know this fact, or even try to deny it, instead multiplying "sources" for Jesus that don't exist or that aren't really sources. So I'll expand on the point a little more for their benefit, and that of anyone else who might be taken in by their con or folly. Throughout all this, though, one basic historical principle must be understood: an author who just repeats what another source said is not a "source" themselves and thus cannot legitimately be counted as such. And an author who never even places Jesus in history obviously can't even *be* a source for placing him in history. And yet outside the Bible, one or the other, that's all we've got.

Of course other Gospels continued to be written, as many as forty altogether. Not a single one exhibits signs of coming from any actual source; they merely embellish prior Gospels with increasing fabrication and fictionalization. Just as the canonical Gospels already appear to do with simply that lone, original Gospel, Mark. Later Christian authors, all dating a hundred years or more after the fact, like Tertullian of Africa or Clement of Alexandria, or Ignatius or Quadratus or Aristides or Justin, reveal they had no sources at all other than those same Gospels—and legends spun out of them later. Even surviving traces from lost authors, like Papias or Hegesippus, reveal they had no other sources to count on, just unsourced legends embellishing again on what the Gospel of Mark had begun—or even later, and wholly absurd, apocryphal tales; also unsourced. They also date a hundred years or more after the fact. Inside the Bible, but outside the Gospels (and Acts, which is just a chronological extension of Luke's Gospel), the only texts that clearly historicized Jesus (like 2 Peter and 1 Timothy) mainstream scholars already agree are second-century forgeries—building, again, on the Gospels. Which leaves only one Christian text we *know* to be written in the first century that isn't already in the Bible—the epistle of 1 Clement. Which never mentions Jesus being a historical man on earth (a point I illustrate in detail, as with nearly all the other authors I mention in this chapter, in *On the Historicity of Jesus*).

So that leaves non-Christian authors. Of those, you'll often hear named Josephus, Tacitus, Pliny, Phlegon, Lucian, Celsus, Suetonius, Thallus, and "Mara Bar Serapion." But Mara just vaguely alludes to existing Christian beliefs; his text is undatable and cites no sources. Completely of no use. Likewise Lucian and Celsus, also writing over a century after the fact, are as late or later than Mara, and simply cite the Gospels—and Christians citing the Gospels—as their only source. Useless. Pliny and Suetonius never mention Jesus being a historical person. And Thallus and Phlegon never mentioned Jesus at all.

That leaves only Josephus, whose text we already saw is useless to us as evidence; and Tacitus, whose surviving text contains the singular line, "Christ, the originator of the [Christian] name, was executed by the procurator Pontius Pilate in the reign of Tiberius." Which, by coming so late and citing no sources, is likewise useless. That Tacitus even wrote this line is doubtable (I explain why in *On the Historicity of Jesus*). But even if he did, just like Josephus, we can establish no source he used for it other than the Gospels or Christian informants relying on the Gospels. As again even Bart Ehrman admits, "Tacitus is basing this comment on hearsay," not "research" (*Did Jesus Exist?* p. 56). So again no matter which way we shake it, Tacitus is as useless a source to us as Josephus. The most you could even attempt to get out of them is evidence the Gospels were circulating by the turn of the century (Josephus wrote around 93 A.D.; Tacitus, 116 A.D.), which we already agree was the case. That helps us not one bit in determining whether those Gospels recorded any real history.

This leaves defenders of Jesus' historicity in a real pickle. It's a very uncomfortable position to be in. Which is why they try to make stuff up, rather than admit the total lack of evidence and what that must mean for them. They "invent" archaeological evidence that doesn't exist, like false claims to have discovered "Peter's house" or the "Tomb of Jesus," or the Shroud of Turin. All baloney. There is no archaeological evidence attesting to a historical Jesus. Many will at least admit that. But then it will be "claimed" that "surely" Josephus and Tacitus "fact-checked" their assertions and thus used sources other than the Gospels or Christians merely echoing them. There is no evidence they did or even would have. So once again, just more assertions without evidence, being cited now as "evidence." Welcome to historicity apologetics. Likewise, it will be claimed Suetonius "must" have meant Jesus when he instead reports that a Jewish man named "Chrestus" stirred up riots in Rome decades after Jesus "Christ" is supposed to have died. Wrong name. Wrong decade. Wrong continent. No recorded death or connection to Christianity. No evidence for Jesus here. Surely, if Suetonius got *every single thing wrong* about "Christ," he can't have had any reliable sources in the matter—and he was writing this *years after* Tacitus. So even if we trusted *made up* evidence, we would get no usable evidence here.

Some will then try to insist Thallus and Phlegon "did" mention Jesus, because a much later Christian author, Julius of Africa, "said" they did. But he didn't. He only said they recorded a noonday eclipse of the sun in what is now northern Turkey in the 30s A.D. and that it coincided with an earthquake there. It was *Julius* who tried to claim this was the darkness and earthquake the Gospels claimed occurred at Jesus' death. They themselves never said that, nor linked this or anything at all to any man named Jesus or Christ. Which makes sense, as northern Turkey is over a thousand kilometers from Jerusalem, and solar eclipses cannot occur at Passover when all Gospels claim Jesus died—so neither the eclipse nor earthquake they record would have been experienced there or then. So again, this is made-up evidence. There is no evidence for Jesus in either author. There isn't even a mention of him, nor any event that could be connected with him. "But Pliny mentions Jesus," we'll then hear. Yes—as the "god" Christians "worshiped." No mention of his ever being a real person. So there's no evidence here either. And even if Pliny *had* mentioned such a thing, he wrote in the 110s A.D., long after the Gospels had been circulating their made-up stories about Jesus; and Pliny tells us his source was a Christian informant. What would that informant have told him? Probably just what "Mark" had put into print a lifetime earlier. So even in that *hypothetical* scenario, Pliny would again be useless. A copy of a source is not a source.

Outside the Bible there are no records of Jesus' existence for sixty to a hundred years. And even within that later period (between sixty and a hundred years after), still no usable references exist: neither Josephus nor Tacitus cite any sources, nor can we establish they had any other than the Gospels (or Christians citing them). Never mind that it's likely neither author actually mentioned Jesus in the first place. Even if we set that possibility aside, still neither is usable. Meanwhile, outside those unusable passages in the text of Josephus, we have no Jewish sources for Jesus at all until the Middle Ages, when we get to mentions in the Talmud—which, as we noted in chapter one, place Jesus a hundred years earlier than the Gospels do, and tell a very different account of him, an even bigger problem for defenders of historicity. Which leaves us with the passages in pagan sources. All of which either are forgeries, don't actually mention a historical Jesus, or (again) only repeat what the Gospels were saying. Not a single one is usable as evidence.

Meanwhile, when we look at Christian literature, including their Bible, we see a culture rampant with the forging of evidence. In fact, if we exclude things like homilies and commentaries, all mainstream scholars agree: most of what Christians wrote were forgeries or contain forgeries. Most Christian Epistles—of the hundred or so we have spanning three centuries—are forgeries. Half the Epistles even in the Bible are forgeries. Most of the forty or so Gospels written over those same three centuries are forgeries. As were most of the half-dozen or so Acts that were written. Indeed, it's not just texts; every surviving manuscript from the New Testament also contains scribal additions, deletions, alterations, or errors. The Gospel of Mark alone was given as many as five different endings—most of which you won't have heard about, because Christians today don't like to talk about all the forged material we've found in Gospel manuscripts.

In fact, in the whole category of Gospels, Acts, and Epistles, *forgery was the normal mode of Christian production*. So why on earth would we trust *any* Gospel as our only real source for the historicity of Jesus? Much less an anonymous Gospel, written a lifetime later, in a land and a language quite foreign to Jesus, citing no sources, and corroborated by no one? And yet that is all we have: just the Gospel of Mark, and later repetitions and embellishments of the Gospel of Mark. That's all we have in the Bible. That's all we have outside the Bible. *There is no other source for the historical existence of Jesus.* And yet, since almost all the Gospels Christians ever wrote are today agreed to be forgeries, or otherwise wholesale fictions, we have no *honest* reason to believe Mark's is anything other than more of the same. That's pretty much the worst evidence you could ever have for anyone's existence.

Why, then, are we so confident Jesus existed?

5

But Isn't Jesus as Attested
as Any Other Famous Dude?

So that's where we are. No contemporary of Jesus ever mentioned him. That means none. No historian. No writer of any kind. No inscriptions. No documents. No letters. With only one sure exception: the Apostle Paul at least knew *about* Jesus. But he admits he never met the man—and Paul isn't even clear on whether Jesus was ever a man one *could* meet, rather than an angel one could only see in dreams or visions. The Gospels, meanwhile, were written a lifetime later, not by eyewitnesses nor even contemporaries, but by persons unknown, in a foreign land and language. And even if we trust the letters of James and Jude and 1 Peter or even Hebrews or 1 Clement to be authentic, the only other letters plausibly dating before the Gospels, none seems to know about a Jesus one could meet in the normal way either. Like Paul, they only know of a guy whose story they had to discover by mystical experience or hidden in ancient scripture. So even these guys—supposedly eyewitnesses—don't give any eyewitness account of Jesus. *There is no eyewitness account of Jesus.*

So far as we can honestly tell, there never was. Because nothing else exists outside Christian propaganda. All other references to an earthbound Jesus, even in pagan histories, merely repeat claims originating in the Gospels. Not a single claim about Jesus in them is corroborated by any other source but them. And they, in fact, all derive from a single Gospel, Mark. It really just all goes back to one single document—and later imaginative embellishments to it.

This is kind of a problem. A big problem, you might say. There are only two ways a historian can respond to this problem, if they want to salvage the claim that there was a historical Jesus. One of those ways is sensible. The other is not.

The sensible way is to say, "Well, okay, Jesus must not have been as famous as the Gospels say." He was not renowned throughout all Judea and Galilee and Syria (Matthew 4:24, Luke 7:17, Mark 1:28). He didn't command the attention of the people of Jerusalem upon marching into it. He didn't clear a ten-acre temple square. He didn't feed thousands of people in the wild or kill thousands of pigs with an exorcism. He didn't draw hordes of Jews calling for his blood. He must have been a very obscure man who did nothing impressive enough for anyone to notice beyond a few followers of limited literacy and some crowds and leaders who took a passing but ultimately minimal interest in him. Maybe he was at best one of dozens of messianic claimants, fringe Rabbis, and Jewish counterculturalists whom we know were roaming the land back then, one of barely any note compared to others who got more attention for having made a bigger splash at the time.

The historian Josephus, for example, tells the stories of several men claiming to be a "Jesus Christ," meaning a new and final Joshua—someone echoing the *original* liberator of Israel in the Old Testament, now come to be the *final* liberator of Israel, a messianic linchpin who would bring on the end of the world. As I already explained, "Jesus" is just an awkward English spelling of Joshua. They're the same name. And "Christ," from *Christos*, is just the Greek word for "Messiah," meaning, "Anointed," as in "Chosen One." These heroes, Josephus tells us, tried to replicate the deeds of the mythical Joshua, like parting the Jordan or magically toppling the walls of a city. So by making themselves out to be a Joshua, and a Messiah, these men were basically marketing themselves as a Jesus Christ. With colorful names like The Samaritan, The Egyptian, The Impostor, and one mysteriously named Theudas (possibly meaning Gift of God), these guys got into actual military battles with Roman soldiers. Hence they made the history books. Some random one of maybe a dozen others who merely got themselves executed would likely never gain any historian's notice.

So it's entirely possible Jesus just wasn't that famous—that he didn't really do anything big or amazing enough to get anyone's attention in the historical record. And it's possible the Christian movement after him was never very large and lacked for literate composers to take down records and memoirs or write many letters—or they all assumed the world would soon end, "So what's the point in writing anything down?" The first writing we know of from any Christian came decades later, some few letters of Paul (though he wrote more than we have now), composed late in his ministry. Letters from other Christians we have (whether authentic or forged) appear to date just as late or later. And these all were occasioned by a new and unexpected need created by decades of evangelism: to reign in and keep under control diverse congregations spread across thousands of miles . . . but still expecting the world to end any minute now. The Gospels only began to be composed when so many decades had passed that the original expectation of the imminent end of the world had long been crushed—a disappointment needing explanation.

So that could be why there are no eyewitness records, no contemporary records, no inscriptions or papyri, no direct documentation for a historical Jesus, nor any references to any, anywhere. If we accept the premise—that Jesus was actually a relative nobody—then we can't conclude he didn't exist merely because there is no recent or reliable record of him. Lots of people in antiquity existed who nevertheless were never, or barely or poorly, attested. Although that's also the same evidence we'd expect if someone didn't exist. So admitting this doesn't *help*, either. To get around this lack of evidence we still have to stick to our guns on this explanation, abandoning all theories of a historical Jesus that imagine him at all publicly remarkable. We'd have to bite the bullet and admit he wasn't. But at least we could then rescue the possibility that he nevertheless did exist in some sense.

That's the sensible thing to say.

Want to know what's *not* sensible to say? What too many historians actually resort to: that the evidence for Jesus is so overwhelmingly good that if we were to doubt his existence we'd have to doubt the existence of even such luminaries as Socrates, Alexander the Great, Spartacus, Hannibal, Julius or Tiberius Caesar, and even Pontius Pilate! "And that would be absurd!" So say those who say this. Which includes a lot of serious, credentialed historians. And yet it's what *they're* saying that's absurd. And it's very curious that even the most distinguished historians feel the need to rely on so absurd a claim to defend the historicity of Jesus. It smells of desperation, as if absurdist propaganda has finally overtaken common sense.

I'll show you what I mean. We'll examine each one of those other guys and the evidence we actually have for them. Because they are all very instructive. For each of them the evidence is actually *vastly better* than we have for Jesus, exposing how little we can trust historians who insist Jesus existed when they actually make wholly false statements like this in their defense. These examples also illustrate what kinds of evidence we actually could have had for Jesus, but don't. And finally, these cases also demonstrate the fundamental key difference between these men and Jesus: none of them were preached to be resurrected savior gods from outer space. Not even at all. Much less from the very first moment we hear anything about them. For all of the following you can find links to lists of the evidence cited for each one in the opening paragraph of my blog article "Okay, So What about the Historicity of Spartacus?"

Case 1: Socrates

"It must be admitted that there are few characters of antiquity about whom we possess so much indubitably historical information, of whom we have so many authentic discourses" as we do for Jesus, whereas, "The position is much less favourable, for instance, in the case of Socrates."

—Albert Schweitzer, *The Quest of the Historical Jesus* (1906), p. 7

Oh really? Let's see how well that holds up.

Socrates was a renowned wise man, a spark that eventually launched philosophy as the discipline we know. He was executed in Athens, Greece, in 399 B.C. for challenging the status quo. He then became the most famous sage in the ancient world. But that makes sense. Because we know the names of numerous eyewitnesses who wrote books about him, including at least sixteen of his disciples. We know of not even one such book ever having been written about Jesus. In some cases we even know the titles of these books about Socrates, and a number of paraphrases and quotations from them actually survive in other sources. In fact, two of them *we actually have*. And they were written within a few years of his death, not nearly half a century or more later (as the Gospels were for Jesus), much less in a foreign land and language. So *already* this is vastly more than we have for Jesus. Those two eyewitnesses? Socrates' own disciples Plato and Xenophon, who together wrote *several* books about him.

We thus have not only multiple eyewitness accounts of Socrates within years of his death, we even have a relatively hostile eyewitness account, from an outside party who wasn't a fanatical follower. The Athenian playwright Aristophanes wrote a comedy gently mocking Socrates and his school and students. That play, *The Clouds*, we still have. Not only did Aristophanes know Socrates personally and base his comedy on direct knowledge of him and his school, but as later historians record (based on eyewitness sources from the time), Socrates even sat in the audience of its first production. If only we had such a priceless source for Jesus! But alas, we do not. There are no neutral or third party records of Jesus at all. We only have late material written by his fanatical and glorifying believers, which is the most biased source one can ever be saddled with. As we just saw in the last chapter, what little mention made it into non-Christian historians was simply just repeating what these late, fanatical Christian sources said—or was even outright forged by fanatical Christians! So even on this point alone, we again have vastly better evidence for Socrates than for Jesus.

And that's not even all we have. We have many *contemporaries* attesting to the historical existence of Socrates. We have none for Jesus—other than as a celestial being. And several historians of Socrates, starting at least a century later, gathered material from these contemporaries and witnesses to compose histories and biographies of the man. Including Idomeneus, who wrote *On the Followers of Socrates*, fragments of which survive. In fact, the surviving attestations and quotations of Socrates and his witnesses and contemporaries fill four volumes of the *Socratis et Socraticorum Reliquiae* assembled by Gabriele Giannantoni in 1990. This is so much more than we have for Jesus it boggles the mind why anyone would think we have more for Jesus than for Socrates!

If Socrates had immediately become worshiped as the resurrected Son of God, the Savior of the Universe, whose story and teachings had to be urgently spread across the earth for the good of humankind, and his followers gained control of the entire machinery of society within three centuries, we would have *even more* of this evidence than we do. The dozens of eyewitness and contemporary accounts we know about but have only mentions or fragments of (and more that we don't) would surely have been preserved by this "Church of Socrates" that controlled all book preservation and production for a thousand years after the third century A.D. *We would have all of that.* As well as everything we already have. So why was no comparable production and preservation of witness and contemporary accounts accomplished for Jesus? Well, we have to suppose, because no one wrote any. Or no one could preserve such accounts long enough even for them to be mentioned. Or someone destroyed them. A, B, or C. Take your pick.

Socrates is much like Jesus in being a supposedly famous man and great and revered teacher who never wrote anything, but who had disciples who took charge of spreading his word, making his fame thus eternal. Socrates' disciples and their successors similarly split into competing sects, leading to different schools of philosophy, from Platonism and Aristotelianism to Cynicism and Stoicism, among others less famed. His influence on Western society was tremendous, touching upon every core aspect of our ideals today, from science to democracy. But Socrates is very much unlike Jesus in that he was never a worshipped savior god claimed to be seen in visions from outer space. Socrates had legends invented about him. But he was never mythologized the way Jesus was. Not even soon. Much less ever. Socrates belongs to the category of men founding schools of thought in a culture very much keen on founding schools of thought. Jesus belongs to the category of salvific gods and archangels on high—in a culture very much keen on inventing salvific gods and archangels on high. Not the same thing. And the evidence matches that difference.

Case 2: Julius Caesar

"The historicity of Christ is as axiomatic for an unbiased historian as the historicity of Julius Caesar."

—F. F. Bruce, *The New Testament Documents: Are They Reliable?* (1960)

Oh really? Let's see how well that holds up.

Julius Caesar was not, of course, "the salad dressing dude," as Bill and Ted would have in it *Bill & Ted's Excellent Adventure*. He was, in fact, "the first of the Empire and the last of the Republicans," as his avatar in *Epic Rap Battles* declares. And for him we have one of the best eyewitness sources anyone can have of someone's existence: we have the very writings of Julius Caesar himself! Caesar wrote about several of his wars, including on his role in the Roman civil war. And we have copies of those books today. Jesus, meanwhile, wrote nothing. We have contemporary accounts of Caesar by people who knew him personally, in many surviving letters written by Cicero and Pompey. No such sources exist for Jesus. Many contemporaries who knew Caesar personally wrote about him, including people whose books survive for us to read today, such as the poets Virgil, Ovid, and Catullus; those of whose writing fragments survive, such as the historian Livy; and many others whose books we know existed. Among mere contemporaries, we have writing by the geographer Strabo and the biographer Nicolaus of Damascus and, of course, by many historians soon after his death, from Velleius Paterculus onward, who consulted those earlier writings and more. No such sources exist for Jesus.

Additionally, we have accounts of Caesar by not just eyewitnesses and contemporaries and subsequent historians but also a close friend and follower, Sallust—not only in Sallust's surviving *Catiline War*, but also in surviving fragments of Sallust's *Histories*, his own account of

Roman history, including the affairs of Caesar. No such sources exist for Jesus. We also have not only fragments of things written about Julius Caesar by his own adopted son Augustus Caesar but also actual physical inscriptions commissioned by Augustus mentioning the existence of Julius, which amounts to having *the approved autograph original text* of an eyewitness. In fact, we have inscriptions written and erected *by Julius Caesar himself*. And, of course, countless coins that he minted, attesting to his existence, appearance, accomplishments, offices, and reign. We even have statues of him carved from life! Not a single one of these amazing proofs exists for Jesus.

The Gospels are not eyewitness sources, name no eyewitness sources, and have no verifiable eyewitness sources. There are no eyewitness sources for Jesus. There are at least nine that survive for Caesar. How again is Jesus as well attested as Caesar? And that's before we get to all the inscriptions and statues, on stones and buildings and coins, composed directly by Caesar or those who personally knew him, which is again vastly more than we have for Jesus. So that claim simply makes no sense. Yet we have Christian scholars like Darrell Bock even still today claiming "Christ's story is just as well attested as Caesar's." Sorry, but, no.

Case 3: Tiberius Caesar

Julius Caesar could readily be recognized as a ridiculous choice for this analogy, being that he was literally the most famous man in the entire history of Rome. His war against his own country ended the Roman Republic and set in motion the Roman Empire itself, despite his futile assassination in 44 B.C. As a great ruler of vast wealth, of course he could create and inspire enormous swaths of evidence of his existence, from coins, inscriptions, statues, and buildings, to his own writings, and the abundant writings of others about him, from friends and colleagues to enemies and contemporaries, and historians in every generation thereafter. Obviously in his own time Jesus was never that famous nor commanded any scale of wealth and power sufficient to leave such evidence.

So it is instead suggested that maybe a better analogy would be a less famous ruler of Rome, Tiberius Caesar, who would be the most famous man *in the time of Jesus*, being the reigning Emperor when Pontius Pilate would have executed Jesus in the 30s A.D. If we have to doubt Jesus due to a paucity of records, we are then supposedly compelled to doubt the existence of Tiberius due to the same paucity of records, "And that's just silly!" As one popular (if not competent) historian put it:

> It would be easier, frankly, to believe that Tiberius Caesar, Jesus' contemporary, was a figment of the imagination than to believe that there never was such a person as Jesus.

—N. T. Wright, *Jesus and the Victory of God* (1996), Preface

Oh really? Let's see how well that holds up.

This claim has already been so thoroughly debunked online by classics scholar Matthew Ferguson, in his extensive article "Ten Reasons to Reject the Apologetic 10/42 Source Slogan" (still viewable through the Internet Archive) that I'm giving him full credit on this one. All I'll be doing is very briefly summarizing what he documents.

Of course many historians of the age, using and citing earlier sources including inscriptions and state documents, wrote about Tiberius in ways and details wholly unlike any historian ever wrote about Jesus. This includes Josephus (who began writing about Tiberius within forty years of his death) and Plutarch, Tacitus, and Suetonius (within eighty years). That's already better than we have for Jesus, about whom no historian wrote for several centuries—outside the Gospels and works wholly reliant on them.

But that's not even close to all we have.

There were also many eyewitnesses and contemporaries of Tiberius who wrote about him. Including a huge number we know about (their names, often book titles, and occasionally quotations from same), but also many we still have *full* writings from that mention Tiberius: government men like Pliny the Elder and Seneca the Younger, the historians Velleius Paterculus, Valerius Maximus, and Cornelius Nepos, the geographer Strabo, the essayist Scribonius Largus, the renowned Jewish theologian Philo of Alexandria, the Roman fabulist Phaedrus, the poets Horace and

Ovid, and Columella the agriculturalist. Fragments mentioning Tiberius also survive from yet more witnesses and contemporaries, including Livy, Aufidius Bassus, Apollonides of Nicaea, Servilius Nonianus, Deculo, and Seneca the Elder. Even the *later* historians mention using good sources for Tiberius, including public inscriptions and state documents created during his life, the actual memoirs written by Tiberius himself, memoirs written by members of his family, and letters written to Tiberius by his predecessors in office. This vast array of evidence just *smokes* anything we have for Jesus. If only we had even *one* of these things attesting to a real Jesus! But we having nothing of the like.

And again, we also have tons of contemporary inscriptions by and about Tiberius, on stones, buildings, plates, and coins. And again, statues carved from life. And actual state documents—not later copies, but the originals, in various papyrus finds, mainly from Egypt, attesting to his existence and reign. Nothing like any of that exists for Jesus.

So the evidence for Tiberius is *vast*—far beyond anything we have for Jesus.

And again there is that one other thing that still differs. Julius and Tiberius Caesar do have one thing in common with Jesus: they were also deified, celebrated as having ascended to and then living in outer space, with some people subsequently claiming to communicate with them in dreams and visions. They also had lots of myths and legends told about them. But the Caesars were never worshipped as personal savior deities, as the key to eternal life through the celebration of mysteries, as ancient archangels born at the dawn of time who descended from outer space, or as gods *only* reported by the first generation of their followers as being met in dreams and visions. Nor were they ever as fully mythologized as Jesus was. Not even after centuries. Much less within half a century.

Case 4: Alexander the Great

"The sources for Jesus are better . . . than those that deal with Alexander [the Great]."

—E. P. Sanders, *The Historical Figure of Jesus* (1993), p. 3.

Oh really? Let's see how well that holds up.

Already from the example of the Caesars we should see where this is going. Alexander was literally the most famous man in the whole of antiquity. Beginning as a mere teenager, and then until his death in his early thirties in 323 B.C., Alexander conquered lands on three continents, extending the borders of Greek power and culture all the way from Africa to Syria, Iran, Afghanistan, indeed all the way to India, founding cities throughout. He literally changed the map of half the civilized world. That's precisely why a statement like Sanders' is so absurd. Yet usually here the claim is astonishingly made that our only sources for Alexander the Great are historians from many hundreds of years later. That's simply false. It's also disingenuous. Because how even those historians composed their histories is very different from how the records of Jesus were composed. And again, those historians *aren't* all we have.

Alexander the Great is discussed in several contemporary or eyewitness sources we still have, including the poetry of Theocritus, the scientific works of Theophrastus, the plays of Menander, and the speeches of Isocrates, Demosthenes, Aeschines, Hyperides, and Dinarchus. Again, we have not a single contemporary mention of Jesus—other than the theological mentions of Paul (and maybe James, Jude, Hebrews, 1 Clement, and 1 Peter, if we imagine they all date early), none of which clearly place Jesus on Earth, unlike contemporary attestations of Alexander. The eyewitness and contemporary attestation for Alexander is thus, again, vastly better than we have for Jesus, not the other way around. And once again, that's only if we count what survives on its own. We *also* have quotations of lost texts in *other surviving texts*— literally hundreds of quotations of contemporaries and eyewitnesses of Alexander. Again, we have not even one such source for Jesus. Even Paul never once quotes anyone he identifies as an eyewitness or contemporary source for any of his information on Jesus.

Also, once again, we have contemporary inscriptions and coins by or about Alexander, sculptures of Alexander (originals or copies of originals done from life), and ample supporting archeology of cities he built and places his armies traveled. We even have something almost like his death certificate: the exact time and day of his death were recorded in contemporary clay records of Persian court astrologers, which survive for us to examine. Other contemporary clay-tablet chronicles record his deeds while still alive.

There is nothing even remotely like any of this for Jesus. So already the statement Sanders made is absurd. But it's absurd even regarding what he thought he was talking about. The much later historians of Alexander are actually modern historians' most trusted sources *not* because, as Sanders mistakenly thought, they are our earliest sources, but because they use the most reliable methods (comparatively speaking— since no author in antiquity is very reliable, just some more so than others). Unlike Jesus, we have over half a dozen relatively objective historians discussing the history of Alexander the Great. Most notably Diodorus of Sicily, Dionysius of Halicarnassus, Curtius Rufus, Pompeius Trogus, Plutarch, and more. These are not romances or propagandists, least of all fanatical worshipers writing holy books like the Gospels. They used some critical thinking and sources contemporary to Alexander. Which doesn't mean we trust everything they say. But we still cannot name even one such source for Jesus, and "none" is not "more" than half a dozen.

And that they all wrote hundreds of years later is not of primary significance, either, because we know historians of this era like them were committed to the principle of using eyewitness and contemporary sources, even if they didn't always adhere to that principle, and even though eyewitness and contemporary sources are also not totally reliable. But let's look at an example so you can see what I mean. Our best historian of Alexander the Great is Arrian of Nicomedia, who wrote *The Anabasis of Alexander* five hundred years later. However, unlike any Gospel, Arrian tells us his methods: he employed three eyewitness sources and wrote down what they agreed on and anything he thought was significant that they didn't agree on. This included books written by two generals, Ptolemy and Aristobulus, and one naval commander, Nearchus, who all served under Alexander. Arrian names and identifies these sources, explains how he used them to generate a more reliable account, and discusses their relative merits and why he chose them.

That alone is quite a great deal more than we have for Jesus. For Jesus we have not a single named eyewitness source in any of the accounts of him. We have no discussion anywhere of how those sources were used or what their relative merits were. Not even for the anonymous witness claimed to have been used by the authors of the Gospel according to John. That claim isn't even credible to begin with, but even so, we're not told who he was, why we should trust him, what all exactly derives from him, or where or if or why his account contradicted anyone else's. Similarly, the author of the Gospel according to Luke claims to have slavishly followed some prior sources who recorded a tradition he claims was passed down from the original witnesses—well, we now know he just means other Gospels, Mark, and probably Matthew—but Luke never names those witnesses, who they passed their stories on to, or even which stories, nor does Luke name any of the written sources he used, or explain how he knows *they* used any sources, or why or how he chose what to believe and disbelieve from these sources, or where and why they disagreed with each other, or he with them.

The historians of Alexander were also rationalists—they doubted miracle stories, and admitted what they found incredible, and discussed their suspicions of certain stories, even mundane ones they found odd, where human motives seem implausible, or behavior does not match the geography or politics of the time. Whereas the Gospels just record every wild story they wanted, exhibiting no doubt at all that anything told them was true, no matter how incredible. Their accounts are indeed *filled with* suspicious and unbelievable stories, with no indication they even bothered to fact-check any of it. Or how. And that's it. So we have nothing like Arrian for Jesus. Not even five hundred years later.

So, for all these reasons, even the *late* historians of Alexander are far better sources to have than any of the sources we have for Jesus. And we have vastly more evidence for Alexander than that. None of which we have for Jesus.

Alexander was also deified. And he may have been worshipped in some capacity. But he never became a celestial savior lord, an archangel from the dawn of time, sent down from outer space to give us eternal life through initiation into his mysteries. And though the wildest of myths did eventually grow up around Alexander's core tale—indeed many were fabricated and disseminated even in his own lifetime—he *still* was not as heavily mythologized as Jesus. Even after centuries. Much less within decades.

Case 5: Pontius Pilate

"Not even . . . the most powerful and important figure of his day,
Pontius Pilate" is "mentioned in any Roman sources of his day."

—Bart Ehrman, "Did Jesus Exist," *Huffington Post* (2012)

Oh really? Let's see how well *that* one holds up.

Philo of Alexandria was a living contemporary of Pontius Pilate.
And he was a Roman in any relevant sense. Though a Greek-speaking
Jew living in the Roman province of Egypt—neighboring the Roman
province of Judea, which Philo reports visiting at least once on a
pilgrimage—Philo was certainly a Roman citizen. Not only was he a
renowned and wealthy Alexandrian, and an ambassador to the Emperor,
but he was the uncle of Tiberius Julius Alexander, a Roman government
official. Philo not only lived during the government of Pilate over Judea
but also wrote an *entire book* about Pontius Pilate. We know, because he
tells us he did in his surviving writings. And the fourth-century Christian
historian Eusebius tells us he had read that book himself (in *History of
the Church* 2.5). Philo also discusses an event featuring Pontius Pilate in
another book we *do* have, written in the 40s A.D., not long after Pilate
committed suicide in the reign of Caligula, which fact Philo had reported
in his lost book about him (as you can confirm in Philo's *Embassy* 299–
305 and Eusebius's *History of the Church* 2.7). So much for Pilate not being
mentioned in any Roman sources of his day.

We also have quite a lot about Pilate in Josephus' *Jewish War*,
published in the seventies A.D., and *Antiquities of the Jews*, published in
93 A.D., the same distance from Pilate's life as the Gospels are assumed
to be from Jesus. Josephus covered him extensively because Pilate's
governance of Judea between 26 and 36 A.D. was one of the most
important turning points leading to the eventual destruction of the
Jewish state. Though of course Josephus, who wrote about these events
a lifetime later, was another Greek-speaking Jew—even once, in fact, the
governor of Galilee—he was also a Roman citizen and served much of
his life in Rome itself. We know he used earlier sources (he often names or
mentions them). Josephus was born just a few years before Pilate died, so

he isn't exactly a contemporary. But we still don't have anything like this for Jesus, a detailed third-party account by a rationalist historian using earlier contemporary sources. (As we've already noted, the real Josephus probably never wrote about Jesus.) Nor do we have anything like Philo, a detailed third-party account written by a neighboring contemporary!

It's very odd, in fact, that medieval Christians did not preserve Philo's book about Pilate. They kept dozens of other volumes of his—but let this one vanish. Why? The most likely reason is that it failed to ever mention Jesus. And a book about the entire rule of Pontius Pilate that didn't take any notice of Jesus was either of no interest or even an embarrassment to later Christian readers.

But for an eminent historian like Bart Ehrman to forget that Philo discussed Pontius Pilate, both in books we have and in books we've lost, and to instead miseducate the public by saying in a major periodical that no contemporary of Pilate mentioned him, is very curious. Why would he do that? Why do historians keep saying ridiculous things like this, just to calm the public into believing the evidence for Jesus is as solid as for all these other guys? This is not an isolated incident. It keeps happening. We've seen case after case. And those cases get echoed and repeated endlessly. So there is some common cause to all this. Whatever it is, it calls into question the judgment and reliability behind the historical consensus backing a historical Jesus. Because that consensus is based on scholars, who should know better, nevertheless resting it on ridiculous claims like these. Which certainly renders that consensus suspect.

Eventually in his book *Did Jesus Exist?* Ehrman admitted Philo does mention Pilate—and there he *also* admitted something *else* he forgot to tell the readers of the *Huffington Post*: that, in fact, we have an inscription commissioned by Pontius Pilate himself, attesting to his own existence! A stone once attached to a building project Pilate undertook in Judea commemorates him. That's not just a contemporary source; it's an eyewitness source. And it's not just an eyewitness source; it's Pilate himself reporting to us. And it's not just Pilate himself reporting to us; it's the original autograph. This inscription is not a copy from centuries later, but the actual chiseled stone commissioned and read by Pilate himself. And on top of all that, you can't get more Roman than a Roman government official telling us he exists, in Latin, on an official state monument!

I hardly need mention that we have no such thing from or for Jesus. Nor is Pilate categorically anything at all like Jesus. He was not a worshipped savior deity or celestial space visitor encountered in mystical visions. He was just an ordinary government official who played a role in the ordinary political history of the ancient world. Precisely the sort of person we always assume exists if we have no reason to doubt it . . . *unlike* worshipped savior deities from outer space.

Case 6: Caligula

> "Jesus is as well established as a figure of history as is, say, the emperor Caligula, his near-contemporary."
>
> —N. T. Wright, Text Message to *Inspiring Philosophy* (April 2018)

Oh really? Let's see how well *that* one holds up.

Right from the start, we have nothing for Jesus even like the account of Caligula written up eighty years later by Suetonius in *The Life of Caligula*, which uses, cites, and quotes multiple eyewitness and contemporary documents, including the correspondence and memoirs of Caligula's own family, the books and poems of eyewitnesses who knew him, and contemporary inscriptions and government documents. Suetonius even discusses their relative reliability.

And we have so much more that's even better than that, as surveyed in Aloys Winterling's *Caligula: A Biography* (University of California Press, 2015); Sam Wilkinson's *Caligula* (Routledge, 2003); and Anthony Barrett's *Caligula: The Corruption of Power* (Yale University Press, 1990). We have busts and statues of Caligula carved from life. Wikipedia even correctly says, "Based on scientific reconstructions of his official painted busts, Caligula had brown hair, brown eyes, and fair skin." Source? The Smithsonian. Do we have anything like that for Jesus? No. We have a huge number of coins minted by and naming and depicting Caligula as emperor. We have a huge number of papyri, actually written during Caligula's life, mentioning him as the reigning emperor, official name Gaius (Julius) Caesar Germanicus Augustus. We have a huge number of contemporary inscriptions, erected by Caligula himself, and eyewitnesses to his reign. We have excavated several of Caligula's most peculiar ships. We have actual wine barrels from Caligula's private vineyard, with his name on them! We have his mother's tombstone, declaring him her child. Do we have anything like *any* of that for Jesus? No.

Pliny the Elder, an eyewitness to Caligula, likewise supplies us a great deal of information directly from his own observations, and from government records and other eyewitness and contemporary sources. Other eyewitnesses and contemporaries who report on Caligula include, again, Philo of Alexandria and Seneca, who both met with Caligula personally, and record several things about him: from Philo's *Flaccus* and *On The Embassy to Gaius* to Seneca's *On Consolation to My Mother Helvia* and *On Rage* and *On the Constancy of the Wise*. We have extensive accounts of Caligula in Josephus—a historian born when Caligula reigned, discussing Caligula within only 35 years of his death, and again more extensively only 52 years after his death. An account, by the way, that is exactly in Josephan style and rich with realistic detail: *The Antiquities of the Jews* 18–19 (written c. 93 A.D) and *The Jewish War* 2.184–203 (written c. 76 A.D.). Do we have anything like *that* for Jesus? No. Not even the *alleged* Josephan mentions of Jesus meet these conditions on any relevant point.

We also know eyewitnesses and contemporaries of Caligula wrote works about him that are lost but that are discussed and used by later writers, including Seneca's own friend Fabius Rusticus; Cluvius Rufus, a senator actually involved in the assassination of Caligula; the memoirs of Claudius, Caligula's successor; the published correspondence of Augustus; and various poets like Gaetulicus. Even Caligula's sister, Nero's mother, Agrippina the Younger, wrote up her own memoirs that were cited and used as a source for Caligula by several later historians. Do we have anything like any of *this* for Jesus? No.

Beyond Suetonius we have several later critical historians writing about Caligula who name, cite, and quote eyewitness, documentary, and contemporary sources for Caligula, including Tacitus, *Life of Agricola* 10 (written c. 98 A.D.) and *Annals* 13.20 (written c. 116 A.D.); and Dio Cassius (c. 220 A.D.). We even have government documents that do this: for instance, we've unearthed a bronze tablet copy (dating c. 168 A.D.)

of a letter personally written by Emperor Marcus Aurelius, discussed by A. N. Sherwin-White in the *Journal of Roman Studies* in 1973, that mentions him consulting the extant register of those granted citizenship by Caligula. There's nothing like either for Jesus.

Oh . . . and we have Caligula him-fracking-self! An inscription recording his own letter, in his own words, to the Achaean League, dated 19 August 37 A.D. (published in *Inscriptiones Graecae* 7.2711 and ll.21–43). We also have declarations of alliance and celebration from many localities at the accession to power of Caligula. For example, the Oath declared by the Aritensians, inscribed on stone shortly after 11 May 37 A.D., elaborately asserting they shall ally with Caligula and declare his enemies their enemies; similarly the Cyzicans; and the Oath and Decree of Celebration of the Assians of the same year, which says they are sending an embassy "to seek an audience with and congratulate him, and beg him to remember" their city "as he personally promised when together with his father Germanicus he first set foot in our city's province" (quoted in Lewis & Reinhold's *Roman Civilization* Vol. 2, § 3 & 9). So here we have the eyewitness, original autograph testimony of an entire city of people. Caligula was with his father at the age of six when he visited their region. So they are trucking rather hard here on the utterance of a toddler. But of one thing we can be certain: you don't say this of, and thus send embassies to, a guy who doesn't exist.

Do we have anything like *that* for Jesus? No.

Case 7: Hannibal

"[We can even employ] the rhetorical strategies of the Jesus Mythologists to 'prove' that Hannibal never existed."

—James Hannam, "Is Jesus Christ a Myth? Part 4" (2010)

Oh really? Let's see how well *that* one holds up.

The vast depth, quality, and range of evidence for Hannibal is so wildly unlike what we have for Jesus I'm astonished anyone would even attempt this one. But you can just compare works on the historical Jesus with works on the historical Hannibal to get a feel for the stark difference, such as Dexter Hoyos, *Hannibal's Dynasty* (2005); John Prevas, *Hannibal Crosses the Alps* (2001); Serge Lancel, *Hannibal* (1999); or J. F. Lazenby, *Hannibal's War* (1998).

Hannibal fought his famous war with Rome just before 200 B.C. and lived to around 180 B.C. Archaeology corroborates the existence of Hannibal in a number of indirect ways—the flow of precious metals, excavated camps and materiel—but anyone could have led the Carthaginian armies into Spain and Italy. And we have coins he himself struck, that *might* have his face on them (in the guise of Hercules-Melqart), with on the other side symbols befitting him, such as the war elephants he famously employed and depictions of his conquest of the Alps, as discussed by M. McMenamin in "Depiction of the Alps on Punic Coins from Campania, Italy" in *Numismatics International Bulletin* 41.1-2 (2012). And we *might* have a marble bust of him carved from life. But neither has his name on them. They only match each other, and their historical date and geographical locations match Hannibal's campaigns. So they attest to some singular man in that role. Which is still unlike anything we have for Jesus.

But even better is a Roman inscription, the epitaph of Quintus Fabius Maximus, who fought Hannibal. Carved in stone at his death in 205 B.C., it boasts of his victories against Hannibal, by name, saying, "he besieged and recaptured Tarentum and the strong-hold of Hannibal" (*L'Année Epigraphique* 1954, no. 216). We also have the epitaph of Felsnas Larth, inhabitant of Capua, Italy, who was one of the soldiers of Hannibal, and mentions his service under him, by name, in the Etruscan language (A. J. Pfiffig, "Eine Nennung Hannibals," *Studi Etruschi* 1967). We definitely don't have marble inscriptions carved by eyewitnesses to the life of Jesus, naming him and attesting to his activity. Not even one. Much less two.

Then we get to textual evidence.

First of all we have the writings of Polybius, a contemporary of Hannibal, being in his late teens or early twenties by the time Hannibal died, and the personal friend of the family of Scipio Africanus, the Roman general who defeated Hannibal. Polybius had access to multiple eyewitness sources to interview for his accounts. Not just the sons and grandsons of Africanus, but also other officers and politicians of the era who prosecuted and documented the war—including Carthaginians, as Polybius operated as an ambassador to Carthage just a few decades after Hannibal's death. Polybius mentions interviewing King Massinissa, a Roman ally who fought Hannibal, and Gaius Laelius, a personal friend and companion of Africanus during the war, and thus himself an eyewitness to Hannibal's existence. Polybius cites and uses eyewitness textual sources, too, like Scipio Africanus's letter to King Philip V of Macedon about his interactions with Hannibal, and Polybius's citation and use of a bronze inscription erected by Hannibal himself in the course of the war (*Histories* 3.33.5-18). We don't have anything like this for Jesus: a contemporary historian researching a critical account of him, within forty years of his death, with direct access to named eyewitnesses and explicitly cited eyewitness documentary and textual sources. Polybius also tells us his preferred method: of only trusting eyewitness sources he interviewed himself or whose own documents or memoirs he read, and using them critically rather than gullibly, a fact explored by Kenneth Sacks in *Polybius on the Writing of History* (1981). We have no author on Jesus naming what sources they had or how they used them.

The same is true of the next historian whose account of the war mostly survives: Livy. Though yet another hundred years after Polybius, Livy nevertheless consulted and quoted state documents on the Hannibalic war, including the treaty signed with the Carthaginians that ended the war, which mentions Hannibal several times—including a specific clause requiring his surrender (Livy, *From the Founding of the City* 37–38; see Polybius, *Histories* 21.42). We have nothing like this for Jesus, either. Livy and other authors also had and used eyewitness literary sources on Hannibal. Accordingly, we have descriptions of these authors and what they wrote and often direct quotations and citations of their lost works. This includes the Roman politician and orator Cato the Elder and the Roman historian Fabius Pictor. Both lived during and wrote about Hannibal's war. Sosylus of Lacedaemon and Silenus of Caleacte, traveling companions of Hannibal, also wrote extensive accounts of his wars. Lucius Cincius Alimentus was a Roman war prisoner who dined with Hannibal during years in captivity, and then wrote of his experiences after the war in his *Annals*. The historian Gaius Acilius wrote a researched account of the Hannibalic war within forty years of his death, and may even have lived during it. We have nothing like this for Jesus: multiple quotations and citations of writings about him by named and explained eyewitnesses. We have, in fact, not even one, once we admit the one mention of a vague "someone" at the end of the Gospel according to John is both nameless and fake.

Then we have the writings of numerous historians within a century or so of Hannibal's death, writing detailed histories using critical and rational methods, *not* composing mythical hagiographies. These include not just Livy but also Cornelius Nepos, Diodorus, Coelius Antipater, Silenus of Caleacte, Valerius Antias, Claudius Quadrigarius, and many others, from whom we have fragments, quotations, or partial texts. We have nothing like this explosion of quotable histories of Jesus within 120 years of his death. In fact, we have exactly zero histories of Jesus. Only a line or two in a few historians nearly a century after the fact or more, who have no identifiable sources outside the Gospels, which in turn are mythical hagiographies anonymously composed by literary propagandists after the lifetime of any known eyewitnesses, all just redacting the first of them, Mark. Exactly unlike Hannibal.

This is why we are so certain Hannibal existed. The evidence is amazing. If we had almost *any* of that evidence for Jesus, we'd be sure he existed, too. But we don't. We have none of it. And whenever you go looking for someone else like that, who isn't as securely attested as Hannibal, you end up only finding someone historians would accept reasonable doubts of, and whose historicity they only maintain (if even they do) because it's some dude or dudette who *doesn't* belong to any reference class of persons who usually turn out to be mythical. Whereas Jesus does.

Case 8: Spartacus

"Almost everything we know about Spartacus is based on the writings of two people writing a couple of decades either side of the two hundredth anniversary of Spartacus' death," and yet, "Despite this paucity of evidence, which is such that his historical existence has to be recognised as a damn sight less well attested than that of

Christ, I've yet to hear even one ancient historian ever claim that Spartacus didn't exist."

—Gregory Daly, "Even If He Wasn't God, He Was Certainly a Man," *The Thirsty Gargoyle* (January 2006)

Oh really? Let's see how well *that* one holds up.

Spartacus was the enslaved gladiator of Thrace (now mostly Bulgaria) who led a nearly successful slave revolt against the Romans in Italy in 73–70 B.C. Just like Julius Caesar, and everyone else in these comparisons, when it comes to determining the probability of his historicity, Spartacus once again differs from Jesus in two respects . . .

First, Spartacus belongs to a different category. He is not a worshiped deity whose only narratives are extensively mytho-fantastical. Spartacus does not belong to any myth-heavy reference classes at all. He is not in any significantly sized sets of persons claimed to be historical, most of whose members are probably mythical. But you know what? Jesus is. As we'll see next chapter, Jesus belongs to the categories of legendary sages and hero kings, worshiped savior deities, mystery-cult sky-lords, dying-and-rising demigods, and ancient heavenly founders. Spartacus belongs to not even one of those categories. Or any category like them—much less *to all of them*. To the contrary, Spartacus belongs to the category of mundane military foes fighting a literate, record-keeping nation's armies, a reference class in which most members by far are indeed historical. So we don't even need more evidence to confirm Spartacus existed. We can trust it's just very likely he did, because in such cases, in such sets of persons, every time we can check, it turns out it usually is the case that those people existed. Not so with the categories Jesus falls into. In those, their members usually turn out to be mythical—or no more likely historical than mythical.

This is why we can't compare Jesus with ordinary people. Ordinary people are not usually mythical. There is little reason to have made them up or to have given them a historical existence. Ordinary people are not worshiped celestial gods with astonishing superpowers. They don't usually have suspiciously convenient names—as, again, Jesus actually happens to mean "God's Savior," so to have God's Savior named God's

Savior is a bit of a pill to swallow. Nor are they usually rapidly surrounded by wildly egregious myths, to serve as invented authorities for promoting new cultural and religious norms. So, already, Spartacus and Jesus aren't even in the same boat. For Jesus, his existence begins already suspect. For Spartacus, it's the other way around. And that's even before we get to the fact that, unlike Jesus, our earliest sources for Spartacus don't claim to have met him in only dreams and visions.

So we have no initial reason to doubt Spartacus existed, as we do Jesus. And yet we *still* have more evidence for Spartacus than we have for Jesus. Leading scholarship collecting it all includes Aldo Schiavone's *Spartacus* (2013) and Brent Shaw's *Spartacus and the Slave Wars: A Brief History with Documents* (2001). It's usually claimed that our earliest references are Plutarch's *Life of Crassus* (written around 100 A.D.) and Appian's *Civil War* (written around 150 A.D.), which date well over a hundred years after the fact (although they both used earlier sources). But that's not true. Those are the earliest *detailed narratives*. And not the earliest *written*; the earliest that *survive*.

It is sometimes claimed that the oldest surviving historical source on Spartacus are some fragments of the histories of Livy—and his full account was indeed a major source for those later authors. Livy was born about ten years after the Spartacus war and wrote probably around the turn of the era, which makes Livy with respect to Spartacus comparable to Josephus with respect to Jesus. But there is a huge difference. We can tell even by extant summaries that Livy wrote extensively and believably about Spartacus (unlike anything in Josephus about Jesus) and had good and detailed information (unlike anything in Josephus about Jesus), and none of that information shows signs of obvious forgery or meddling (unlike everything in Josephus about Jesus). So even just on this count, with Livy we already have better evidence for Spartacus than anything we have for Jesus.

But that's actually *not* the oldest thing we have. We also have fragments of Sallust's *Histories*, which covered Spartacus—and was *another* major source used by later authors like Plutarch and Appian. Sallust was born about ten years *before* the Spartacus war, and later shared the Senate with persons who fought Spartacus. So he would have personally known the likes of Crassus, Julius Caesar, and Pompey, who were in the army at the time. And Sallust wrote around 40 B.C., just thirty years after the Spartacus war, making this a better source than we have for Jesus in any form at all. This would make Sallust comparable to the letters of Paul. But unlike Sallust, Paul does not treat Jesus as a subject of narrative history or give any specific earthly details about him or write anything biographical about him at all, other than vague theological statements. So once again, in Sallust we have *even better* evidence for Spartacus than we do anywhere for Jesus.

And that's just the earliest *account* we have pieces of. If we want just mentions attesting to Spartacus *existing*, then we are even better off than that. We have mentions of Spartacus from several of his contemporaries. We have him attested in the letters of Cicero—in *Response to the Haruspices* written in 57 B.C., just fourteen years after the Spartacus war. Cicero also mentions details of the Spartacus war, albeit without naming Spartacus, in *Against Verres*, written and orated to the Senate just *three years* after the war. Cicero was in his thirties and in the Senate and serving in Roman government during that war. So he certainly would have known that the man and his war weren't made up.

Spartacus is also attested in fragments from the *Library of History* by Diodorus of Sicily (s. 39.22). That passage also reveals that Diodorus had written *a whole section* on the Spartacus war. Diodorus was a Greek, in his twenties during the war, and wrote his histories between 60 and 30 B.C., so a living contemporary historian, writing about Spartacus earlier than any narrative we have for Jesus (apart from maybe the Gospel of Mark). We also know the erudite Varro, who was in his forties during the Spartacus revolt and was thus in the Senate during the war, also attested to the existence and treatment of Spartacus. We know that because Varro's books are quoted doing so by a later reader, Sosipater Charisius, a scholar of the fourth century A.D. (he quotes Varro mentioning Spartacus in *Grammatical Arts* 1.133). Once again, we have nothing at all like that for Jesus.

So, altogether, what we have for Spartacus is very much better than we have for Jesus. He is not "a damn sight less well attested than . . . Christ." He is, to the contrary, a damn sight *far better* attested than Christ.

This is, of course, only in respect to establishing the bare fact that Spartacus *existed*. We don't trust that all the surviving sources providing us details about him are wholly reliable in every detail. For example, it's generally agreed that the later Appian makes identifiable errors, and thus probably made several unidentifiable ones as well. Plutarch seems to have more reliably used Sallust and Livy and other sources, but he's also known to be prone to sensationalism. But there were also other historians of the same period who cover or mention Spartacus: Suetonius (writing around 120 A.D.), Tacitus (writing around 115 A.D.), Florus (writing around 100 A.D.), Frontinus (writing around 90 A.D.), and Paterculus (writing around 20 A.D.). Possibly more. We don't have this for Jesus: numerous objective historians researching his history from earlier sources and discussing it, all within one to two centuries after the event. Even the one lone case we might claim for Jesus, the single mention in Tacitus discussed in the last chapter, cannot be traced to any source other than the Gospels—and might never have been in Tacitus to begin with.

We know historians in antiquity who used contemporary sources well—or were or knew contemporaries or witnesses—usually get major public facts correct, like the names of generals, the season and year of a campaign, things like that. Because there was good data for them to use to do that, including public inscriptions, state gazettes, and the letters and memoirs of generals. And we know they were held at least to minimal standards of reliability and fact-checking by their peers among the Senatorial elite. Whereas, by contrast, the more gossipy or elusive stuff these same historians often *can't* be trusted on—because we know they were prone to believing uncheckable rumors, or even making them up, or treating inferences and conjectures as reported facts. This is true across the board. There is no historian in antiquity whose account of anything we trust entirely. There are just some historians we trust more than others, or more on some things than on others.

So there is plenty that is legendary or uncertain about Spartacus. Or Pilate. Or Alexander. Or the Caesars. Or Socrates. And all scholars acknowledge this. And we all analyze the data in terms of probability and the likelihood or traceability of eyewitness or contemporary sourcing. But if all you want is to be assured of historicity, even the evidence *for Spartacus* is vastly better than for Jesus. As, too, all the others.

And So On

Historians keep trying to find a winning example of what I now call "The Argument from Spartacus," some person we're all sure existed, yet whom we'd have to doubt if we applied the same standard to them as we do Jesus. But we can never find someone who meets both conditions: someone we are sure existed who is as attested as Jesus, or more poorly than Jesus. Always, when we find someone that poorly attested, we *aren't* so sure they existed; and when we find someone we *are* sure existed, we quickly find that's because we have for them tons of the very evidence we *don't* have for Jesus! So why are we so sure about Jesus?

It's been claimed Jesus is better attested than Roman emperors like Trajan, Hadrian, or Antoninus Pius. They are, in fact, massively more attested than Jesus. It's been claimed Jesus is better attested than lesser figures, too, like Herod Agrippa. Alas, we have multiple inscriptions and coins attesting to Agrippa's existence, and a contemporary account (again from Philo), and details from a historian writing a generation later using nonmythological, firsthand sources: Josephus, who personally knew Agrippa's son, and clearly describes the elder Agrippa as a regular earthly person. Which, again, we have nothing like for Jesus. We could perhaps pick on some even more obscure people, like Caiaphas the High Priest mentioned in the Gospels . . . except we have his inscribed casket, and researched accounts in Josephus, which is still more than we have for Jesus. Maybe we can pick on those messianic heroes documented only in Josephus . . . except, they are plausibly documented in Josephus. Jesus isn't. And should we choose to dial up our doubts about Josephus as a source *on them*, or anyone else "only he" mentions, we just end up doubting their existence! We don't end up increasing our confidence in it. That would be the opposite of sense.

Why Do We Have *None* of This for Jesus?

The tendency of historians not to admit or reveal this disparity in the evidence to the public—even to try telling the public the disparity is the other way around!—is strange.

Paul is our only contemporary who has any plausible connection to any witnesses, and he is hopelessly vague about the reality of Jesus—was his Jesus seen only in visions, or someone who once walked the earth? As I've already noted, and as we'll soon see, we honestly can't tell. And yet Paul can't have been the only one writing. There had to be *many* more Christian leaders and evangelists doing so, if he was. Yet we don't even have all that *Paul* wrote; nor any of the letters he mentions were written *to him*. After that all we have is a wild, late, unsourced and foreign legend, and later authors embellishing it.

The only reason we could have no more letters from the early churches and apostles, and no memoirs from anyone and no investigated historical accounts and no third-party records or documents and no examples of any of the first Christians ever citing or disputing or asking after the facts of Jesus' life, can only be because later Christians had to have chosen to throw all those other materials away. We then must ask why. We also must conclude Jesus just wasn't famous or remarkable enough for anyone to write things about him, or preserve even a *mention* of anything written about him. Sure, Christians may have thought it was pointless because the end was nigh—but that doesn't really explain much, because obviously Paul didn't think that; he wrote quite a lot. Nor did the several churches who wrote *him* letters think that. But rather than admit this, too many historians seem keen instead on snowing the public with false claims, about "how much better attested" Jesus is than every other famous dude of the day. Why?

One thing we've seen to be a good source of evidence in many of the cases we've examined are inscriptions, which somehow historians forget exist when they want to claim Jesus is better attested than even the greatest of rulers and kings. And yet, one scholar, James McGrath, in his desperate need to convince the public that Jesus existed, actually said that "the obvious reason why we have no inscriptions referring to Jesus" is that only "prefects and procurators and governors and kings made inscriptions, as did other public functionaries," so "when, where, and why would a figure like Jesus have made an inscription, or had one made that referred to him?"

I nearly fell out of my chair reading that. And not because, in fact, I'd never implied Jesus would erect an inscription. But rather, I was so startled because McGrath's claim about who erected inscriptions in antiquity is false. It's bad enough that a professor like James McGrath, who claims to be an expert and represents himself to the public as an authority they should trust, didn't know what he just said was false. What's so much worse is the fact that *it didn't even occur to him to check this claim before making it.* That McGrath doesn't even know the rudimentary methods of an expert, *and* lacks basic expert knowledge, is why he should stop claiming to be an expert. But what's *weird* about this is that he could have simply said *this*: "Yes, private individuals and religious congregations erected inscriptions all the time, but it took money and motive, neither of which the Christians had." The earliest Christians, one could propose, were too poor, and were so certain the whole world would be vaporized any day now—the cosmos was to be literally melted into a plasma according to 2 Peter 3:10–12—that the carving of words in stones may well have seemed pointless. But that obvious explanation eluded the expert McGrath. Why?

It still remains true that we could have had early Christian inscriptions. And that could have changed the debate. In fact, the vast majority of ancient inscriptions were made by private citizens. Not just in graveyards—though we do have tens of thousands of funerary epitaphs, by all manner of not just wealthy but also middle-class folk, celebrating their freedom from slavery or success in their trade or even, in many cases, their philosophy or religion. There is also a vast amount of graffiti. But even after leaving all that out, we still have inscriptions by practitioners of nearly every major religion in antiquity. Pick your god, there is probably an inscription somewhere, by someone, celebrating them. Likely hundreds.

The inscriptions attesting the miracles of the god Asclepius at Epidaurus in Greece, commissioned by those healed by them, is just the most famous example. We also have thousands of inscriptions by Mithraists, and Bacchants, and Isis worshippers, and those of countless other cults—including Jews. The *Revelation of Gabriel* is a recently discovered example, a whole Jewish scripture carved in stone, an example of precisely the kind of thing we have from a fringe Jewish cult that we don't have from Christianity, *also* a fringe Jewish cult. We have inscriptions celebrating visions and revelations across the whole empire, from an Egyptian wizard named Harnouphis who "saw" the goddess Isis in what is now the Czech Republic, to tourists who heard a miraculous talking statue in Egypt, to inscribed accounts of a spate of visions of the gods along the coast of what is now western Turkey. We also have inscriptions by philosophy enthusiasts, celebrating and broadcasting their philosophy to the public—something you'd think Christians were most keen to do, being evangelistic missionaries and all. (On all of the above examples and those to follow, see my blog article "McGrath on the Amazing Infallible Ehrman.")

I'll tell you about three pertinent examples—of dozens I could discuss—that illustrate what the earliest Christians *might* have done had they pooled their resources and had time been kind enough to preserve their labor.

Diogenes of Oenoanda, a private citizen and a disciple of the Epicurean philosophy, commissioned a massive public inscription in what is now Turkey detailing his philosophy for the good of mankind, declaring as its purpose "to help those who come after us" by publicizing "the remedies of salvation." As an Epicurean, he didn't even believe in such vitally urgent matters as an afterlife or a coming end of the world to warn people about, yet he spent his own money to publish his gospel.

We have an inscription in Lanuvium, Italy, stating the rules of a private dinner club, as part of a communal burial society. These religious associations are one of the models that early Christianity followed, mimicking the same gatherings and procedures in their eucharist feasts. In most burial clubs members would have their burials charitably assured by their membership, as well as other charitable aims from the pooling of member resources. Members also often shared fictive kinship—they were all each others' "brethren"—and shared communion in the form of regular divine meals—often of fish, bread, and wine—in celebration of their own pagan Lord and Savior. The Lanuvium inscription preserves the rules of order for one of these clubs, which reflect some of the same concerns Paul faced with *his* dinner clubs—those rowdy Christian eucharist parties (see 1 Corinthians 11:16–34)—and for which Paul voiced some of the same solutions, which must only have become more elaborate and codified over subsequent decades, just as happened at Lanuvium.

Robin Lane Fox, in the fourth chapter of *Pagans and Christians*—an engaging history of Christianity in its pagan context—discusses an example of a private cult erecting an inscription to record the fact that they had recently been having a spate of revelations from the gods, and had consulted an oracle about it, and now were publishing its reply. This was in the city of Miletus; the cult was that of Demeter; and the celebrant who commissioned it was the priestess Alexandra, who was in a position similar to that of Peter, as leader and prime revealer to the cult. The inscription in part reads, "Ever since she has taken on her priesthood" the "gods have been appearing in visitations as never before" either to or in the form of "girls and women, but also, men and children." The inscription asks, "What does such a thing mean? Is it the sign of something good?" The oracle's answer was basically yes. Here we have visions, seen as an exciting new event, being celebrated in stone. And the gods' message about it permanently displayed.

And yet Christians never erected any inscriptions like these, for at least two centuries. Well, except heretics. Because, evidently, a Valentinian Christian in the late second century finally got around to it. They commissioned a stone plaque that read:

> Co-brothers of the bridal chambers, celebrate with torches the baths for me; they hunger for banquets in our rooms, lauding the Father, and praising the Son; oh, may there be flowing of the only spring and of the truth in that very place.

Not much useful information there. But no one else did this? Never for a hundred and fifty years? Christians must have been too few. Or had too little to say.

Of course this Valentinian inscription is a direct refutation of McGrath's generalization that no Christians would ever do this. But it's also a good example of a relatively cheap production. Hence a Christian inscription might not have been as elaborate and expensive as that of Diogenes, for lack of funds. But it could have been as simple as this. Obviously Christians might have been unable to do this in Judea, but they would have been free to in pagan cities for at least a couple of centuries. Contrary to what you usually hear, Christianity was not actually outlawed, and was rarely persecuted by Romans, as Candida Moss demonstrated in her book *The Myth of Persecution* (2013). Even the Christians' own book of Acts routinely demonstrates this. Indeed, if we accepted the account in Tacitus, Christians had to be accused of arson even to prosecute them. Their merely being Christians wasn't enough to make a case. By the time we find government officials like Pliny the Younger prosecuting Christians, almost a century after the religion began, it's only because of general laws against illegal assembly in his province, not against their beliefs. To avoid that fate one could simply have gotten a license from the state to congregate for worship, as every other religion did—including the Jews. Or you could worship alone with your family, and pronounce any belief you wanted publicly.

So, why? No Christians, in a hundred years of practicing, across many dozens of churches, ever once thought to post their gospel or celebrate a miracle or vision or write up their rules on a house wall like pagan dinner clubs had? Nor even so much as to carve or scrawl "Jesus is Lord" on anything, anywhere? Christians could easily have erected all manner of messages, in honor of their god, or to advertise their gospel, or to warn people to repent, or anything else. So why didn't they? Or did they, but so rarely that every example has been lost? Whatever explanation we give for this, it cannot be yet another falsehood like McGrath's claim that only the state erected inscriptions. The same goes for the greater plethora of letters, memoirs, and church documents that must have existed in the first decades. All gone. We can imagine explanations why. *But we still don't have any of them.*

Historians really need to stop making things up—to stop making false claims—in defense of the historicity of Jesus.

Conclusion

Jesus is *not* as well attested as Socrates or Julius Caesar or Tiberius or Alexander the Great or Pontius Pilate or Caligula or Hannibal or Spartacus. And certainly not *better* attested. He is vastly *less* attested than any of them. In fact, the evidence we have convincing us they did exist does not exist for Jesus *at all*.

Now, all that this shows is, again, that if Jesus existed, he must have been a nobody—some obscure figure no one in his time wrote about, and whom no one really much noticed other than some scant few fanatical followers, and even they struggled to produce or preserve anything about him. So we can't conclude Jesus didn't exist *because* he wasn't anywhere near as well attested as all these other guys. But what all this does show is that historians today feel so desperate to defend the existence of Jesus that they will make wholly false claims like these, confidently resorting to rampant hyperbole, misinforming all their students and readers, in pursuit of keeping their peers and the public quiet about it. And that suggests the case for Jesus really is disturbingly weak—and that the consensus is not built on sound reasoning. Otherwise, historians would have been consistently honest about the actual evidence gap. They wouldn't be making ridiculous claims like these. *That instead they do* is why they can't be trusted. When the consensus appears founded on desperate bluster contrary to obvious facts, it's time for that consensus to go.

6

More Like All the Other Dying-and-Rising Savior Gods of Yore

We saw in chapter two how the Jesus cult could have been a lot like a Jewish version of what Osiris cult had become. Osiris was a dying-and-rising savior god, who never really existed, but whose public gospels placed him on Earth anyway, as a historical pharaoh. And yet his priesthood secretly taught that he was never such a person, but only ever a celestial being who endured a celestial death at the hands of the Egyptian equivalent of Satan, in outer space below the orbit of the moon, then rose from the dead in a supernatural body to reign from the heavens above. We also saw that Christianity resembles this and other ancient savior cults in countless details and clearly is a Jewish version of them. We've since seen there is no good historical evidence that Jesus was ever real, any more than Osiris was, or any of the other savior gods, who likewise were all portrayed as historical, yet none were. But here we'll see it's worse than that. Not only is evidence lacking, but evidence is abundant that Jesus was invented using numerous mythical archetypes.

If All We Have Is a Gospel . . . ?

I've already noted that since the Christian Jesus looks so much like all other mythical savior figures, it would be *remarkable* if he, alone among them, *actually* existed. We therefore need some evidence that he is, indeed, the exception to the rule. And that's precisely the evidence we lack. We can't point to "the Gospels," as all other savior gods had "Gospels" like them, placing them in human earth history, in every case *mythically*. So we can no more use the Gospel of Mark to argue Jesus really existed than we can use Plutarch's biography of Romulus to argue Romulus really existed. Or Hercules. Or Osiris. Or Bacchus. Or any other savior god. *All mythical gods had biographies written about them pretending they were real historical people.* So the probability we'd have one for a mythical Jesus is one-hundred percent expected even if he didn't exist, which is already the highest probability any evidence can have. So merely having a biography of him cannot increase the probability he existed—at all. That would require some evidence that is *more* likely if he existed than if he didn't. But as we've already seen in previous chapters, we have no such evidence in the Gospels, and we have no such evidence outside the Gospels—other than maybe some vague passages in the authentic Epistles of Paul, which we'll look at in the closing chapters of this book. But even there, the evidence is weak tea. Which ought to warrant considerable uncertainty—not obsessive certitude.

In this chapter we'll look at just how starkly this is the case, by exposing just how mythical the Gospels are, and how unlike actual researched histories they are; and how much Jesus looks like just another mythical culture hero—a revised Moses or Elijah—and just another savior god—a revised Romulus or Bacchus or Osiris. We already saw before how the stories told about him in the Gospels are invented tales serving a purpose—or at best we can find no evidence they aren't. That they are just the random recording of oral lore is by contrast an assumption without evidence, indeed even contrary to the evidence we have; and even if true, gets us nowhere closer to history, as made-up myths can be circulated and passed on orally just the same as in writing. Similar lore was built around every other nonexistent hero, Jewish *and* Gentile. So no argument to historicity can proceed from this, either. Attempts to argue that at least *something* in the Gospels more likely derived from a real history than mythography, we already saw, simply don't succeed, ignoring either logic or the actual facts of the case. Here we'll see why it's worse than even that.

When we look at how the Gospels are constructed, and compare them with how actual biographies of real people and genuine histories of the period looked, the fact that they are myths becomes all the clearer. Real histories and biographies exhibited some critical awareness of problems with their sources or with the intrinsic believability or uncertainty of at least some events. They admitted when something sounds amazing, or when their sources contradict each other or are not completely reliable. They were concerned to understand causality and why things happened as they did, and they strove to make what they report understandable as history. Myths, by contrast, show little awareness of sources at all, will report the incredible as if it were ordinary, will rarely even mention alternative accounts of the same event even when we know they exist; they'll even just change the story, without mentioning that they are, or why; and then they build their stories symbolically and cryptically, with minimal regard for intelligibility or causal sense. Real histories and biographies also tended to engage in logical historical argument, at least occasionally addressing their evidence and assessing its merit. Mythographies usually didn't; they'd simply tell stories as if not a single event or fact is doubtful or uncertain. At most they might admonish their readers, 'You'd better believe, or else' (John 20:29–31)—the surest giveaway that what you are reading isn't true. Comparing the Gospels with ancient histories and biographies makes undeniably clear: they belong to mythography, not historiography.

A Popular Fashion for Dying-and-Rising Gods

All across what was then the Roman Empire, well before and during the dawn of Christianity, there were many dying-and-rising gods in popular myth and literature—not just Osiris. And yes, they were gods. Some even half-god, half-human, of divine or magical parentage, just like Jesus (as we learn in Philippians 2:6–8; Romans 8:3; Matthew 1:18–25; Luke

1:26–35; John 1:1–18). And yes, these gods died. And yes, they were then raised back to life, living on, even more powerful than before. Some returned in the same body they died in; some lived their second life in new or even more powerful and magical bodies, just like Jesus (as we learn in 1 Corinthians 15:35–50 and 2 Corinthians 5). Some left empty tombs or gravesites, or their corpses were otherwise lost or vanished. Just like Jesus. Some returned to life on "the third day" after dying. Just like Jesus. Most went on to live and reign in heaven—not on Earth. Just like Jesus. Some still even visited Earth after being raised from the dead, to deliver a message to disciples or followers, before ascending again into the heavens. Just like Jesus. And all these gods were depicted as historical people. But none of them really existed.

There were likewise countless mythical gods who were miraculously conceived, sometimes even born to women who were still virgins. Just like Jesus. But this notion is never made explicit for Jesus in the earliest Christian texts, whereas his death and resurrection was. So the dying-and-rising god, particularly the dying-and-rising *savior* god, is the mythotype most descriptive of original Christianity. But the parallel is still essential to understand: every "miraculous conception" story flourishing in the ancient world at that time, indeed even every "virgin birth" story, is different from every other. They differ from each other in nearly every particular detail: Ra, Hephaestus, Mars, Attis, Perseus, Romulus, for each at least one version of their myth imagines their conception was miraculous. Hence all share one common theme: in at least one known version of their myth, their mother became pregnant without sexual congress; and in some cases, had never had sex at all. This is how mythic parallels always operate: differences across these myths *always* exist; what they share in common is the underlying theme: a miraculous or virgin birth. It is therefore irrational to claim, "But they all differ from each other, therefore they aren't at all connected." Of course they're connected. They are linked by a singular, powerful idea that inspired numerous different instantiations of that same idea. Likewise for death and resurrection: how a god dies, irrelevant; in what body they rise from the dead, irrelevant. Because the common idea inspiring them all is *dying* and *returning to life*. That's the underlying mytheme. The rest is simply variation on the theme. As such, the developing myth of Jesus is clearly part and parcel of this same widespread trend. Every death and resurrection differed from every other. And thus so did the death and resurrection of Jesus. But all shared the same mytheme of *death* and *resurrection*.

Some real people had later legends attached to them of miraculous conceptions, too, like Alexander the Great. And there were real historical people claimed to have risen from the dead in some sense, like Julius Caesar. But most such heroes never really existed; and none who became the central figures of savior cults did. Thus for anyone who had this claimed of them, we definitely need to double-check the evidence before being certain they actually existed; because usually, they didn't. When we do that for historical people—like Alexander or Caesar (as I demonstrated in the last chapter)—the evidence we find is overwhelming, so we *know* they're exceptions to this "myth-making" rule. But when we do this for Jesus, we don't get the same results. Not even at all. *So we should not be as confident in Jesus' existence as we are in Alexander's or Caesar's.*

Ideas that ancient people witnessed as pervasive (many different kinds of miraculous conceptions; many different kinds of resurrections) were readily then seen as bearing a cultural commonality ("a" virgin birth; "a" resurrection), and that commonality could then be adapted to any specific belief system, creating a new religion, or a new variant of an old one. The process always involves transformation: the creation of differences. A new and different miraculous conception story; a new and different resurrection story. Those differences are what is brought by the native adopting culture. But the underlying idea is what is adopted from the outside culture—often a dominating imperialist culture—and transformed into a new religious idea by the local native religion. This is how Christianity developed within the Roman Empire.

The second-century Christian writer Justin Martyr was well aware of this, and that his peers understood it too, admitting that:

> When we say the Word, who is the first-born of God, was produced without sexual union, and that He, Jesus Christ, our Teacher, was crucified and died, and rose again, and ascended into heaven, we propound nothing different from what you believe regarding those whom you esteem the sons of Jupiter.

And for this reason, Justin had to *deny* this meant cultural influence by claiming Satan invented all these earlier versions of those Christ mythemes to trick us. "When I hear," Justin wrote, "that Perseus was begotten of a virgin, I understand that the deceiving serpent counterfeited this" idea. We know cultural anthropologists have a much more likely explanation. And indeed, all mainstream scholars now agree: already-popular mytho-heroic ideas were simply added on to Jesus over time. Only, the death and resurrection mytheme *wasn't an add-on*. It's fundamental to the whole origin of Jesus as an idea. Paul, after all, appears to say no one ever saw or met Jesus until *after* his resurrection, in visions spawning the entire Christian religion (1 Corinthians 15:3-8). Could that be in fact what actually happened? *Tales* of his death and resurrection arose later, and *were* mytho-heroic add-ons, built out of prior resurrection and hero stories, reworked into new ones by the creative minds and rhetorical purposes of the Gospel authors. But Jesus being *in essence* a dying-and-rising God is how Jesus appears to have begun. And that makes it reasonably likely he did indeed *begin* that way. Without evidence to rule that out, we cannot honestly *claim* to have ruled it out.

Like miraculous conceptions, every dying-and-rising god is different. Every death is different. Every resurrection is different. The common mythic feature is that there is a death and a resurrection. Everything else is a mixture of syncretized ideas from the borrowing and borrowed cultures, to produce a new and unique god and myth. Nearly every culture in the Mediterranean created and popularized one: the Egyptians had one, the Thracians had one, the Greeks had one, the Romans had one, the Syrians had one, and so on. The Jews were actually late to the party in constructing one of their own, in the form of Jesus Christ. It just didn't become popular among the Jews, and thus ended up a Gentile religion. But understanding the structure of this new addition to the family of dying-and-rising saviors still requires understanding its Jewishness: all the "differences" between Jesus and every other dying-and-rising god are entirely the Jewish contribution, transforming the general mytheme into their particular cultural and religious understanding.

Now, that there were dying-and-rising god myths in antiquity is often ignorantly denied. So I will catalog why we are certain this religious phenomenon was real. Detailed source citations and scholarship you'll find, as always, in *On the Historicity of Jesus*. I've also cataloged even more evidence than is cited there in an article on my blog, "Dying-and-Rising Gods: It's Pagan, Guys. Get Over It." But in summary, here we go . . .

Plutarch said both Dionysus and Osiris were clearly understood to have died and been resurrected. He tells us in chapter 9 of his book *On the E at Delphi* that many religions of his day "narrate deaths and vanishings, followed by returns to life and resurrections," citing as his principal examples the Egyptian cult of Osiris and the Greek cult of Bacchus-Dionysis. And as I already noted, in chapter 35 of his book *On Isis and Osiris*, Plutarch outright calls this a "return to life" and a "resurrection," using the same word for resurrection found in the Gospel of Matthew. Plutarch also described Osiris physically returning to Earth after his death in chapter 19 of that same book, telling us that "Osiris came to Horus from the other world and exercised and trained him for the battle," and taught him other lessons, and then "consorted with Isis after his death and she became the mother of Harpocrates." And his ascending to heaven I likewise demonstrated from Plutarch's discussion of the teachings of the Osirian priesthood. (All this I covered in chapter two.)

In every version of his myth, Osiris only comes back to life after Isis reassembles and reanimates his corpse. Again, some want to deny this. But the physical resurrection of that corpse is explicitly described in pre-Christian pyramid inscriptions. There we find etched on the walls declarations of one or another divine agent (often Isis):

- "I have come to thee . . . that I may revivify thee, that I may assemble for thee thy bones, that I may collect for thee thy flesh, that I may assemble for thee thy dismembered limbs . . . [so] raise thyself up, king, [as for] Osiris; thou livest!" (Pyramid Texts 1684a–1685a and 1700; Utterance 606 and 670);

- "Raise thyself up; shake off thy dust; remove the dirt which is on thy face; loose thy bandages!" (Pyramid Texts 1363a–b; Utterance 553);

- "[As for] Osiris, collect thy bones; arrange thy limbs; shake off thy dust; untie thy bandages; the tomb is open for thee; the double doors of the coffin are undone for thee; the double doors of heaven

are open for thee . . . thy soul is in thy body . . . raise thyself up!"
(Pyramid Texts 207b–209a and 2010b–2011a; Utterance 676).

That sure sounds like a physical resurrection of Osiris's body to
me. And this is confirmed by the most recent translation of these texts
by James P. Allen: these spells, he explains, are sung to and about the
resident Pharaoh, but in the role of Osiris, because the Pharaoh was
expected to receive *the same resurrection as Osiris*. For instance, one such
inscription declares "there has been done for me what was done for my
father Osiris on the day of tying bones together, of making functional
the feet"; another says "do for him that which you did for his brother
Osiris on the day"; and so on. Thus the physical resurrection of the dead
Osiris was a well known mytheme long before Christianity arose.

As I noted already, by the time Christianity appeared this had been
reimagined as a cosmic event. Osiris was "really" killed in outer space
by the Egyptian equivalent of Satan, is there resurrected, and ascends to
rule from above, as was said of the risen Jesus, who no more remained
on Earth than Osiris did (as we learn most assuredly in Hebrews 9).
Osiris even rose from the dead "on the third day" after a full moon,
just like Jesus. If you didn't know, Passover, when Jesus dies, always
occurs during a full moon, and Jesus is raised two days later, making
three days altogether; likewise Osiris (*On Isis and Osiris* 13, 39, 42). Sure,
all the incidental particulars are different between them. But in the
abstract, really, the difference between them is that Judaism preferred
not a cyclical-eternal but a linear-apocalyptic conception of theological
history, so when a Jewish version of this mytheme was constructed, they
converted the god's continual dying and rising into a singular apocalyptic
event: Jesus dies and rises once and for all, not every year. Otherwise, in
essentials it appears all the same.

And that's just Osiris. Clearly raised from the dead in his original,
deceased body; visiting people on Earth in his risen body; and then ruling
from heaven above. In later accounts, he rises in a new supernatural
body, just like Paul said of Jesus (1 Corinthians 15:37–49). And either
way, that myth defined a whole nation directly adjacent to Judea, well
known to a major Jewish population in Alexandria, and popular across
the whole empire.

Osiris was already by then recognized as eerily similar to Dionysus—also popularly known as Bacchus—who had many different tales told of him, just as Osiris did. In one of which Dionysus is killed by being torn apart as a baby, and then resurrected by a human woman, Semele, conceiving a new body for him in her womb after drinking a magic slushy made from bits of his corpse. This is a literal resurrection—just by an elaborate mechanism. The god definitely dies, and then returns to life by acquiring the same kind of body he once had, assembled and "regrown" from parts of his old one. In this version of his myth, he is a full god (son of Zeus and Persephone) but still mortal (capable of being killed by dismemberment, like a vampire); he then is "reborn" a demigod (from the womb of a mortal human woman). This was the savior god central to the Bacchic mysteries, one of the most widely known and celebrated in the Western world at the time. Those baptized into his cult received eternal life in paradise; and as I already noted, just like Paul told us about Christians (in 1 Corinthians 15:29), Dionysians could even baptize themselves on behalf of deceased loved ones, and thus rescue those already dead, who would gain a renewed life eternal in another world.

Zalmoxis was also a resurrected savior, from a region adjacent to the mythic homeland of Dionysus. We know this from Herodotus writing hundreds of years before Christianity. Greeks making fun of the Thracian cult worshiping him made up the polemic that he didn't really die, he just hid in a cave, and thus pretended to have resurrected from the dead. But this mockery tells us the Thracians *did indeed* believe Zalmoxis had died and rose from the dead and appeared to disciples on Earth to prove it. The real teachings involved no cave (that was made up by Greeks poking fun at the Zalmoxians), but they did clearly relate his outright return and declaration of having died and risen from the dead, and a promise to grant the same to all who shared communion with him. His disciples thus believed they would benefit from his power to bring them into eternal life in paradise, and that they would live forever. Accordingly, Celsus, the earliest known critic of Christianity, included Zalmoxis in his own list of resurrected deities, in his own demonstration of how popular this trope was before Christians adopted it.

Zalmoxis cult was clearly quite ancient. But the earliest known resurrected god is Inanna of Sumer. For her, a clear-cut death-and-resurrection tale exists on clay tablets inscribed in Sumeria well over a thousand years before Christianity, plainly describing her humiliation, trial, execution, and crucifixion, and her resurrection three days later. After she is stripped naked and judgment is pronounced against her, Inanna is "turned into a corpse" and "the corpse was hung from a nail" and "after three days and three nights" her assistants ask for her corpse and resurrect her (by feeding her the "water" and "food" of life), and "Inanna arose." And this was according to what had been her plan all along, because she knew her father "would surely bring me back to life," exactly as transpires in the story. This cult continued to be practiced into the Christian period, Tyre being a major center of her worship, though we've lost all textual sources to confirm what it was then like. There is some evidence though that her resurrection tale had by then shifted to her consort Tammuz, one of several resurrected deities the Greeks called "Adonis."

Adonis was the title of possibly several different gods by the time Christianity began. He was sometimes equated with Tammuz, or possibly only confused with him, but either way certainly a resurrected god. Tryggve Mettinger's detailed 2001 study *The Riddle of Resurrection: "Dying and Rising Gods" in the Ancient Near East* includes discussion of the pre-Christian manuscript of a private letter in which a man likens his ability to survive several deadly uprisings to Tammuz's ability to always return from the dead (p. 201), which would certainly suggest Tammuz had by then become the center of his own resurrection cult. This is the same god for whose death even women in Jerusalem mourned (Ezekiel 8:14–15), so his cult was certainly well known to the Jews. And there is no evidence the Tammuz being mourned remained dead. That pre-Christian letter alone attests it was commonly known he returned to life. And in the third century A.D. the Christian scholar Origen says in his *Comments on Ezekiel* that Tammuz was still worshiped even then under the title of Adonis, and as such "certain rites of initiation are conducted" for him, "first, that they weep for him, since he has died; second, that they rejoice for him because he has risen from the dead" (*apo nekrôn anastanti*, the same Greek phrase popularly used of Jesus). This is confirmed over a century later in Jerome's *Commentary on Ezekiel* 3.8.14.

Recent pre-Christian finds attest that indeed a period of rejoicing followed mourning the death of Tammuz, which matches Origen's description. Benjamin Foster discusses this new evidence, for example, in the "Descent of Ishtar to the Netherworld" (which you can find in the 3rd edition of *Before the Muses: An Anthology of Akkadian Literature*). And we have this similarly described by a pagan author shortly before Origen, who describes national ceremonies of mourning for Adonis's death that are followed the next day by celebrations of his returning to life and ascending into outer space. Killed by a beast, we're told, he becomes "a dead person," then he is buried and mourned; and the next day "they proclaim he lives," and he ascends into the skies (as written by either Lucian or Pseudo-Lucian, *On the Syrian Goddess* 6–8).

I shouldn't have to explain that it's far more likely the resurrection of this Adonis had been celebrated long before Christianity began than that it would be a recent innovation. Surely Origen would have known if it were, and made obvious sport of the fact. It would likewise be incredible that even at this early stage major pagan cults celebrated by entire nations would have fundamentally changed their entire religion in emulation of Christianity, which was a little known, wholly uninfluential cult that was rarely liked even when anyone had heard of it. This conclusion is assured when combined with the pre-Christian evidence linking Tammuz to that same returning to life, and other evidence, such as the pre-Christian poem of Theocritus (*Idyll* 15), which describes an Adonis celebration in Egypt in which the death of Adonis is mourned, but then anticipates his return, concluding, "Goodbye, Adonis darling; and I only trust you may find us all thriving when you come next year!"

And that's still not all.

Asclepius was another popular resurrected god. Christian apologists again try to deny this by saying Asclepius merely, like Caesar, "rose to heaven" like a ghost upon his death. But that is not what his ancient worshipers said. Celsus reported that "a great many Greeks and Barbarians claim they have frequently seen, and still see, no mere phantom, but Asclepius himself" (Origen, *Against Celsus* 3.24). By all ancient accounts Asclepius was killed by lightning and buried. He was then restored from death to become a living god. As Ovid put it, "by a god he was turned into a bloodless corpse, and then from a corpse became a god, twice renewing his fate" (*Metamorphoses* 2.647–648).

That's a resurrection. And that this was considered a resurrection is fully confirmed by the narrative. Zeus killed Asclepius for resurrecting the dead, but when the slain's father Apollo complained, Zeus relented and restored Asclepius back to life, this time as an immortal god. Ovid thus remarks that "Zeus did for his son's sake that which he forbade be done" (*Fasti* 6.761); in other words, Zeus forbade raising the dead, but made an exception for Asclepius. So clearly it was understood Zeus rose Asclepius from the dead. He had been a corpse, and so he would have remained, but by a miracle of God, by which he became alive again, eternal and immortal, and supernaturally powerful. Just like Jesus.

Baal (or "Ba'al") is, like Adonis, the name of several deities (essentially meaning "Lord"), including as an epithet of the god Marduk. And we know one of the gods so-named was among the most ancient of resurrected gods. His death is probably the same mourned under the name Hadad-Rimmon in Zechariah 12:11. But whether or no, in pre-Christian texts Baal's "corpse" is found by Anat, so in his myth the god is definitely dead; one text even outright says "and the gods will know that you are dead," and multiple gods actually declare him dead; he is then buried, and funeral rites performed (as cataloged by Mettinger in *Riddle*, pp. 60–62). There are also clear references to Baal's resurrection. His returning to life and then living forever are even used as analogies in pre-Christian immortality spells (Mettinger, *Riddle*, pp. 69–71). Only at that time he was not yet a personal savior god but his myth was intended as a metaphor for communal agricultural salvation. But that was all prior to Hellenization, when he was transformed, like Osiris and Bacchus and Adonis and all the others, into one of the many popular personal savior gods of the era: this time under the name Jupiter Dolichenus. But owing to Medieval Christian destruction of pagan evidence we have little surviving about that sect, a problem we ought to be concerned about. The third-century Christian scholar Hippolytus devoted two entire chapters of his *Refutation of All Heresies* to such mystery cults and their savior deities, yet curiously those are the only two books thereof that were wholly destroyed. What were the Christians who destroyed them trying to hide? What did they not want us to read? I'll let your imagination ponder. But this still isn't the last of the list.

Melqart is another of the most ancient of resurrected deities, akin to Baal in both his origins and possible future co-option into later Hellenistic mystery cults. His legend became fused with that of Hercules. Centuries before Christianity, and later attested by authors of the Roman period, Eudoxus of Cnidus wrote that Hercules was "killed by Typhon, but Iolaus brought a quail to him, and having put it close to him," and ritually burning it, "he smelt it and came to life again" (as reported in Athenaeus, *The Dinnersages* 9.392d–e; see Mettinger, *Riddle*, p. 86). Even the first-century Jewish historian Josephus attests to ongoing celebrations of the "Resurrecting Hercules" (*tou Hrakleous egersin*: in *Jewish Antiquities* 8.146; mistranslated in Whiston: see Mettinger, *Riddle*, pp. 88–89). In both accounts, this is explicitly said to be a story of the Tyrian Hercules, which we know from other sources meant Melqart, whose base of worship was also centered at Tyre just like the cult of Innana-Tammuz.

Diodorus tells a different story of Hercules being killed by fire— dying of poison, he is burned on a pyre. Because his bones then vanished when Iolaus tried to collect them, the story goes, it was concluded Hercules had been resurrected and ascended to heaven (*Library of History* 4.38.5). The supposition of resurrection upon the vanishing of a corpse was not only a common motif in antiquity; it is essentially the story told of Jesus (as thoroughly examined in Richard Miller's 2017 book *Resurrection and Reception in Early Christianity*; and supported by examples in Ava Chitwood's 2004 book *Death by Philosophy*). The addition of appearance narratives to seal the deal also accompanies many of these tales (as we'll see with Romulus, for example). And there may have been such for Hercules. But in any event, it was clearly believed he had died, and had been raised from the dead, and then ascended to heaven with divine power. Just like Jesus.

Mettinger finds a slew of pre-Hellenistic evidence referring to the "raisers of Melqart" and to Melqart as "the risen" and his ceremony as "the rising" (*Riddle*, pp. 90–97). Which is the more telling in context— because other evidence for a resurrected Tyrian Hercules, the Hellenistic Melqart, remains conclusive. Perhaps the best evidence is a votive object actually depicting the death, burial, mourning, and resurrection of Melqart (Mettinger, *Riddle*, pp. 98–100), wherein again a three-day sequence is implied (p. 102). As the second-century wit Lucian observed, the popular belief is that upon death "all bodily things" a man "strips off and abandons before he mounts up, just like Heracles burning on Mount Oeta before deification: he too cast off whatever of the human he had from his mother, and soared up to the Gods with his divine part pure and unalloyed, sifted by the fire" (Lucian, *Hermotimus* 7). Thus again, though his "resurrection" is portrayed as a direct ascent into outer space, nevertheless he died, was dead, and then cast off his corpse, and rose back to life, ascending, in his superior divine body, after its mortal material was sloughed off into the pyre. Much like Jesus.

Thus it is that Mettinger concludes there were many "dying gods" who were "gods that rise or return to new life" (p. 217) and these were indeed "gods who both die and return long before the Christian era." He confirms this for Tammuz, Baal, and Melqart; and even Osiris; and probably, he admits, the Levantine Adonis (p. 218). Add to these the indisputable examples of Asclepius and Zalmoxis and Dionysus and (as we shall see) Romulus, and there simply is no possible way to honestly deny that this was a widespread cultural phenomenon. Sure, Mettinger concludes they aren't all of the same exact "type" (for instance, they aren't all "storm gods"), but they do all exhibit the same trend of "association and syncretism" (p. 218), each influencing the development of the others. And indeed, he confirms, these "dying and rising gods were known in Palestine in New Testament times" (p. 220). So there is no explaining that away. Everything that Mettinger then says is different between Jesus and those other dying-and-rising gods he examines (p. 221) is all explicable as either the common framing of Hellenistic mystery religion (which followed the period Mettinger focused on), or the Jewish element of the resulting syncretism.

For example, Jesus' death and resurrection is a singular apocalyptic event rather than part of an eternal cycle . . . because that's the Jewish contribution fused to the dying-and-rising motif. It's exactly how a dying-and-rising god would then be Judaized. Likewise, the role of sacrificial atonement blood-magic in framing his death, which is exactly a replication of Jewish temple atonement magic—Jesus thus becomes the Yom Kippur, foundational to Jewish soteriology. So we can already expect *that* in the creation of any Jewish savior cult as well. Meanwhile, the Hellenistic contributions include the role of Jesus as incarnated divine being—and thus demigod and not fully human nor fully god. In this respect he most closely models Romulus, who was also a preexistent celestial who flew down from outer space and assumed a mortal body, even arranging for himself to be born to a human woman. But as we've seen, many other resurrected mortals and demigods abounded to inspire the same concepts. Likewise, the abandonment of the communal agricultural context and its replacement with an interpretation of future individual salvation is exactly what happened to many other resurrected gods—such as Osiris, Adonis, Dionysus, Baal-Dolichenus—precisely in consequence of the influence of the Hellenistic mystery religions.

Many of these gods had other myths, with different stories and fates imagined for them. But this was also true of Jesus, for whom competing Christian sects (as well as anti-Christian polemicists) wove and taught different stories of what actually happened to Jesus, of how his resurrection was actually effected, and so on. In some versions, Jesus's soul escapes his body at his death (as per the teachings in the *Second Treatise of the Great Seth*). In some versions, Jesus leaves his flesh behind in the grave (as per the teachings in the *Gospel of Philip* or the *Gospel of Thomas*). But just as we can choose to focus on one popular version of his myth that we want to explain (the one in which he is an actual dying-and-rising god—either rising in his restored corpse, per the Gospels, or a newly made super-body, per Paul), so we must do the same for all the other dying-and-rising gods we are tracing the same motifs to.

The resurrection of Jesus, for example, has more in common with the reanimated Dionysus born of Semele from a potion, than from the Dionysus born by a second sexual conception by Zeus—in which account (known only from Late Antique fabulists) *Zeus* is the one who ate the dead heart of the slain Dionysus, and thereby imbued with the requisite atoms to pass on again, he reinseminated Semele sexually rather than asexually, and Dionysus is thus reconceived from atoms of his corpse and reborn, through this much more exceedingly complex chain of events. These stories are very different, but when looking for elements of influence upon the construction of the myth of Jesus (like the idea of an asexual conception of a demigod by a mortal woman), it's the *actual* precedents we want to examine—not the stories that *didn't* have an influence. Jews abhorred the idea of divine beings engaging in sexual reproduction. So when any Jew was constructing his own resurrected savior god, "born of a woman," he needed to look around for ideas of gods conceiving by a mortal woman that didn't involve sex. There were many such models around to inspire the idea (just see my blog article, "Virgin Birth: It's Pagan, Guys. Get Over It"). Having a demigod slain and resurrected as a baby *also* didn't suit the needs of the messianic model a Jew would prefer, so obviously other models were looked to there as well—*other* gods, whose death-and-resurrection tales would better suit the final apocalyptic atonement sacrifice that Jewish soteriology required. But Dionysus is nevertheless one of many widely known instantiations of a common motif of the miraculously born, dying-and-rising savior god—each, like Jesus, just as unique as the next: from Dionysus and Osiris and Zalmoxis to Inanna, Dolichenus, and Adonis, and likewise Romulus, Hercules, and Asclepius.

It simply cannot be claimed that the Jewish authors of their own miraculously born, dying-and-rising savior, were in no way aware of nor at all influenced by the widespread instantiation of exactly that kind of savior figure all around them, in practically every culture they knew. That's simply absurd. The coincidence is impossible. Which is why even ancient Christian apologists were not so foolish as to claim this—or even more absurdly, claim that no such dying-and-rising savior model *even existed*. Of course it existed. And they well knew it. They chose to blame it on the Devil. They preferred to believe Satan had plagiarized the idea in advance, to try and set up a culture that would then dismiss the Jesus story as just another myth akin to all the others the Devil had conjured. This is a ridiculous defense, akin to claiming evolution is obviously false because the Devil "planted all the fossils." And yet, such a defense proves there are fossils. Just as Justin's defense proves there were dying-and-rising gods. They all knew it. So let's admit it already.

It follows that the only plausible reason why some Jews ever came up with a *Jewish* dying-and-rising savior god in *precisely* that region and era, is that everyone else had one. It was so popular and influential, so fashionable and effective, it was inevitable this idea would seep into some Jewish sect's consciousness, and erupt onto the scene of "inspired" revolutionizing of a perceived-to-be-corrupted faith. They Judaized it, of course. Jesus is as different from Osiris as Osiris is from Dionysus or

Inanna or Romulus or Zalmoxis. The differences are the Jewish tweaks. Just as the Persian Zoroastrian system of messianism, apocalypticism, communal resurrection, an evil Satan at war with God, and a future heaven and hell effecting justice as eternal fates for all, was Judaized when *those* beliefs were imported into Judaism. None of those ideas existed in Judaism before that. You won't find them in any part of the Old Testament written before the Persian conquest. And yet no one claimed they were "corrupting" Judaism with those pagan ideas (even though, in fact, they were). They simply claimed these new ideas were all Jewish, and always had been, ordained and communicated by God, through inspired scripture and revelation. The Christian sect did exactly the same thing, with the equally popular religious ideas of *their* conquerors.

It's time to face this fact, and stop denying it. It's time to get over it already. Resurrected savior gods were a pagan idea. All Christians did was invent a Jewish one.

So Many Heroes Alike

In fact Jesus belongs to numerous categories most of whose members are mythical: legendary kings, founders, and culture heroes; worshiped savior deities; mystery-cult sky-lords; dying-and-rising demigods; even conveniently named godmen. In fact, Jesus belongs to more myth-heavy reference classes than any other purportedly historical figure I know. This is why I'm deeply suspicious of his historicity, as much as I am of any other member of those same categories. True, some members of those reference classes really were actual, historical people, but we only know that—our suspicion is only overcome—because of an exceptional amount of evidence in their case, evidence I don't find anywhere for Jesus. We should respond to that fact the same way we do for every other member of these mythotypes: if we lack good evidence to show Romulus or Hercules or Moses existed, we should doubt they existed. And we do. All mainstream experts agree their historicity is dubious. The fact that Jesus is in exactly the same evidential state should warrant the same response. Why, after all, should it not?

From the very first moment any narrative gets recorded placing his life on Earth, Jesus is not only then or already a legendary king and culture hero, a worshiped savior deity, a mystery-cult sky-lord, a dying-and-rising demigod, an ancient heavenly founder, and a conveniently named godman, but also a preexistent incarnated superbeing—literally a mystically revealed space alien (as we learn in Philippians 2, Galatians 1, 2 Corinthians 12, Romans 16:25–26), whose earthly history is only ever claimed in sacred, mythic literature, where he conveniently fulfills numerous prophecies, and works improbable wonders never elsewhere recorded. His biography, from the very first, is substantially built out of prior religious heroes he is meant to supersede, including Moses, Elijah, Romulus, and others, and is rife with fabulous and improbable events. This biography names no sources, discusses no sources, and has no known sources. Instead, it emulates known counter-cultural hero narratives and popular ascending-sage legends—with even miraculous birth and appearance narratives added on later. And not one detail about Jesus in any of those biographies is demonstrably true.

It's not as if we first had more mundane memoirs or scattered accounts or discussions or mentions of his life that only later became embellished into all these extraordinary tales. No. We go directly from "revealed space alien" in Paul to completely fictional mythographies in the Gospels. No intermediate stage. No evidence backing anything in the latter. No evidence attaching the former to a real person. That the first biographies setting Jesus on Earth make Jesus look so much like so many other mythical, nonexistent persons should concern you. It should affect your assessment. The only debate should be about *how much* doubt it warrants—not whether it warrants any.

Improbable from the Start

Let's just look at the Gospel of Mark for a moment. It's easy to see how subsequent Gospels added even more absurdities. Everyone pretty much agrees the Gospels get more fabulous over time. But often it's claimed the first Gospel isn't fabulous at all, that Mark is more like the mundane memoir we ought to have if Jesus really existed. That couldn't be more inaccurate. Mark is wholly fabulous from its first chapter to the last. I demonstrate this quite thoroughly in *On the Historicity of Jesus*. Here I'll just walk you through some of the highlights.

Already, in its very first chapter, this is how Mark's story goes:

A historically famous Holy Man conveniently endorses Jesus as his successor and superior for no explicated reason. At which the sky rips apart, God's voice echoes from heaven declaring Jesus his son, and a magical spirit descends upon Jesus in the form of a dove. Jesus is then immediately magically attended by angels and animals in the desert, where he meets and overcomes Satan. Then he walks up to some random fishermen who never met or heard of him before, and with but a single sentence he immediately converts them to slavish followers who abandon their work and families to join him without explanation or settling of affairs. He then amazes whole towns with his extraordinary teaching, not one line of which teaching we are ever told about. In fact, it is never explained what was so amazing about anything he taught or why anyone was so impressed by it. He repeatedly talks to and commands demons who publicly proclaim him the Son of God—and again everyone is amazed by this, even though exorcists running such acts across Palestine were commonplace, not extraordinary. In fact, all throughout Mark's narrative, *no one* ever acts like any real person of that time and place actually would. This is clear chapter after chapter.

Jesus goes on exorcizing and healing countless folk and has whole towns gathering at his door. He instantly cures leprosy. These marvels continue into chapter 2, where now Jesus starts arguing with the authorities. We still aren't told what his amazing teachings are, and none of his arguments with the authorities are about anything he taught, only things he did: miraculously healing the ill on a Sabbath; hanging out with Gentiles and sinners; not fasting when he was supposed to. When challenged on these things, his responses are either too cryptically bizarre to have impressed anyone, or else he makes exactly the same arguments his opponents *in real life* actually made. For example, the very Mishnah law the Pharisees then defended *already declared* that healing was permitted on the Sabbath (*Yoma* 8:6), and so in the real world they would never have challenged Jesus on that. Even if a more conservative Pharisee had tried quibbling over whether Jesus' healings were "necessary" enough to override the Sabbath (the only point on which they'd actually have ever challenged him), the majority of Pharisees, who followed the more popular school of Hillel, *would have stood up in defense of Jesus*. Instead, Mark has completely erased the most influential school of the Pharisees from history, got entirely wrong what even the most conservative Pharisees would have argued, made Jesus voice the actual arguments of the Pharisees themselves as if he was arguing against the Pharisees, and pretended any Pharisees who would have opposed him had never heard those arguments before, from their own Mishnah tradition and majority of peers.

Every chapter thereafter is like this. Implausible stories, unexplained developments, unrealistic behavior from everyone involved, improbable events that could never have actually happened. Instead we get stylized fables exhibiting whatever Mark wants Jesus to have said or his readers to believe. Every chapter contains convenient teachings that don't make much sense in their supposed historical context—but only in Mark's fabricated literary context. Nearly every chapter portrays people behaving oddly. Every chapter includes one or more miracles that are ridiculous outside any other context than a myth, and that have a literary, moralistic, or symbolic purpose, just as one finds in every other myth. In Mark alone we get Jesus not merely summoning angels, rending the heavens and conjuring the voice of God therefrom, meeting Satan, curing the blind and the lame, and casting forth and conversing with demons, but also withering trees, mystically murdering thousands of pigs, calming seas, walking on water, raising the dead, rising from the dead, predicting the future, imbuing his clothes with a radiant glow, summoning ancient dead heroes on mountaintops, rending gigantic temple curtains from afar, feeding thousands with a single basket of food, blotting out the sun. Please. This is myth, not history.

Even the scenes depicting Jesus teaching are made up. For example, we know Jesus never taught anything about paying taxes, because Paul practically wrote a whole chapter on the subject (in Romans 13), yet he knew of no such teaching to cite as guide or authority. Instead, Mark takes what Paul said and converts it into a clever story about Jesus saying it (in Mark 12). Mark does this quite a lot; in fact, Mark appears to be mythologizing Jesus by building stories out of things taught by Paul, not Jesus. I quite thoroughly survey the evidence and scholarship establishing this point in my blog article "Mark's Use of Paul's Epistles." But here's just a sample . . .

Mark takes Paul's account of seeing Jesus explain to him the Eucharist in a vision (1 Corinthians 11:23–26, which Paul says he received directly "from the Lord"), and relocates that event to Earth, and populates it with an earthly audience (the Disciples, who are nowhere mentioned in Paul's account), whom now (in this new version) Jesus interacts with, and so Mark invents the Last Supper. Mark takes Paul's rebuke of Peter (in Galatians 2) and converts it into Jesus' rebuke of Peter (in Mark 8). Mark takes from Paul's letters the idea of a messianic secret (such as in 1 Corinthians 2:6–10) and implausibly weaves that theme throughout his narrative of Jesus—a theme so unrealistic it was gradually abandoned by later redactors of Mark. Mark gets the idea from Paul that Jesus was actually present with Moses during the desert Exodus (in 1 Corinthians 10:1–5), and from that invents a whole sequence of Jesus leading Jews around in the desert, recreating new versions of the miracles of Moses (Mark 4–8). For instance, Moses' parting of the sea is split into Jesus commanding the sea and walking across it; Moses feeding thousands with manna from heaven is split into Jesus twice feeding thousands with manna from his own hands; Moses healing the people is split into stories of Jesus healing people, just as Moses miraculously defeating hostile soldiers is split into stories of Jesus miraculously defeating hostile demons.

Mark likewise borrows from Paul the idea of interacting with Gentiles as much as Jews, and thus invents a Rabbi Jesus touring a Galilee "of the Gentiles," thereby reifying exactly where Isaiah 9 said the gospel would arise. This Jesus then has an excuse to implausibly interact with Gentiles as much as Jews. Mark describes Jesus being wrongly chastised by Pharisees (in Mark 2) for eating and drinking with "sinners and tax collectors" (in other words, Gentiles), just as Paul describes Peter being wrongly chastised by conservative Jews for doing the same thing (in Galatians 2). Conveniently, Mark's and Paul's message is the same here, yet Paul never cites Jesus as precedent or authority for this—Mark's story was thus invented later, crafted out of *Paul's* story, and is therefore obviously a fiction intended to make Paul's position that of Jesus.

And so on. This is all myth. Not memory.

Mark also takes prophecies and scriptures and turns them into history. His crucifixion narrative is built out of Psalm 22, with further details lifted from Amos 8:9, Isaiah 53, Wisdom 2, and other scriptures. His triumphal entry narrative is built out of prophecies from Zechariah 9 and 14 and Psalm 118. As we saw in chapter three, Mark takes from Paul the idea that Jesus and his sacrifice replicate and replace the Passover lamb and the goat of Yom Kippur, and builds his entire narrative around these two themes with the made-up Barabbas narrative—and as we shall see, with a whole lot more. All of this illustrates how much Mark is inventing a narrative to sell an underlying message, leaving little reason to believe anything he includes ever really happened. Why should we think so? If all the ridiculous things in it didn't happen, why should any of it have?

Consider even Mark's narrative structure. According to the Torah the Passover lamb had to be singled out and set aside on the tenth day of the month (Exodus 12:3), and then is slain at twilight on the fourteenth day (Exodus 12:6), when "the whole congregation of Israel must slay it together." And then the lamb is eaten when Passover begins on the fifteenth. This is essentially what happens to Jesus. On the tenth of the month he is singled out and set aside—by his triumphal entry into Jerusalem (Mark 11). Then on the fifteenth of the month Jesus is symbolically eaten in place of the Passover lamb—since at the Last Supper, he declares the food and drink there to be his body and blood. He is killed the next afternoon. Mark has thus deliberately arranged his narrative to symbolically represent Jesus as the Passover lamb.

Jesus was also known as the "firstfruits" of the general resurrection (1 Corinthians 15:20–23), and the Torah commands that the Day of Firstfruits take place the day after the first Sabbath following the Passover (Leviticus 23:5, 10–11). In other words, on a Sunday. Thus Mark has Jesus rise from the dead on Sunday, the firstftuits of the resurrected, symbolically on the very Day of Firstfruits itself, likewise satisfying Paul's declaration that Jesus rose again "on the third day" after he died. So the whole choice of what day to have Jesus crucified on is decided here by literary symbolism, not historical plausibility. Indeed, since executions would not be performed on holy days, Mark's narrative has no historical credibility at all. As we learn from the Mishnah tractate on the Sanhedrin, Jewish law also commanded that trials for capital crimes had to be conducted over the course of two days and could not be conducted on or even interrupted by a Sabbath or holy day—nor ever conducted at night. Mark's account violates every single one of these requirements and is therefore not at all what would actually have happened. In reality had Jesus been arrested at Passover he would have been held over in jail until Sunday, and could only have been convicted and executed on Monday at the earliest. So as history, Mark's narrative makes zero sense. But as symbolic myth, every oddity is explained, indeed expected.

It's therefore telling that the overall structure of Mark's closing narrative is centered on this Passover symbolism. As I explain and show in *On the Historicity of Jesus*, Mark's chapter 11 corresponds to the singling out of the Passover lamb; chapters 12 and 13 recreate a Passover seder in narrative form (Mark 12 recreating the haggadah where four sons ask four questions, in a particular sequence Mark has emulated; and Mark 13 recasting the seder elements of keeping watch for the messiah and recounting the tribulations endured and the salvation promised); chapter 14 depicts an actual Passover; and chapter 15 transforms Jesus' figurative death as the one eaten at Passover into Jesus' literal death ensuring our salvation. Mark even makes the time of his death, "the ninth hour," identical to that of the slaying of actual Passover lambs the day before. And finally chapter 16 symbolizes the very rescue from death that the Passover represents. On the original Passover, the angel of death "passed over" those who were protected by the lamb's blood and killed the "firstborn sons" of those who were not; in Mark, *the* firstborn son is *rescued* from death, and *his* blood protects those who share in it. This is all obvious mythic symbolism. It is not remembered history.

Then, to also represent Jesus as the sacrifice of Yom Kippur, Mark invented the Barabbas narrative, as I already mentioned in chapter three. In that tale, in Mark 15, we're told there was a "custom" of Romans releasing a criminal on the Holy Day, and the Jews demanded the rebel and murderer Barabbas be released instead of Jesus. No Roman magistrate, least of all the infamously ruthless Pontius Pilate, would let a murderous rebel go free, and no such Roman ceremony ever existed, nor could have. Mark made it all up, so he could emulate the Yom Kippur through this invented fable. In the real Yom Kippur, every year two identical goats would be selected, and upon one all the sins of

Israel would be cast, and it would be released to die in the wilderness, while the other would be sacrificed and its blood atone for those sins. This is obvious when you learn Barabbas means "Son of the Father," and in some manuscripts this Barabbas is even named "Jesus" as well, as if the point wasn't already obvious enough. Of course Mark's Jesus was *the* "Son of the Father." So we have two sons of the father here, and one is released into the wild mob bearing the sins of Israel—murder and rebellion—while the other is sacrificed so his blood may atone for the sins of Israel.

Had this story appeared in any other book, of any other religion, we would readily identify it as myth and not history. This is what Mark is doing in literally every chapter and section of his book. It's all just one, big, made-up story, a parable of parables, which if taken literally will ensure your damnation, and only if understood symbolically can you be saved. As Mark has Jesus himself say, "The secret of the kingdom of God has been given to you, but to those on the outside everything is said in parables so that they may be ever seeing but never perceiving, and ever hearing but never understanding, otherwise they might turn and be forgiven" (Mark 4:11–12). Mark is cluing you in to the function of his entire Gospel. If you are reading it as history, you are the outsider; you are the damned. Those who "get it" and will thus turn and be forgiven are those who read these stories as signifying deeper truths about reality—as symbolic, and not as events that "actually" happened; just as Mark's Jesus instructs that we approach *all* parables. It was only the later redactors of Mark who increasingly tried to market their rewrite of his Gospel as a history—first Matthew purports it all happened to fulfill prophecy (to make Mark's fable resemble the Pentateuch); then Luke tries to rewrite it all to look and sound like a rational Greco-Roman history (albeit only with vaguely formulated assertions); and finally John insists it's all literally true—and implies anyone who doesn't believe it will be damned (John 20:29–31). Thus, what Mark told his readers, through the voice of Jesus, has by then been completely reversed. This is how the whole Jesus narrative came to be transformed from myth to history.

Just as Mark's chapters 11 through 16 all fit this whole Passover–Yom Kippur structure that is obviously not historical, Mark's chapters 1 through 10 are similarly artificially constructed. Of course Mark's birth narrative for Jesus (1:1–13), portrayed as an adoption by God and imbuing of the Holy Spirit, reverses Mark's death narrative for Jesus (15:34–39)—both John the Baptist and Jesus cry out with a loud voice; in both narratives an allusion is made to Elijah; in both, the heavens are torn apart (at Jesus' baptism, literally; at his death, symbolically, in the magical tearing of the temple curtain, which famously had the heavens depicted upon it); in his baptism the Spirit descends "upon" Jesus, and in his death that same Spirit "departs" from him (the verb often translated "he gave up the ghost" literally means "he exhaled the Spirit," which means it entered into him at his baptism); and in both stories, Jesus is declared to be God's son—at his baptism, by God himself; at his death, by the Roman official standing watch. This is all mythical parallelism—symbolical fable, not historical memory.

For all the rest of Mark we get a system of concentric circles organizing his Gospel's entire ensuing narrative, which starts with *the beginning* of a peripheral ministry (1:14–34) and ends with *the concluding* of a peripheral ministry (10:46–52); then at first people are looking for Jesus to be healed, but Jesus says he needs instead to teach more people (1:35–38), concentrically paralleled by people looking to Jesus for boons, but Jesus instead teaches them the error of their ways (10:17–45); then Jesus ventures out "throughout all Galilee" (1:39–45), concentrically paralleled by Jesus venturing out to expand his ministry *beyond* Galilee (10.1–6); then Jesus stops at Capernaum and explains he can forgive sin (2:1–12), concentrically paralleled by Jesus returning to Capernaum to explain the dangers of sin (9:33–50); then we hear of problems and controversies (2:13–3.12), concentrically paralleled by once again hearing of problems and controversies (9:14–32); then we're told of an important gathering on a mountain (3:13–19), concentrically paralleled by another important gathering on a mountain (9:2–13); then Jesus is accused of being in league with the Devil, and preaches those who reject Jesus are damned (3:20–35), concentrically paralleled by Jesus accusing Peter of being in league with the Devil, and preaches those who blaspheme the Holy Spirit are damned (8:27–9.1).

In the center of these concentric rings of structure is an entire, similarly organized Sea Narrative (chapters 4 through 8), in which we get three repetitions of the exact same sequence: Jesus meets with crowds by the sea, with an uneventful trip in a boat; followed by an eventful crossing of the sea; and after landing, healings and exorcisms. Separating those three sequences are two repetitions of another identical sequence, each the reverse of the other: two stops and a tour ("going around" the villages); followed by a tour ("going around" the villages) and two stops. Throughout this repetitious sequence we are given competing examples of the gospel brought to Jews and the gospel brought to Gentiles, and we see Jesus reimagining the five miracles of Moses in pairs of events that make a decalogue of ten miracles.

History does not have structure like this. Only fictional narratives do. In ancient literature, the only histories that employ this kind of ring structure were achronological (lists of events by subject rather than in temporal order), for this very reason—actual events don't line up like this. *Only ancient fiction sequenced narratives this way.* And here we have seen every single chapter and verse of Mark is explicably part of an artificial symbolic structure, neatly organized, all with an apparent message, reifying the teachings of Paul in an imagined life of Jesus; it is not a random collection of memories or recollected stories. So why should we think any of it comes from any memory at all?

We see this kind of messaging structure all over Mark.

For example when Mark tells the fable of Jesus withering a fig tree: as history this tale makes no sense at all, not only because it defies the laws of physics, but also because Jesus' behavior would be wholly illogical even if such a thing actually happened—he curses a fig tree because it isn't bearing figs for him to eat *even though it wasn't the season for figs* (Mark 11:12–14). The fig tree promptly withers to death before nightfall (Mark 11:19–22). Obviously this story is completely made up. But why write such a bizarre fable? Well, to illustrate a point. This is a parable about Jesus and the gospel, a bit of fiction Mark has composed to communicate something he wants to say. As here, so everywhere else in Mark's Gospel: Mark is writing parables about Jesus as a mythical character; he is not recording anyone's memories of a historical man. And here, key to understanding Mark's point is to look at the seemingly unrelated tale Mark has wrapped this other absurd story around: in between Jesus cursing the tree (11:12–14), and confirming it's ensuing fate (11:19–22), Jesus attacks the temple cult in Jerusalem (11:15–18). So the beginning and end of the fig tree story is wrapped around (and thus contains within its center) the clearing of the temple. This was a common device in ancient literature: when one story is wrapped around another, each is meant to illuminate the meaning of the other. And here, the fig tree and its fate are a metaphor for the temple and its fate. It was no longer the season for the temple to bear fruit, because of its corruption and the coming end of the world; it therefore had to be destroyed and replaced with faith in Jesus. So Jesus' attack on the fig tree deliberately parallels and thus explains his attack on the temple, and vice versa, which is all meant to explain why God allowed the Romans to "wither" God's own temple and cult (as they did in the year 70, probably shortly after which Mark wrote). This is all fable, not history; allegory, not memory.

Mark does this again with the similarly implausible (and thus obviously made-up) tale of the raising of Jairus's twelve-year-old daughter, which Mark wrapped around a symbolically related story of a woman who had bled for twelve years. The coincidence of the number twelve is a dead give away: both stories are fable, not fact. They are meant to convey a point, not record history. In both tales, Jesus is explicitly asked to touch the girl (Mark 5:23) and does (5:41), while in between the woman seeks to touch Jesus (5:28) and does (5:27), and by this means both are "saved" (5:23, 28, 34) by "faith" (5:34, 36) in spite of "fear" (5:33, 36). Both the girl and the woman are called "daughter" (5:23, 34). Moreover, the woman has bled for twelve years, which is not only the same age as the girl, but also at which menstruation was thought typically to begin, and thus the point at which a girl becomes a woman. We can see symbolism here of the twelve tribes of Israel and how they shall be saved by evolving from the old Israel to the new, through faith in Jesus Christ. Whereas in no way is either story believable as history.

In fact, the Jairus tale is one of many examples throughout Mark where he has rewritten another mythical story told of Moses or Elijah or Elisha (in this case Elisha, in 2 Kings 4:17–37), recasting Jesus as the hero, and updating the messaging and historical context—a common technique of composing fiction taught and applied across antiquity. I list or discuss numerous examples in *On the Historicity of Jesus*. But this one will suit as exemplary of them all. In Elisha's story, a woman of Shunem (meaning "place of twice rest" in Hebrew, where Elisha would often take his rest, per 2 Kings 4:8–11—coincidental names being a common indicator of mythmaking) seeks out the miracle-working Elisha and to beg him to resurrect her son. After looking for Elisha she falls at his feet, begging his help; then someone checks on the boy and confirms he's dead. But Elisha is not deterred and goes into her house himself and works his magic, by word and touch, resurrecting the boy. In Mark's version (5:22–43), the same things happen: Jairus comes looking for Jesus and falls at his feet and begs his help; someone then comes to confirm his daughter is dead, but Jesus is not deterred and goes himself into the petitioner's house and works his magic, by word and touch, resurrecting the girl.

Several elements have been conspicuously reversed in Mark's version, producing even more telltale coincidences: instead of a woman begging for her son, a man comes begging for his daughter; and while in the Old Testament version an unnamed woman comes from a named town that means "rest," in Mark's version a named man comes from an unnamed town, and the man's name (Jairus) means "awaken" (*yair*, "to bring light, enlighten, awaken" in the Hebrew). Mark even borrows from the Greek edition of Elisha's tale: the clause *exestēsan euthus ekstasei megalē*, "immediately they were amazed with great amazement" at what Jesus had done (Mark 5:42) is an allusion to *exestēsas hēmin pasan tēn ekstasin tautēn*, "you have been amazed with all this amazement for us" (2 Kings 4:13), which is how the woman had earlier reacted to having Elisha as a guest, and for which he blessed her with a miraculous conception— of the very son he would later resurrect. Thus Mark accomplishes another literary reversal, switching the placement of this reaction (of double amazement) from the child's miraculous conception to the child's miraculous resurrection, and from what *earns* the miraculous reward to what *follows from* it.

Mark does this again and again, creating stories about Jesus by rewriting stories of other past heroes, updating and transforming them in intentionally meaningful ways. Even, sometimes, real people. You heard in chapter four the example of Mark employing the unrelated tale of Jesus ben Ananias as a framework for his own tale of Jesus Christ. In fact their passion sequences have over twenty parallels, in identical order. And in *On the Historicity of Jesus* I showed how the myth of Jesus as already first conceptualized in Mark models his narrative after storylines already told of *many* other persons, historical and mythical. Which is not typically how you record the lives of real people, whether from memories handed down from one person to the next, or direct eyewitness informants. It is, rather, indicative of a *mythical* person—particularly when *the first* narrative of that person ever to exist operates this way, rather than only *later* narratives adopting that style.

Besides Moses and Elijah and Elisha, and figures like Jesus ben Ananias, Mark's tale of Jesus also models the fake biography of the similarly mythical Aesop, whose own story structure had *already* been borrowed from legends developed around the historical Socrates. This mythotype includes over eighteen features, seventeen of which Mark borrowed for constructing the legend of Jesus:

1. They all came from a humble background (Socrates was the son of a stonemason; Aesop was a slave; Jesus, a carpenter's son).

2. And yet all were exalted as a moral hero and exemplary man, who was in the right all along, and whose teachings one ought to follow.

3. And that despite all of them having opposed and denounced the established religious authorities and having challenged the received wisdom of their people.

4. All of them were also given a "gift of the spirit" from God before their ministries began.

5. All attacked the sin and greed of the religious and political elite.

6. All attended the parties of sinners and ate and drank with them.

7. Yet all consistently denounced sinners, and sought to reform them.

8. All taught with questions, parables, and paradoxes.

9. All taught to love truth, despise money, and live with compassion for others.

10. All taught that they wanted to save everyone's soul.

11. All were despised by some and beloved by others for their teachings.

12. All were publicly mocked in some way.

13. All were executed by the state for blasphemy, a crime their tales affirm they did not commit.

14. All were *actually* executed for speaking against the sin and greed of the authorities.

15. All voluntarily went to their deaths, despite all having had the power to escape.

16. All prophesied that God's wrath would befall their killers; and all were right.

17. And all were subsequently revered as martyrs.

The eighteenth feature Jesus soon acquired as well, thus illustrating how readily he continued to be conformed to mythotypes: Aesop, Socrates, and eventually Jesus were all renowned to be ugly or deformed. Though not found in our extant Gospels, for Jesus this idea is affirmed (even derived from scripture) in Tertullian, Irenaeus, and Clement of Alexandria; even the critic Celsus took it as standard Christian belief decades before them. But even at seventeen features the model Mark followed in constructing a tale of Jesus is clear. That Mark's whole account would be built out of tropes from the *Lives of Aesop* is evidence of his mythographic designs from the very start.

But Mark didn't stop there. His tale also emulates over twenty tropes from a commonly repeated mythotype of the betrayed but celestially vindicated hero who ascends to heaven in glory—indeed, in many cases this mythotype already featured an outright dying-and-rising godman. But many of the same features were also commonly found in earlier Jewish myths of "abused and vindicated" righteous men, which Jesus' narrative also looks quite a lot like. As noted scholar George Nickelsburg explains, in Jewish myths and legends, "tales about a wise" or righteous man, or sometimes even woman, "who, as the object of a conspiracy or plot, is persecuted, consigned to death, rescued, vindicated, and exalted to high position in the royal court" were commonplace; as were Jewish wisdom tales that feature a righteous man "who is put to death but exalted in the heavenly courtroom, where he confronts his enemies as their judge." But what is aways shared across both genres is "the rescue and vindication of a persecuted innocent person."

Nickelsburg of course finds that the Markan Passion Narrative is just another rewrite of this same mytheme. Every similar sequence begins with an introduction of the characters and situation, a tale of provocation of the authorities by some act of or for the hero, the arising of a conspiracy in which the authorities look for the right moment or means to dispose of the hero, which is interwoven with a subplot of decision (wherein the hero must choose between obeying God or the authorities), and trust (wherein the decision to obey God is described in terms of trusting God's will, often voiced in a prayer for deliverance), and obedience to God and acceptance of the hero's fate (which is usually death). Just as for Jesus, many versions of this tale accomplish these elements with a trial at court. Formal accusations are brought against the hero, which are usually false or distorted; they then face a trial or the equivalent and are condemned; attempts are made to save them (Mark, for example, imagines Pilate attempting to let Jesus go, despite its historical implausibility); but those fail, so the hero undergoes an ordeal, and they are then rescued, vindicated, and exalted. As in Mark, these stories usually narrate the different reactions of those witnessing the key events, and often involve the hero being invested with royal power. God is then praised, the hero's new status acclaimed, and the persecutors punished (by the hero, or at his or her decision, or on his or her behalf), a feature Mark implies with Jesus' repeated promises to return and destroy those who killed him. These tales sometimes even contain allusions or links to God's suffering righteous servant in Isaiah 53, the very passage the "gospel" of Jesus is based on.

Mark's narrative follows this entire generic storyline. As Nickelsburg explains, "these stories have emplotted a common theme in a highly consistent series and sequence of narrative components," yet "each story has its own particular inner consistency and storyline that runs through its major elements and differentiates it from other stories in the genre." Just like Mark's story of Jesus. But Mark also merged this Jewish mythotype with that already-popular pagan mythotype of similar construction, one of the most prominent examples of which is the Roman national hero myth of their founding godman, Romulus.

By the time Matthew and Luke had embellished Mark's narrative, the passion narratives of Romulus and Jesus would share twenty features in common (fully cataloged with cited scholarship in *On the Historicity of Jesus*). But already in Mark several features of this trope appear. Shared by Romulus and Jesus: the hero is the Son of God; he is killed by a conspiracy of the ruling council (the Senate, for Romulus; the Sanhedrin, for Jesus); his death is accompanied by prodigies; and the land is covered in darkness; the hero's corpse goes missing; he then receives a new immortal body; which on occasion has a bright or shining appearance (for Jesus, prefigured in his transfiguration; and symbolized by the boy in a bright white garment at his grave); the names of those present at these events are given (even though none of these events happened, and none of those witnesses existed); and those witnesses are frightened by the hero's appearance or disappearance, or both; in response to either, some witnesses flee the scene; and though his followers are initially in sorrow over the hero's death, it is soon revealed, indeed "at the break of dawn" (just as in Mark), that the hero has risen from the dead, and that his body is "no longer here" because he has ascended to godhood; which event occurs outside of their capital city. Does this all sound familiar?

Public Romulus passion plays of the time even included the recitation of the names of those who fled his vanishing in fear, and who thus "remained silent" out of fear for a long time, just as Mark ends his tale of Jesus. Indeed, one of those witnesses named in Romulus's passion play is none other than . . . Mark. Though that name appears to have been added to the Gospel later. Within the *anonymous* text, after the author of that Gospel names the three women in mourning—the two Marys and Salome—and depicts them discovering that the body of Jesus has vanished, "trembling and bewildered," Mark concludes, those "women went out and fled from the tomb," and "said nothing to anyone, because they were afraid." The similarity to Romulus's passion plays would have been evident to any Roman reader of the time. Indeed, this myth enacted of Romulus declared him a preexistent eternal being, a god *become incarnate*, to die for the good of Rome and be raised to glory and divine power. So we here have a model of the same story: a great man, founder of a great kingdom, is actually an incarnated god, but dies as a result of a conspiracy of the ruling council, then a darkness covers the land and his body vanishes, at which the witnesses flee in fear, after seeking his body but being told he is not here, he has risen. There are many differences, surely. But the similarities are too numerous to be a coincidence. It certainly looks like the Christian passion narrative is a deliberate transvaluation of the Roman Empire's ceremony of their founding savior's incarnation, death, and resurrection. What Mark changes, are all the things he wants to say differently than the Roman myth, all the ways he imagined his Jesus the superior of their Romulus.

Matthew and Luke borrowed even more features from the passion plays of Romulus than Mark did. In Plutarch's biography of Romulus we are told he was the son of god, born of a virgin; an attempt is made to kill him as a baby; he is saved, and raised by a poor family, becoming a lowly peasant; then as a man he becomes beloved by the people, hailed as king, and killed by the conniving elite; then he rises from the dead, appears to a friend on a road from the city to tell the good news to his people, and ascends to heaven to rule from on high. All as happens in Matthew or Luke.

Indeed, in the Romulus myth claims are made of "dubious alternative accounts" of what happened to his body—which claims were obviously fabricated, there never having been a true account of Romulus's vanishing body to begin with. And yet, lo and behold, Matthew borrows exactly this same trope, inventing a "dubious alternative account" of what happened to Jesus' body: the Disciples stole it away! Which, as with Romulus, we are told was a lie. Matthew also borrows the idea that some followers doubted the hero was really resurrected ("but some doubted," Matthew 28:17), just as was said of Romulus. Similarly Luke borrows the ascension scene (where Jesus, like Romulus, flies up into the clouds) and inverts the geography of Romulus's post-resurrection appearance myth, imagining the risen Jesus appearing to Cleopas (whose name means "All-Glory") on the road from Jerusalem to Emmaus, just as the risen Romulus appears to Proculus (whose ancient name most resembles the Latin Proclamator, "Proclaimer") on the road from Alba Longa to Rome; in each case the pair of cities were a similar distance apart, both roads ran northeasterly and downhill, from an elevated location to a plain, both toward Rome. Luke also inverts the appearance of the god from the glorious (Romulus) to the humble (Jesus), to illustrate how the Christian message, and Kingdom they were offering, was greater. And by switching the risen savior's appearance from eminent (Romulus appears in mighty regalia) to indiscernible (Jesus appears in disguise), Luke conveys the point that the Kingdom Jesus is selling is likewise invisible.

It's hard to imagine these are coincidences. These authors are getting their ideas not from witnesses or recollections, but from other tales, of other gods and heroes. This further includes a type that spans both pagan and Jewish mythology, a story-framework that Jesus was conformed to that contains so many recorded members that we can actually estimate some frequencies from it: the so-called Rank-Raglan hero class, named after the two scholars long ago who proposed different ways of defining the category and found all its members still visible to us in extant records. Their work was most recently updated by Alan Dundes, and even further by myself, revising the definitions of the several shared features to match the actual myths that include them. Mark already co-opted more than half the features of the Rank-Raglan hero; Matthew would add nearly all the rest.

The most peculiar thing about this hero type is that though we have found fourteen heroes who fit in extant records more than half the twenty-two shared features of this hero category, not a single one of them is known or likely to have been historical—including the two Jewish members of the set, Moses and Joseph. Though some real kings nearly scored as many features in the legends that later grew up around them—most notably Caesar Augustus, Alexander the Great, and King Mithradates—none score above half; and thus none are in the fourteen counted as fully within the set. Jesus would make fifteen.

The full course of shared features ran thus:

1. The hero is conceived by a virgin.

2. His father is a king or the heir of a king.

3. The circumstances of his conception are unusual.

4. He is said to be the son of a god.

5. An attempt is made to kill him when he is a baby.

6. To escape which he is spirited away from those trying to kill him.

7. He is reared in a foreign country by one or more foster parents.

8. We are told nothing of his childhood.

9. On reaching manhood he returns to his future kingdom.

10. He is crowned, hailed, or becomes king.

11. He reigns without war or national catastrophe.

12. He prescribes laws.

13. He then loses favor with the gods or his subjects.

14. He is driven from the throne or city.

15. He meets with a mysterious death.

16. He dies atop a hill or high place.

17. His children, if any, do not succeed him.

18. His body turns up missing.

19. Yet he has one or more tombs (in fact or fiction).

And . . .

20. Before taking a throne or a wife, he battles and defeats a great adversary (such as a king, giant, dragon, or wild beast).

21. His parents are related to each other.

22. He marries a queen or princess related to his predecessor.

I'm not even counting four other features many of these and other mythical figures also conform to—performing miracles (in life or as a deity after death); having been a mortally incarnated preexistent superbeing; being subsequently worshiped as a savior god; and fulfilling ancient prophecies in their lives. Jesus conforms to all four of those as well. But even if we just count the twenty-two enumerated features of the Rank-Raglan hero narrative, Mark's Jesus scores no fewer than fourteen: "His father is a king or the heir of a king" (Mark 10:47–48, 11:10, 12:35–37); "He is said to be the son of a god" (Mark 1:1, 3:11, 5:7, 15:39); "We are told nothing of his childhood" (Mark 1–16); "He is crowned, hailed or becomes king" (Mark 11:7–10 and Mark 15:2, 9, 12, 18, 26); "He reigns without war or national catastrophe" (Mark 11–14); "He prescribes laws" (Mark 7, 10, 12); "He then loses favor with the gods or his subjects" (Mark 14:27–15:33); "He is driven from the throne or city" (Mark 15:16–24); "He meets with a mysterious death" (Mark 15:37–44); "He dies atop a hill or high place" (Mark 15:22–24); "His children, if any, do not succeed him" (Mark 1–16); "His body turns up missing" (Mark 16:4–6); "Yet he has one or more tombs (in fact or fiction)" (Mark 16:4–6); and, "Before taking a throne or a wife, he battles and defeats a great adversary" (Mark 1:12–14). Matthew would add six more. Jesus thus accumulated all but two of the total twenty-two features, making him one of the highest-scoring members of this mythotype known to us.

Many historians are indignant that the Gospel Jesus could possibly have been based on a widely recognized and repeated hero trope of the ancient world. But alas, there is no denying he must have been. The only alternative explanation is to posit "extraordinary coincidence." And that's always less likely an explanation than so obvious a conclusion as emulation: the authors of the Gospels were building their hero to match or transcend other popular heroes. For my analysis in *On the Historicity of Jesus* I combined and updated the wording of the twenty-two criteria developed by Rank, Raglan, and Dundes to fit the actual matching data they all cited, and then I double-checked the scoring myself. In result I even downscored some members I believe Rank and Raglan overscored. And yet after all that, I found their discovery held up: Moses and Joseph, Oedipus and Theseus, Dionysus and Romulus, Perseus and Hercules, Zeus and Bellerophon, Jason and Pelops, Osiris and Asclepius all score over half the twenty-two criteria.

That so many criteria would match so many heroes (fourteen in all; fifteen counting Jesus) is not credibly explained as an accident. It's impossible for a modern observer to invent it (try extending the ridiculous Lincoln-Kennedy coincidences circulating on the Internet to *twelve other people* and you'll start to realize why this can't be done). And it's likewise impossible that being in this set isn't indicative of mythic origin. For were that the case, *there should be a lot of historical persons in this set.* And yet *there are none*—to a probability of chance accident near enough to zero that we must dismiss that explanation as implausible.

No historical person on record was ever so heavily mythologized as to majority-match the Rank-Raglan pattern. Which means even from this one indicator Jesus is among the most mythologized figures in history;

and has been from the very first moment any narrative was composed of him. That should worry us. It's only worse that Jesus had numerous *additional* mythotypes grafted into this first-ever tale of him. Mark's construction emulates not only the Rank-Raglan hero type but also the mythotypes of Aesop, Romulus, Moses, Elijah and Elisha, the dying-and-rising personal savior, even the Jewish mythotype of Nickelsburg's suffering but vindicated wise men. Mark also reifies in his narrative of Jesus what actually began as the sayings or stories of Paul. Mark then builds the rest out of scripture, allegory, and convenient symbolism. You won't find any historical person this mythified—who doesn't also come with exceptional evidence of their existence. And that's why we should be ready to doubt Jesus existed, as much as we do every other figure as mythologized as this—without some good evidence that he's the lone exception in history. And as we've already seen, for Jesus, such evidence is wanting.

This should be recognized as an obvious truth: the more mythical features a figure has from the very earliest narrative of them, the more likely they are to be mythical and not historical. Anyone who would gainsay this has to produce evidence to the contrary: they have to collect all the just-as-highly mythologized persons in history, and count how many are historical, and how many not (or at least, not plausibly). I am quite certain you will never get a result above half a chance of such a figure being historical, or even a third. Count up everyone in history who from their earliest record is all at once a worshiped savior-lord, a dying-and-rising demigod, a culture hero and heavenly founder, a conveniently named godman, a miracle-working sage, a preexistent incarnated being, a revelatory space alien, appearing only in sacred literature, who dies and rises from the dead, and whose life improbably fulfills numerous prophecies, and whose only biographies build him out of prior religious heroes he is meant to supersede, and are rife with fabulous and improbable events; whose biographies name no sources, discuss no sources, and have no known sources; and who becomes *that mythologized* in under forty years time . . . and who actually existed.

Good luck.

Even if you found one such person (did you?), how many did you also find who *didn't* exist? The ratio between those two groups (all persons just as mythologized as that who existed, in ratio to the number who didn't), makes the prior odds Jesus existed. The odds aren't good. And though prior odds aren't final odds, the only way to get those odds up, and up enough to leave a balance of probability favoring his having actually existed, is to find some evidence that is very unlikely unless Jesus existed. And there just isn't any. That's the problem here. And anyone who doesn't acknowledge this isn't being honest with themselves—or with you.

It gets you nowhere to say "but a historical person *could* have had that much mythology piled onto them in just forty years." Because that still doesn't tell us *how probable* that is. You need a frequency: how often does that happen? Because that's then the prior probability it happened to *any* such person, including Jesus. And if you can never show any evidence that that frequency is high, you have no business declaring that it is. Likewise for the power of any evidence that could turn this around for Jesus. Can you find anything that is so unlikely, unless Jesus existed, as to *restore* the probability of his historicity? And if you think you have, can you explain why your belief that this evidence is "so unlikely" is credible, and not just a probability you made up in your head to avoid the cognitive dissonance of admitting you actually have no reason to believe that?

To Such a Degree of Mythologization

When we look closely at the Gospels, even the original Gospel, "according to Mark," we see just how fantastically mythologized Jesus was from the very moment anyone recorded any narratives about him at all. Yes, his myths became even more elaborate afterward, with more fantastical things added to his story by Matthew, Luke, and John, and then yet more as dozens more Gospels continued to be written. But even before that Jesus was already almost as mythologized as any person could be. So adding *yet more* myth on top of Mark's tale can't have any further effect on the likelihood of the conclusion: that all biographies ever written about Jesus were wholly mythical, or at best, *cannot be known to be otherwise.* We can locate no history about Jesus in them, other than by pure speculation or with no rational confidence.

We therefore cannot use the Gospels to argue Jesus existed, any more than we could use the biographies of any other mythical, non-existent hero of antiquity to argue *they* existed. They didn't. Ergo, we should suspect, neither did Jesus. There is no basis for granting Jesus an exemption from so obvious a conclusion. If Jesus were not the central figure of a powerful, influential religion today, we wouldn't hesitate to class him with all the others. Because he looks just like them. Jesus, like Bacchus or Romulus or Osiris, was probably always mythical, known "for real" only ever through mystical means, never an actual historical person in the ordinary sense. We don't hesitate to admit this of all the others. Why do we hesitate for Jesus? All Rank-Raglan heroes, including Moses, all heroic savior figures, from John Frum and Ned Ludd to King Arthur and Moroni, even the Roswell aliens: all mythical; all portrayed as historical; all eventually even believed historical—some even within the same span of time. This is what typically happened. And what typically happens is by definition not even implausible, much less improbable.

The manner in which Osiris came to be historicized, moving from being just a cosmic god sometimes manifest spiritually, to being given a whole narrative biography as a pharaoh set in Egypt during a specific historical period, complete with collections of wisdom sayings he supposedly uttered, is an apt model. Jesus appears to have been historicized in just the same way. Of course it's not an exact model, because it's distinctively Egyptian, whereas Christianity's savior-lord is distinctively Jewish. Both were constructed out of the tropes of their respective founding cultures. That explains all their differences. The myths contrived for Jesus model him after previous mythical Jewish heroes like Moses and Elijah, and all his tales and sayings likewise derive from Jewish sentiments rather than Egyptian. Myths about Jesus adapted qualities from Gentile heroes like Romulus or Osiris or Aesop only in very abstract and fully Judaized ways. But the similarities, even at the abstract level, are unmistakable; and they are not rationally explicable as anything other than a countercultural sect of Jews adapting those same general ideas from their Gentile milieu into a new sectarian construct, just as Jews had previously done with their Persian-Zoroastrian milieu, from which much that became distinctive of Judaism derived—including messianism, apocalypticism, hellfire, a linear view of history, resurrection of the dead, even the role of a Satan as the enemy of God and originator and sustainer of death in the world.

As I've noted, Romulus, too, began as a celestial deity—Quirinus, one of the three principal gods of Rome—who was later historicized, and given a convenient name (just as "Romulus" more or less means "Seedling of Rome"; "Jesus," remember, means "Savior of God"). Then biographies were written, falsely setting his death and resurrection in Roman history. If such could happen to him, obviously it could happen to Jesus; likewise every other dying-and-rising savior deity. And among them all, Osiris is geographically and conceptually closest to Christianity: his death and resurrection were portrayed as historical events on Earth but in secret truly believed to have occurred only in outer space, where Osiris is there killed by the Egyptian "Satan," just as the original *Ascension of Isaiah* appears to have imagined Jesus being killed by the Jewish Satan, only to rise again, in triumphant glory, in a new body. Osiris cult certainly establishes a proof of concept. It is in essence what all mythicists are saying happened to Jesus. So why can't it be what happened? If our earliest sources only speak of Jesus—and indeed they do only speak of him—as a revealed being, and never clearly place him in earth history, never discuss his having a life or ever meeting anyone but in visions from on high, and the first time we ever hear otherwise is only in a later sacred mythology, shouldn't we admit to the obvious conclusion here?

This is why it's reasonable to suspect that, just as for many other celestial deities, Jesus began as a revelatory celestial being. This appears to be what Paul said. And it certainly looks like it was only a lifetime later an allegorical story of this same Jesus was then composed and told in some Christian communities—a myth that placed their savior on Earth, in history, as a divine man, with an earthly family, companions, and enemies, complete with deeds and sayings, and an earthly depiction of his ordeals . . . just as happened to every other savior hero—Moses included. That this *was typical* is the important point to realize here. All savior heroes like Jesus had this happen to them. *All of them.* At least so far as we can tell—we know of not a single exception. So it's not even unusual. To the contrary, *Jesus being the lone historical one* would be unusual.

So let's not pretend anymore. Even from the moment of his first mythologization, Jesus belongs to numerous mythotypes—possibly more than any other mythical savior. The Rank-Raglan class is simply the largest and most detailed of those categories of myth known, and thus the most informative. But it is not merely because Jesus was fashioned after it that we suspect he didn't exist, just as we suspect none others in that class did. It's that Jesus was fashioned after *so many* mythical categories, immediately upon being mythologized at all, without any intermediate development, that signals he was mythologized entire. We should have expected some mundane recollections, evolving over time into increasingly mythical fantasizations. Instead we get one-hundred percent myth, right out of the gate. And that myth is preceded only by texts wholly unaware of any distinctive content of that myth, instead only declaring Jesus to be known by private revelations and secret messages planted in ancient scriptures. That sequence is precisely what we expect if Jesus didn't exist. Whereas it's a little odd to find things that way if he did. Don't you think?

7

How Did Christianity Switch to a Historical Jesus?

Okay. So the evidence Jesus existed is pretty scant. Plus, he really looks a lot like a mythical person. But if Jesus didn't exist, if he was originally believed to have lived and died in outer space, how did *our* Christianity come to exist? How could an earthly Jesus just get invented like that, and the original view of him be forgotten? The answer is obvious when you consider a different debate over what is and isn't historical that the mainstream consensus has already landed on the other side of: the resurrection of Jesus. The mainstream consensus among experts today fully accepts that the same transition happened for the historicity *of the resurrection*: from private, subjective visions (or even just claims of such) to fully reified historical encounters with a reanimated corpse. And that change happened in exactly the same timespan, with exactly the same lack of evidence of how or when exactly it occurred. Yet scholars have no difficulty proposing how it happened and accepting that it did. Those same scholars therefore cannot object to the same transition occurring for historicity *as a whole*. If you can invent the one, you can invent the other.

Analogy in Resurrection Apologetics

Weirdly, when it comes to the historicity *of Jesus*, secular historicists act just like Christian fundamentalists. Yet they switch roles when it comes to the resurrection narratives in the Gospels.

It's quite clear that in Paul's day the risen Jesus only appeared in fleeting, inner visions. Paul says the teaching and message of Christ was known only through revelation and scripture (Romans 16:25–26). The voice of Jesus was heard only by apostles (Romans 10:14–18). Jesus was only seen by apostles (1 Corinthians 9:1). Paul only ever mentions people meeting and conversing with Jesus mystically (2 Corinthians 12; 1 Corinthians 11:23; Galatians 1:11–12). Paul says Jesus made someone an apostle by appearing "within" them in a "revelation," and not in an encounter with a "flesh and blood" man (Galatians 1:11–17). Indeed Paul clearly signals it would make one a fraud to claim otherwise (Galatians 1:8–12). When he lists the original revelations in the creedal summary in 1 Corinthians 15:1–8, the very way they are listed there entails momentary, fleeting events, not Jesus hanging around for days. To the contrary, only one of those events, Paul says, occurred "all at once" to more than one person, which means every other such event was a single, brief, isolated experience claimed by each individual apostle. Even to "the twelve" (verse 5) and "all the apostles" (verse 7), as in neither *of those* cases does Paul add that this took place "all at once." Meanwhile, that one, single mass experience only matches in later narrative the ecstasy of the brethren described in Acts 2, where each saw an ambiguous light above and felt the spirit of Jesus inside themselves, just as Acts 9 reports of Paul's revelation of Jesus, which Paul himself portrays as just like everyone else's (in 1 Corinthians 9:1 and 15:8 and Galatians 1:11–17). These people did not converse with a reanimated corpse. They did not have dinner with him or hang out and inspect his wounds. Paul had never heard of such a thing. In Paul's knowledge there was no finding of empty tombs, no eating together, no touching of hands and body, no living in a house with the risen Jesus for days on end as Acts 1 would absurdly imagine.

Pretty much all mainstream scholars now agree Christianity began exactly that way, with private revelations—whether hallucinations, visions, dreams, or pious inventions thereof—and that only *a generation later* Christians invented the wild tales in the Gospels of Jesus appearing as an animated corpse, leaving behind a tomb verified to be empty that no one had heard of before, confirmed to be physically the same man by touch and sight, and hanging around and having dinners with the Disciples—by some accounts for over a month! And not only that . . . but the original claim disappeared. Completely. We still see it evidenced in the few letters of Paul preserved for us. But after that, all writings by any Christian still maintaining what Paul originally reported, vanished. Their narratives survive neither in mention, refutation, or quotation.

The later victorious Church that gained control of all documents and doctrine entirely "disappeared" the original teachings of the sect, which had been of private revelations as Paul relates; it then entirely replaced them with those bizarre Gospel teachings about a reanimated, touchable, dinner-eating corpse-Jesus. That transition began within mere decades and was completed in under a hundred years. We don't have any surviving documentation as to exactly how or when or by whom this was accomplished. But we can plainly see that it was. No one can dispute it. So if that could happen to a *post*mortem Jesus, why couldn't the same thing happen to a *pre*mortem Jesus? What, honestly, would even be the difference?

Yet as soon as we mention that, suddenly secular historians take up like Christian fundamentalists and deny such a thing could happen, immediately after having just admitted it not only could, but did. Just like after any rational person calmly explains what most likely happened to launch the false belief that Jesus rose from the dead, a fundamentalist will ask, with outraged incredulity, "How did the religion go from internal visions to detailed narratives of physical on-earth encounters in the Gospels? You can't explain that!" And when we offer totally reasonable explanations of how that could have happened, the fundamentalist declares, "All your explanations are implausible!" When really, they're all far more plausible than reanimated corpses. Just as is our visions-to-history account of the Gospels altogether.

Internal visions were the only experience Paul talks about anyone ever having of the risen Jesus back in the first twenty years or so of the religion. And he's quite emphatic about that. But by the time the Gospels appear, the only experience we *then* hear about are all their reanimated corpse tales instead. We have no record of how Christianity's preferred narrative shifted from internal visions to the elaborately historicized appearance narratives in the Gospels. Does that mean the latter are therefore true? No. To the contrary, most mainstream scholars agree they are quite false and insist—correctly—that the first apostles only had personal inner visions of a risen Jesus from on high and that the Gospels wholly fabricated all those historical "on earth" encounters. Yet that still became the solely attested belief thereafter, with believers even "reading it back in" to the Epistles of Paul, just as Christian fundamentalists now do. Which is just like other fictions invented by the Gospels that get "read back in" to Paul, such as his references to the Lord's "brothers" or Jesus being killed by the "archons of this eon." What the Gospels invented is simply assumed to be what Paul was talking about all along. Yet we have no evidence that's the case.

Nothing you could possibly think of that would stop that from happening for historicity belief, stopped it happening to resurrection belief. So clearly no such things *could* stop such an outcome, any more for the historicity of Jesus than the historicity of his resurrection. All the sects that kept teaching the original version—that Jesus was seen only in inner visions, not touched and handled and eaten with on hills and in homes—were overrun and driven extinct, and all their literature thrown away or destroyed. At best only stuff they wrote that was suitably ambiguous was preserved—like, for example, the few Epistles of Paul we are allowed now to read. We don't get to hear anything anyone had to say about this complete radical change in how the resurrection of Jesus came to be understood. We don't get to see how that change came about and overwhelmed the church, eclipsing every other view. Instead, every source we get to see insists Jesus was touched and handled and eaten with on hills and in homes, and *not* simply experienced in inner visions—or else, vaguely doesn't specify either. "Gosh. How could that happen?? It's so implausible!! Jesus must be risen!! God be praised!!"

If you don't buy that reasoning for the resurrection, neither should you buy it for Jesus. "You can't explain how that switch happened" is simply not a logically valid objection to the conclusion that, in fact, *it happened*. Resurrection belief did, in fact, radically switch from "inner visions" to "historical-physical encounters, complete with veridical details and elaborate conversations." It happened in the exact same time frame; in exactly the same documents. We get to see no one gainsaying it or calling foul. We get to see no evidence of how that change came about or even why; much less of how it drove extinct what the original witnesses were actually preaching, and consumed the entirety of extant Christian literature. And yet that is exactly what happened. And however that happened, is exactly how it would have happened to historicity *altogether*.

Phenomenologically, the historicity of Jesus, and the historicity of the Gospel resurrection narratives, are the same. They started as visions of celestial beings and ended as fictional narratives of events on earth. Fiction just like all the public miracles that were made up yet never gainsaid either: the sun going out for three hours, stars wandering and hovering over cities, the temple square ravaged by a single unstoppable man, the eighty-foot-tall temple curtain magically torn from top to bottom, hordes of zombies descending on Jerusalem, hundreds of babies slaughtered, thousands of pigs drowned, thousands of people miraculously fed with magic food. All made up. Never gainsaid. We never get to hear from anyone who was really there what *really* happened. So why should we expect to hear such for anything else? All of this the Gospels' authors invented without any surviving protest. Inventing *a mere man* is far easier.

In *On the Historicity of Jesus* I provided extensive background knowledge on this—specifically, on which facts are the same whether one is speaking of how this transition from visions to history occurred in resurrection belief, or historicity belief. The third-century Christian scholar Origen gave this away, for example, when he let slip the Christian principle of two truths—that literal stories were invented to save the ignorant masses, while educated elites know the real truth lies only within the allegory, and dare not expose this to the rank and file lest they lose faith and become damned. Pretty much exactly as Plutarch said how the Osiris cult reasoned, as we saw earlier. All of the records we would need to test and know what happened in the transition period of about fifty years (then an average human lifetime)—literally *all* those records, every single last one—were destroyed, and are never mentioned, quoted, or referenced by anyone, ever. Whatever the original witnesses and their faithful successors had to say about the newfangled versions of events suddenly appearing, negative *or* positive, we never get to know. And yet some hints survive of there having been Christians who preached the earthly Jesus was indeed mythical. But we aren't allowed to see how ancient that view was or when or how it started. Was it in fact the original view? Honestly, we have no evidence it wasn't.

This holds for historicity as firmly and plausibly as it holds for the resurrection. There is nothing implausible about this having happened, or about its matching exactly the evidence we now have. Because all the evidence that would expose it having happened would have indeed been destroyed, or thrown in the trash, or otherwise kept from us. And that's not conjecture. *We know it for a fact.* Christians didn't just stop writing letters and homilies and polemics for a whole human lifetime— the entire period between Paul in the mid-first century and the early-to-mid-second century. So it had to all have been destroyed. What else could have happened to it? Even whatever they were arguing by word of mouth—as they must have been—is totally lost. Also a fact. But all the *literature* is gone too.

The treatises that 2 Peter was forged to rebut? Destroyed. The original edition of the *Ascension of Isaiah*? Destroyed. The original collection of Paul's letters? Destroyed. All the cosmic-Jesus literature Irenaeus says he was attempting to rebut? Destroyed. All the supposedly "Docetist" treatises *of early date* we have no good reason to trust their opponents like Ignatius were representing accurately? Destroyed. Everything written by every Christian for a hundred years who would have had even a dogmatic reason (much less a genuinely informed reason) to challenge anything in the Gospels—literally *anything* in the Gospels? Destroyed. And this is why we don't know how, when, or why *resurrection* belief shifted from personal inner visions to physical earthly encounters. Which means that's also why we won't know how, when, or why *historicity* belief shifted from personal inner visions to physical earthly encounters.

Brief Summary of What's Most Likely

Here's what I think we can conclude happened given the surviving evidence. It's what I present evidence for in *Historicity*. Between the 30s and 70s A.D. some Christian congregations gradually mythicized the story of their celestial Jesus Lord, just as we've already seen other mystery cults had done for their gods, eventually representing him rhetorically and symbolically in overtly historical narratives, during which time much of the more esoteric truth of the matter is reserved in secret for upper levels of initiation.

Right in the middle of this process the Jewish War of 66–70 A.D. destroyed the original church in Jerusalem, leaving us with no evidence that any of the original apostles lived beyond it. Before that, persecutions from Jewish authorities, and famines throughout the empire (and, if it really happened, the Neronian persecution of 64, which would have devastated the church in Rome) further exacerbated the effect, which was to leave a thirty-year dark age in the history of the church, from the 60s to the 90s A.D., a whole generation in which we have no idea what happened or who was in charge. In fact, this ecclesial dark age probably spans fifty years, from the 60s to 110s A.D., if 1 Clement was written in the 60s and not the 90s A.D., as I and many other scholars think is almost surely the case. For then we have no record of *anything* going on until either Ignatius or Papias, both of whom could have written anytime between the 110s and 140s A.D.

It's during this early "dark age" in Christianity's history that the canonical Gospels appear to have been written, by persons unknown. And it is in that same age that at least one Christian sect started to sell the myths those Gospels contain as real, and thus began to believe (or for convenience claim) that Jesus was an earthborn man, and then preached and embellished that view. And we can expect someone would; because having a historical founder represented in controlled documents was a significant advantage. As a result, this "historicizing" sect gradually gained political and social superiority, declared itself "orthodox" while condemning all others as "heretics," and preserved only texts that agreed with its view, and forged and altered countless texts in support—as we know for a fact they did. As a result, almost all evidence of the original Christian sects and what they believed has been lost or doctored out of the record; even evidence of what happened during the latter half of the first century to transition from Paul's Christianity to second-century "orthodoxy" is completely lost and now almost wholly inaccessible to us.

No element of the theory I just outlined is ad hoc. Every single element of it rests on indisputable evidence. The letters of Paul corroborate the hypothesis that Christianity began with visions (real or claimed) and novel interpretations of scripture, and this is not a fringe proposal but is actually a view shared by many experts. The idea of a "celestial savior" is corroborated by documents such as the *Ascension of Isaiah* and has precedents in theologies like the continual death-and-resurrection of Osiris, and is found even in the Dead Sea Scrolls. The "euhemerization" of ahistorical god-men by placing them in historical contexts was commonplace in antiquity, a process so-named after the ancient Euhemerus who did that very thing with the gods Zeus and Saturn (albeit he did that for different reasons than most, for all manner of other reasons the practice became popular afterward). That ancient texts could have symbolic and allegorical content is well established in classics and religious studies, has ample support in the sociology of religion, and was common practice in ancient mystery cults and Judaism. Christianity did possess the central features of ancient mystery cults. And the fact that such "mysteries" were kept secret and revealed only to initiates, who were then sworn to secrecy, is a well-known fact of ancient religion. Everything else is an undeniable fact: the Epistles do reveal the constant vexation of novel dogmas; the devastating events of the 60s did occur; the history of the church is completely silent from then until the mid-90s or even decades later; a historicist sect did later gain supreme power and did decide which texts to preserve, and it did doctor and meddle with numerous manuscripts and even produced wholesale forgeries to that same end—and not as a result of any organized conspiracy, but simply from independent editors and authors widely sharing similar assumptions and motives.

The only element of the basic myth theory I just outlined that is even incredible (at least at first look) is the idea that a transition from a secret cosmic savior to a public historical one happened within two generations, and without a clear record of it occurring. But we already know exactly that happened—for the historicity of the resurrection. So we cannot claim it didn't, much less couldn't happen. It clearly did, for that belief. So why could it not for others? The unusual circumstances of a major disruption in the church had clearly opened the door to rapid developments in its dogmas (just as we see with the historicizing of Jesus's resurrection), and the complete silence of the record in the following period blocks any attempt to argue "from silence" that there was no transition from myth to legend. That this development did not get recorded is because *nothing* got recorded. And we cannot argue from the silence of documents we don't have.

When we consider the prospect of newly evangelized Christians handed a "euhemerized" Gospel, but not yet initiated into the full secret, and then being set loose to spread their unfinished beliefs and founding their own churches and developing their own speculations, the idea that a myth could be mistaken as and transformed into "history" in just a few generations is not so implausible as it may seem, particularly given that the geographical distances involved were large, lifespans then were short, and legends often grow with distance in time and space. There may even have been a "transitional" state of the cult in which the historical narratives were seen as playing out what was simultaneously occurring in the heavens (so one could believe both narratives were true), or in which certain sect leaders chose to downplay or reinterpret the secret doctrines and sell the public ones as the truth instead (just as Origen seems to have thought was a good idea).

Any number of possibilities present themselves. Without any data from that period, we cannot know which happened, or didn't happen. For comparison, even if we granted historicity to Jesus, then we do not know how some sects transitioned to a cosmically born Jesus in the Christianities that Irenaeus attacks as heresies, or a cosmically killed Jesus in the *Ascension of Isaiah*, or to a Jesus who lived and died a hundred years earlier, as we find in the Talmud. Thus, our ignorance in the matter of *how* the cult transitioned is not solved by positing historicity. Either way, we're equally in the dark on how these changes happened.

So, what in all that is implausible? By which we mean *implausible in context*. Nothing. So why are we resisting the conclusion?

What Happened Looks Really Suspicious

Ask yourself, how did the creed go from this:

I want to remind you . . . By this gospel you are saved, if you hold firmly to the word I preached to you. Otherwise, you have believed in vain. For what I received I passed on to you as of greatest importance: that Christ died for our sins according to the Scriptures, that he was buried, that he was raised on the third day according to the Scriptures, and that he appeared . . . [*by revelation to a select few*]. (1 Corinthians 15:1–8)

To this:

Stop your ears when anyone speaks to you at variance with the Jesus Christ who was descended from David, and came through Mary; who really was born and ate and drank; who really was persecuted under Pontius Pilate; who really was crucified and died in the sight of witnesses in heaven, and on earth, and even under the earth; who really was raised from the dead, too, His Father resurrecting Him, in the same way His Father will resurrect those of us, who believe in Him by Jesus Christ, apart from whom we do not truly have life. (Ignatius, *Trallians* 9, written between 110 and 160 A.D.)

How did the creed change so radically, into so conspicuous an assertion of historicism, in just 60 years? That's as weird on historicity as it is on mythicism.

Note what's changed:

- Paul said Jesus "came into being from David's sperm" (*genomenou ek spermatos Dauid*, Romans 1:3). Ignatius now insists we have to say Jesus came "from the descendants of David" (*ek genous Dauid*). Conspicuously, precisely the thing Paul never said.

- Paul said Jesus "came into being from a woman," and his surrounding argument implies that by this he meant from the woman "Hagar . . . an allegory" (Galatians 4:4, 24–26). Ignatius now insists we must say Jesus came from an actual woman named "Mary," not some generic "woman" in an argument about allegorical women. Notably Paul never mentions a Mary. Not in any creed he attests. So why is her name now important to affirm in the creed? When did that happen? Why?

- In both places Paul said Jesus was "made" (*ginomai*) not "born" (*gennaô*), by choosing the same word Paul uses to signal divine manufacture (of Adam and our future resurrection bodies), and never of human birth, in conspicuous contrast to the word Paul *does* always use of human birth. Ignatius conspicuously *reverses* the vocabulary, and insists we now must say "born" (*gennaô*) not "made" (*ginomai*). Exactly the same way we know Christian scribes tried doctoring the manuscripts of Paul—in both Romans 1:3 *and* Galatians 4:4 at the same time, thus proving they were well aware of the problem I'm pointing out. Hence though both words *can* mean birth, Christians were *aware* Paul's usage, uncomfortably, did not.

- Paul said Jesus ate and drank *in a vision* (1 Corinthians 11:23). Ignatius now insists we must say Jesus ate and drank *for real*. Why is that important? How did that get into the creed? Why?

- Paul said, "the archons of this eon crucified" Jesus (1 Corinthians 2:8), language evocative of celestial demonic powers, while essentially saying the Roman authorities never would have done that (Romans 13). Ignatius now insists we must say *Pontius Pilate* crucified Jesus, and shun anyone who says otherwise as an agent of the Devil. So who was saying otherwise? Indeed, why did the *name* of the crucifier become important to the creed? And why does that only happen well *after* the Gospels chose to place Pilate in the story?

- Paul essentially says there were no earthly witnesses to Jesus before his resurrection (1 Corinthians 15:3–8; Romans 10:14–16; Romans 16:25–26). Ignatius now says we must say there were. Why did that become necessary? Why did that enter the creed? When? How? What did other Christians this new maneuver was designed to exclude have to say about it?

Historicists have theories to explain all this. But are they correct? They'll say, for example, that "Docetism," a modern category of heresy that supposedly taught Jesus only "appeared" to do or suffer things on earth, was the threat Ignatius is retooling the creed to combat. But Ignatius never mentions Docetists. And the only texts we have that show anything like Docetism date a century later, and they don't say anything like what's in Ignatius. So this is a really poor theory.

For instance, some of those later "Docetic" texts say Jesus switched places with Simon of Cyrene, which is clearly not what Ignatius is talking about or arguing against. So how do we know what *those whom Ignatius is responding to* were actually teaching? We don't get to read anything they actually wrote, not even in quotation. Ancient Christian apologists were notorious liars and misrepresenters of their opponents, so we can't trust them. And they only wrote anything half a century later anyway. Since none of the later documents that survive that are now called Docetic reference the doctrines Ignatius is concerned about, Docetism cannot really explain what he means. So who were the folks Ignatius is writing against? Were they really those later, unrelated Docetists we have some writings from and that later apologists opposed—or were they actually mythicists? We aren't told. But it sure sounds a lot more like mythicists, the same ones 2 Peter was forged to rebut. And since we can't show otherwise, we have no business declaring otherwise.

What we are left with is a creed—in fact, *several* creeds—quoted by Paul, that never references any historical detail placing any of Jesus' activity on earth; then we have a blackout of fifty to eighty years, during which the Gospels get written; and suddenly, a lifetime after the Gospels began circulating, which was already a lifetime after the religion began, we find the creed has been retooled to include details that only first appear in those Gospels—Mary, Pilate, a human birth associated with Davidic ancestors, dinner parties, earthly witnesses to the Crucifixion. Not only do these things suddenly get added to the creed, but they also become *essential* to the creed: we are told we must condemn any Christians who *reject* them. Which means . . . *there were Christians who rejected them.* And we don't get to hear from them. Think about that.

Plausibility Derives from Context

What makes a theory plausible or implausible is not what we *now* in the modern age think is normal or weird, but what was normal or weird *in the era and region this actually happened in*. Too many scholars today seem to be relying on their modernist intuitions, balking at all the weird things the ancients believed—which is exactly backward. All that weird stuff they believed back then *was normal*. So anything that coheres with it *is plausible*. That's how plausibility operates in historical reasoning. Anything else is anachronism.

The manner in which Osiris came to be historicized, moving from being just a cosmic god to being given a whole narrative biography set in Egypt during a specific historical period, complete with collections of wisdom sayings he supposedly uttered, is still an apt model, if not by any means an exact one. Which is to say, it establishes a proof of concept. It is in essence what all mythicists are saying happened to Jesus. That's the model from which the hypothesis of minimal mythicism is derived, particularly the last two of its five basic components, as I laid out in my peer-reviewed study. There I outline it as follows: after Jesus originated as a revealed, celestial savior . . .

- As for many other celestial deities, an allegorical story of this same Jesus was then composed and told within the sacred community, which placed him on earth, in history, as a divine man, with an earthly family, companions, and enemies, complete with deeds and sayings, and an earthly depiction of his ordeals.

Which was typical. All savior deities like Jesus had this happen to them. *All of them*, so far as we can tell. We know of not a single exception. So it's not even unusual. To the contrary, Jesus being *the lone historical savior deity* is what would be unusual. Likewise for several other myth-heavy sets Jesus belongs to—as I document in *Historicity*, and just surveyed in the last chapter: Jesus actually belongs to more myth-heavy reference classes than any other purportedly historical figure I know. So there is nothing implausible or even unusual about his being historicized as all other such beings were.

Which leaves only one more feature to explain:

- Subsequent communities of worshipers believed (or at least taught) that this invented sacred story was real (and either not allegorical or only 'additionally' allegorical).

This was likewise the case for all other mystery cult saviors, all Rank-Raglan heroes, including Moses; just as also for John Frum and Ned Ludd and King Arthur and the Roswell aliens. Again, it's what typically happened. And what typically happens is by definition not implausible.

Hence we have a precedent not just in Osiris but also in every other mystery religion, all of whose saviors are of dubious historicity yet were placed in history in fake tales or biographies, the functional equivalent of "Gospels" for their respective religions. We also have the precedent of Moses himself. Made up. Complete with history, named siblings and parents, teachings, deeds, birth and death, and so on. We do not need to explain "how" all these people got made up and believed real. We know that's what happened. So it's not really all that sensible to demand a specific account of how the same thing happened to yet another Jewish lawgiver and mystery savior. There are a dozen ways it can have happened to Moses, or Osiris, or Bacchus, or John Frum, or Ned Ludd. To all of whom it happened. There are likewise a dozen different ways it can have happened to Jesus. And we can't know which, because all the evidence from the very period in which it happened was erased. So we don't get to find out.

Imagine arguing that a resurrected Jesus must really have shown his wounds to Thomas and eaten fish with Peter because it's "implausible" that the whole religion could transition from inner visions to such detailed narratives without anyone on the extant record noticing or mentioning it. Unless you're a Christian fundamentalist, you couldn't argue that and still keep a straight face. You well know that transition without a record of it surviving is simply *not even implausible*. It is, indeed, obviously what happened. So, too, for every other made-up tale about Jesus, from murdering thousands of pigs to snuffing the sun out for hours. And thus, so, too, for Jesus altogether—who only first clearly appears in earth history in the Gospels.

All the Contributing Factors

In *Historicity* I discuss numerous factors that could have contributed to this transition. And they are as applicable to how *Jesus* became historicized as to how *his resurrection* did.

For example, I discuss the Noll Thesis: historicizing mythical founders is actually anthropologically normal, and is driven by its polemical advantages. We see this in the Cargo Cults, the Mystery Cults, the Hadith, the Torah, the Mishnah, and beyond. A religion that converts its disparate revelations and inspirations into the singular deeds and teachings of a made-up "historical founder" is inherently more successful in the marketplace of ideas, quite likely to drive extinct its less-adapted ancestor. As in fact happened: the original mystical resurrection teaching was driven extinct by the physical dinner-buddy resurrection teaching.

I also discuss Origen's Confession: that controlling the masses *requires* feeding them literal stories, because they won't be moved (and thus won't be saved) by allegory or esoteric cosmologies. And his confession to this is so detailed and frank, it's even possible (but not necessary) to imagine Origen knew or suspected Jesus never walked the earth, but would never admit it for fear of destroying his religion by causing the illiterate masses to abandon it and thereby fall into the clutches of Satan. There was therefore a strong incentive among the church elite to push historicity.

I also discuss the role of historical accident: the sect that just happened to be positioned by the fourth century to gain the Emperor Constantine's ear, and thus secure total power on his lucky coattails after he won a civil war to reunify the Empire, was the most fundamentalist and literalist sect of them all, as we can see from the absurdist idiocy of Constantine's closest Christian advisor, Lactantius (as I discuss in *The Scientist in the Early Roman Empire*), and the questionable honesty of his favorite Christian scholar, Eusebius. Had the dice rolled the other way, *mythicist* Christians might have been the ones suppressing the "heresy" of historicism. But for the very reasons Origen and Noll point out, that may have been causally improbable. The historicist heresy was the most innately adapted for success and dominance. And once it was secure in absolute power, it decided all document survival for a thousand years.

One might object and say, "Well, they didn't destroy the collection at Nag Hammadi." But the collection at Nag Hammadi is late; no manuscript in it even dates before Constantine. Even by the most favorable conjectures, none of the texts those manuscripts preserve were composed any earlier than the second century, and most were composed in the third. Useless. If we had a comparable find for first-century Christianity, indeed it probably would decide this debate once and for all. But alas, we don't get to see anything like that. And that's the problem. *Why don't we get to see anything like that?*

The bottom line is, all the sects of Christianity we hear about by the end of the second century, including what became "orthodoxy," were evolved elaborations that did not match the original teachings of Peter or even Paul. And yet every sect declared the others heresy. But which teachings of which sects were the late aberrations, and which still resembled the original sect? It's statistically impossible that the sect that won total power "just happened" to be the only one with true beliefs, that *no* other sects retained some true facts of the original sect that were abandoned by the sect that became politically victorious. So what is *actually* the heresy? The cosmic Christ doctrines the "orthodoxists" condemned, as we see in Irenaeus and the subsequent editing of the *Ascension of Isaiah*? Or are those self-proclaimed *orthodoxists* the heretics? It's as likely one as the other. *We have no evidence by which to prove either.* So we can assume neither.

That leaves us back at square one: we know the Christianity that decided what documents we get to see was nothing like the original, and therefore certainly underwent radical transitions that we have no record of. So we can't balk at there having been radical transitions that we have no record of. Therefore, balking at that is a non sequitur. It has no logical effect on the probability of *any* hypothesis. Historicists have as many radical transitions to explain as the mythicists. They simply differ on which details were "transitioned."

What We Learn from Pliny the Younger

Consider what we discover about Christianity from the one letter about it we find in Pliny the Younger's government correspondence, the first time in history anyone ever noticed Christianity in any known literature (given that Josephus, as we've already seen, probably never really mentioned it): Christianity appears to have experienced a first-century bottleneck of failure and subsequent revival. In a letter Pliny wrote to Emperor Trajan around 112 A.D. he reveals two interesting facts: he had never been present at any trial of Christians and had no idea what they believed or what was criminal about it; and most of those reported to be Christians in his province had left the faith, years or decades before.

The second fact is telling. The first fact is peculiar. By the time he wrote that letter, Pliny the Younger had been a Roman Senator for 25 years. He had served as the ancient equivalent of the Chief of Police at Rome, the very Capitol of the Empire, with a population above a million. After that he had served as the ancient equivalent of the Attorney General for the whole Empire. Then as Consul (akin to being both Secretary of State and Secretary of Interior). Then served as the governor of Bithynia (a portion of what is now Turkey) for two years before any Christians were brought to his attention. And he had also governed that same province a decade *before that*. So he wasn't even *new* to the province or its legal matters. And yet, somehow, this most legally experienced man in the Empire had never once ever seen a trial of Christians and knew nothing about them or even why it was illegal to be one. That entails Christianity was recruiting so poorly as to be *almost nonexistent*—even after eighty years, nearly two average lifetimes, of evangelizing across three continents. That most of those who could be rousted up as Christians had already left the religion only verifies the conclusion: people were losing interest; membership was scarce and dwindling.

Put those two facts together, and we must conclude Christianity almost died out. It was so uninfluential, so small, so unsuccessful, that by the end of the first century, and dawn of the second, they had never even appeared on Pliny's radar, anywhere, ever, in *several decades* of his legal and administrative experience across the whole Empire. In fact, it was so unsuccessful, that it was even *losing* membership. Sure, Pliny expressed worry that, all of a sudden, Christians could be found everywhere, but it's evident this was hyperbolic alarm based on no actual facts or statistics, akin to McCarthy's fear of Commie Spies infiltrating the government and social elite in the 1950s. Yes, probably a few Christians could be found in many a city or town. But it's clear from Pliny's own account that most of those accused were never Christians or had long ceased to be. Only but few maintained their confession of faith. And they were so rare, it was a labor even to find them, and until he was pressed to search, he'd never encountered a single one in all his career.

It's notable that this apparent failure in the fortunes of the religion corresponds exactly with when a new batch of missionaries attempted to revive it with new, exciting doctrines and texts: the Gospels. When else is a radical reformation of a cult going to be most successful, but when most of its old believers had left, its founders were all long dead, and the sect is so small and anemic no power existed to stop or gainsay any development—and when you could easily dismiss any of the old guard still around as *themselves* being the revisionist heretics! We hardly need any further explanation of how the religion could transition from mystical to historicist doctrines—for the resurrection just as much as for the existence of Jesus. Same difficulty. Same opportunity. Same causes and mechanisms of success. If the one happened—and it unquestionably did—the other could have happened, *with nothing else having to be posited* but what we *already know for a fact happened.*

Conclusion

By 110 A.D., even most adults who had read the first edition of Mark would be dead. The original witnesses and founders would have been *long* dead. In fact, they would likely have been dead *before Mark was even written*—there is, after all, no evidence of any apostle still alive after 70 A.D. And Pliny's report entails Christian converts were a scattered few; most had even abandoned the religion altogether. And this was for a mystery religion with secret doctrines, the easiest to alter without anyone noticing or being able to prove them altered.

So just think about this. If someone started selling the Gospels as real histories, who could prove that untrue by then? The witnesses were all long dead. Anyone who knew them could be gainsaid by liars claiming to have known them—and who could tell the difference? The celestial theory could be claimed the heresy and condemned, and people ordered to shun anyone still advocating it as of the Devil . . . precisely as we see Ignatius and the author of 2 Peter doing. After all, who by then could prove the celestial doctrine the original even if it was? If it was never written down, if it was a mystery only transmitted by word of mouth to initiates, no evidence would exist that what they were told, and thus what they were teaching, was actually the truth. And if it *was* written down, who could prove *that* was not the forgery? Faced with competing copies of the original text of the *Ascension of Isaiah* and the Gospel of Matthew, who could prove which was written first? Who could prove which preserved the doctrines predating the War? Anyone who gainsaid the historicists could be condemned a heretic. And no one would be the wiser. From there on out, it was all just a matter of mere politics which "version" of the church's history would win out. It was in no way anything anyone could decide with evidence. And we don't get to hear any of that debate anyway. Just as it was all erased for the resurrection, so it would have been erased for historicity. Indeed, it would have been the very same documents and statements being erased!

If anyone then "knew" (despite it being impossible to know) that the religion really began with inner visions, and that the absurd narratives in the Gospels of angelically occupied empty tombs and meeting and eating with a risen Jesus were fabrications, how would we know? Anything they said or wrote to call that out was erased. It is not extant, quoted, cited, or mentioned. And if meeting and eating with a risen Jesus could be fabricated that easily, and never be gainsaid in any extant records, and win over the entirety of the subsequently surviving church, why couldn't *the exact same process* result in just as easily fabricating meeting and eating with Jesus *altogether*? What would stop it from never being gainsaid in any extant records and winning over the entirety of the church? Fabricating a dinner with someone *after* they died is no easier than fabricating a dinner with someone *before* they died. So if the one succeeded—and it did—then just as easily could the other have. There is therefore nothing else we have to explain.

8

The Cosmic Seed of David?

There are really only two arguments for Jesus being a real historical person: that Paul said he met Jesus' brothers; and that Paul says Jesus had a mom and a dad and was therefore an ordinary descendant of David. Neither argument is well supported by the evidence. Because in truth, Paul is far more vague than this—in fact, weirdly so.

Every other argument just doesn't carry any water. As we've well seen by now. There is no evidence for Jesus outside the Bible that doesn't derive from the Bible. So nothing corroborates the Bible's claim that Jesus existed. And that really just means, the Gospels and the Epistles. But the Gospels are heavily and demonstrably mythical; every passage in them is just as likely invented to a purpose as reflecting any real source or true event, and we can't tell which is which. So we can't get any evidence out of them. And that leaves the Epistles. And they don't say anything that clearly links anything about Jesus to Earth's real history. They say he descended from the heavens to become a mortal man and be killed and buried, but they never say where any of this happened. They say people saw him spiritually after his death, but by that point he was an exalted celestial being again. They say Jesus told the apostles various things, but when they ever do say at all where or how, they only mention his doing that through revelations from his exalted station in outer space—or through secret messages he channeled through ancient prophets. And that's it.

That leaves only those two things asserted in the Epistles that carry any water at all, and that very little. In the next chapter we'll examine the first of these, whether Paul really said he met Jesus' biological brothers. Here we'll examine the second of these, Jesus' parentage.

Jesus Came from the Seed of David

In Romans 1:3 Paul says Jesus "came from the seed of David according to the flesh," which many historians insist proves Paul knew Jesus was an ordinary man once living on Earth. Because, they say, this verse proves Paul believed Jesus was a descendant of David—and a cosmically incarnated Jesus could hardly be descended from David.

But there is a problem with that. Paul does not say Jesus descended from David or was a descendant of David. Paul never says anything about his even having a father, or even being born. To the contrary, when we look at what his chosen words actually mean, and what he elsewhere says, it's no longer so clear. In another place altogether Paul says Jesus came from outer space:

> When Jesus Christ existed in the form of a god, he did not try to be equal to God. Instead he cast off everything and took up the form of a slave, being made to look like men. And in appearance indeed he was found to look like a man. Thus he humbled himself, becoming obedient all the way to death, even death on a stake. For which God exalted him to the highest station, and bestowed on him the name above all names, so that in the name of Jesus *every* knee would bow—celestial, terrestrial, and subterranean. (Philippians 2:5–10)

There is nowhere here where Paul can imagine Jesus *descended from David*. Jesus was a divine being in outer space, and *then* put on a human body to pass as human, just to die, for which sacrifice God grants Jesus ultimate celestial power—and even, it *might* seem, bestows upon him *then* the name Jesus: for only at his exaltation did God "give him **the name** above every name, so that in **the name** of Jesus" all would bow. Whether that's the case or not, when Paul says here that Jesus had a body manufactured for him to wear briefly to carry out his mission in, Paul uses *the same verb* ("**made** in the likeness of men") that he uses in Romans 1:3 ("**made** from the seed") and Galatians 4:4 ("**made** from a woman")—*and* of Adam's body (1 Corinthians 15:45) and our future resurrection bodies (15:37), neither of which bodies are born or descend from anyone, but all of which are manufactured directly by God.

So we know for a fact that Paul can only mean that his Lord's flesh, upon his incarnation, was "made from the seed of David," and was therefore Jewish and messianic flesh. But he does not here explain what he means by "made from." The word Paul uses can sometimes mean birth in some other authors, but it is not the word Paul himself ever uses for birth (which is *gennaô*); instead, as just noted, it's the word Paul uses for God's manufacture of Adam's body from clay, and God's manufacture of our future resurrection bodies in heaven (which is *ginomai*). In short, Paul says in Philippians he means God *made* a body for Jesus to occupy. So when Paul says the same in Romans 1:3, that's simply weird. It's weird even if Jesus existed. As Bart Ehrman points out in *The Orthodox Corruption of Scripture*, Christians even found it so weird themselves that they tried doctoring later manuscripts to replace this word that Paul only uses of manufacture and "coming to be," with Paul's preferred word for actual "birth." So saying this passage is *also* weird if Jesus *didn't* exist leaves us at a wash. It's weird either way. Even ancient Christians knew it was weird. So what on earth *or in heaven* could Paul have meant?

Probably What Prophecy Said

In the very Holy Scriptures the first apostles believed contained the Word of God we learn that the prophet Nathan was instructed by God to tell King David the following:

> When your days are done, and you sleep with your fathers, I will raise up your sperm after you, which shall come from your belly, and I will establish his kingdom. He will build for me a house in my name, and I will establish his throne forever. I will be his father, and he will be my son. (2 Samuel 7:12–14)

This prophecy, read literally, plainly says God promised this of David's own son, not a distant ancestor. It would be *David's son* whose throne will last forever, and who will be called the Son of God, and build a "kingdom" and a "house" of God. Of course, when originally written, this was speaking of Solomon. But later Jews were already taking it as referring to some future messiah—because otherwise it had long been proved false: Solomon's throne did *not* last forever. And what Paul says in Romans 1:3 was surely derived from this passage, as this is the only prophecy in scripture that speaks of the Son of God coming specifically from "the semen" of David.

If this passage were read like a pesher—an ancient Jewish method of reinterpreting scripture, thinking it had been coyly composed to convey hidden and cryptic meanings only the wise could discern, a method of reading scripture we know the sectarian Jews resembling Christians at Qumran were obsessed with—we would most readily conclude that God was here saying that he extracted semen from David and held it in reserve until the time he would make good this promise of David's progeny sitting on an eternal throne. For otherwise God's promise was broken: the throne of David's progeny was not eternal; it had ceased to exist for hundreds of years by the time Christianity arose. Nathan's prophecy originally meant an unending royal line, and not just biologically, but politically: it is the *throne* that Nathan prophesies would be eternal. Yet history proves it was not. So how could a messianic Jew have read this passage as still telling the truth? There is only one possible way to do that: God must have meant he would raise up a son for David *who will rule eternally*, instead of a royal line that had long since ended, and that "his" will be the kingdom God establishes, and "he" will build God's house—meaning to Paul, of course, the Christian church. And thus *this son of David* will be the one to sit upon a throne forever—and be declared *the* Son of God.

That sure sounds like Jesus. And it's clear from Paul that the first Christians thought it was. Thus they could claim God predicted that Jesus, Son of David, will sit on an eternal throne. Exactly as early Christians taught. Taking the prophecy literally this way is to read it with the fewest assumptions. It's therefore the simplest reading available. Any other reading requires stacking up assumptions not in the text to get the prophecy still to be true. We can be sure messianic Jews would have accepted any elaborate stack of assumptions to get that result, so I don't assume no one was attracted to more elaborate readings. Rather, I am saying the literal reading of this prophecy is the simplest and easiest solution to the problem history had created for it, and thus is the most likely way many Jews would understand it. *Even if Jesus really existed.* All the more so if the earliest Christians thought Jesus had only been incarnated on high.

This is the most parsimonious way to fit Nathan's prophecy to historical fact and messianic Jewish belief. And it seems clear that's what the Christians actually did—even if Jesus existed, they saw the eternal throne in Nathan's prophecy as sat by an actual son of David, and not by an unending line of his descendants. This is as true on historicity as on ahistoricity. So there is nothing unexpected in Romans 1:3 either way. It's the most plausible way to rescue God's prophecy: God could not have been speaking of David's hereditary line, since no such line sat on an eternal throne; so He must have been speaking of *a special son* who will be born of David's sperm *in the future*, using sperm God took up (as indeed God declares) "from his belly," when David still lived. Nathan's prophecy does not say God will set up an eternal throne for someone born of sperm from *a subsequent* heir's belly, but of sperm from *David's own* belly. It's unmistakably clear on this point.

This "cosmic seed" hypotheses actually rescues this prophecy from failure better than any historicist interpretation could. God promised the throne would be eternal. It wasn't. So how could God have been telling the truth? It's not a very good fit to say God didn't mean "throne" but meant that some dethroned scions hiding out for centuries uncrowned would be the thing that's "eternal," and *then* set up an eternal throne with an immortal king, which God could simply have done directly, and (through Nathan) outright said he would. Whether Jesus existed or not, of course, in the conception of Paul's Christians, Jesus only ever rules from outer space. He never sat on or established any real, earthly throne. And he wasn't expected to. The world would soon be burned up, and Christians snatched up into the sky, to share in Christ's "kingdom" above. So there is nothing peculiar about the mythicist alternative here. It's essentially identical to any plausible historicist belief.

If anyone read Nathan's prophecy as saying what it literally says, that the seed God took from David's "belly" will indeed itself, without cessation or break, sit an eternal throne and be "the Son of God," then their belief in what it says *requires* their believing in a cosmic sperm bank of sorts, simply because history left a huge gap of no throne sat. The cosmic seed hypothesis is thus the *only* interpretation of this passage that makes God tell the literal truth. So that very idea surely would have been attractive—indeed, it surely would have felt so brilliant as to be divinely inspired—to anyone who needed it. And the Christians absolutely did, both historicists as well as mythicists. Since they *all* appear to have imagined God directly manufactured the body of Jesus. What then did they think he manufactured it from? Well, Nathan told them.

Literally or Allegorically?

That's why I think it's most likely Paul means what the first Christians he is echoing probably meant: that God manufactured Jesus out of sperm taken directly from David's belly exactly as prophecy declared he would—a concept already more rational than God manufacturing Eve from *a rib* taken directly from Adam's *side*, or storing already-manufactured superhuman bodies for us in heaven (as Paul says God is doing in 2 Corinthians 5). And if Jesus didn't exist, this manufacturing of a Davidic body for Jesus to wear would most likely have occurred in outer space. Although that's not necessarily the case—a mythical Jesus is also compatible with earthly events imagined in distant mythical places, like the Garden of Eden. But, like many Jews, Paul believed even the Garden of Eden (also known as "Paradise") resided in outer space—somewhere in the vicinity of Venus or the Sun in the ancient geocentric scheme, otherwise known as the third sphere of heaven, as

Paul reveals in 2 Corinthians 12, alluding to the same lore preserved in the apocryphal tale of the *Life of Adam and Eve* from back in Paul's time, where Adam is created, and from which he later falls, and then some version of him is taken back up and buried or stored in this same Garden in outer space. There is no evidence in Paul's letters that he thought Jesus had descended *all the way to Earth* to assume human form. Or, even if he did, that it was to any realm humans had access. So we have no reason to assume he thought either of those things.

The best response a historicist can make to Paul's choice of phrasing in Romans 1:3 is that Paul must be echoing an early belief in some kind of virgin birth theology that was somehow already being attributed to Jesus, that he is describing God manufacturing Jesus' body *in the womb of Mary* using Davidic seed. Though Paul never says that. He never mentions Mary, and only mentions Jesus having a mother in an extended argument elsewhere (in Galatians 3–4) that declares the mothers he is speaking of are *also* allegorical and not meant literally. But regardless, cosmic manufacture is exactly what the Gospel nativities give us as well. For in neither Matthew nor Luke is Jesus biologically descended from Davidic seed. In both their accounts, Joseph never imparts that seed to Mary. Instead Jesus is directly manufactured in the womb of Mary by God. Out of what?

Think about it. How can even *the Gospels* mean Jesus was born of the seed of David? They must have been assuming exactly what I am saying here: that God took the seed of David, stored it in heaven until the last days, and used it to manufacture a body for Jesus—whether he took it from David directly or from Joseph or wherever these authors imagined he took it from. Either way, they mean, took it miraculously; not biologically. And if *they* could imagine God doing that, *Paul* could imagine God doing that. And what Paul says in Philippians 2 clearly indicates he *did* imagine God doing that. And if Paul imagined God doing that, he could as easily imagine God doing it in outer space as on Earth. Because *where* a miracle happens is no longer bound to reality. Being a miracle, no one would then have thought such a deed was limited to terrestrial biology. So there would be nothing to stop them imagining it happening in space, as they imagined so many other things happening there, from the storing of the deceased Adam to Satan claiming a throne. Even the author of the book of Revelation seems to have believed Jesus was born in outer space, describing his mother as a celestial being, who was pregnant *in heaven*, and while in labor had to escape Satan's clutches *in heaven*, and whose baby was snatched up to be hidden near God's throne *in heaven* (Revelation 12:1–5).

Of course it's just as possible Paul meant "came from the seed of David" in some allegorical way instead, just as he clearly meant Jesus "coming from a mother" in some allegorical sense in Galatians. Or as he meant for everyone—as in Galatians 3:29, where Paul declares, "If you are Christ's, then you are Abraham's seed, and heirs according to the promise." Meaning, even non-Jews become born "of the seed of Abraham" at baptism. And if Paul can thus say we "come from the seed of Abraham" allegorically, not literally—spiritually, not biologically— then he could as easily mean the same about Jesus having "come from the seed of David." After all, as Paul goes on to explain, what he means is that the seeds and mothers he's talking about are allegories, code words, for the world order we are subject to:

> It is written Abraham had two sons, one by a slave woman, another by a free woman. The one, the child of the slave woman, was born according to the flesh; the other, the child of the free woman, was born through the promise. Now this is an allegory: these women are two covenants. The one woman, in fact, is Hagar, from Mount Sinai, bearing children for slavery. Now Hagar is Mount Sinai in Arabia, and corresponds to the present Jerusalem, for she is in slavery with her children. But the other woman [Sarah, the other legendary mother of the Jewish line] corresponds to the Jerusalem above; she is free, and she is our mother. (Galatians 4:22–26)

Paul outright says the allegorical meaning of being born of Hagar means being born "according to the flesh" (Galatians 4:23 and 4:29), and thus of this world, just as he says of the seed-body of Jesus in Romans 1. And he says we can switch mothers, from this world to the next world on high, by accepting the risen Jesus. Which means Jesus must also have accomplished this feat, as obviously he is no longer made of flesh (per 1 Corinthians 15:37–50 and 2 Corinthians 5), and obviously no longer subject to the law, no longer a slave trapped below, but a son now of the celestial Jerusalem, and hence allegorically of Sarah, just as those who join him will be. That's Paul's entire theory of salvation: as for Jesus, so for us. So here it's quite clear Paul understands the phrase "born of a woman, born under the law" allegorically, not literally. He is talking about cosmology, not biology. And so likewise he could be in Romans 1.

We can even tell Paul is talking about all this same stuff in Romans 1, because this allegorical argument in Galatians 3–4 about Abraham's seed being spiritually meant, and the coming from different women being code for subjection to either the earthly or celestial world orders, all parallels Romans 1:3, where Jesus is, like us, also born both ways: "according to the spirit" (becoming God's heir and viceroy, and thus a son of Sarah), and "according to the flesh" (becoming incarnate, and thus, temporarily, an ordinary mortal man, a "son of Hagar"); and in the same order: first, by the flesh; then, by the spirit—just as Paul says in respect to God's various manufactured bodies in 1 Corinthians 15:44–49. In Galatians 3–4 Paul reveals that these people, and thus their names (Hagar, Sarah, Abraham), are allegorical, not literal actual women, and not literal actual Abraham— nor literal actual semen. So, when Paul says Jesus was born according to the flesh and from the seed of David, he can just as easily mean allegorically here in Romans as there in Galatians, when he says this *of us* being born to Hagar and the seed of Abraham. It's thus telling that already in the early to mid-second century, Ignatius would be complaining in his letter to the Smyrnaeans of Christians who were *not* taking this "seed of David" literally—which means, there *were* Christians who understood it allegorically. And as we saw in the last chapter, in his letter to the Trallians Ignatius warns against even listening to those Christians; his Christians had to newly *insist* this "seed of David" was meant literally. Which suggests originally, it wasn't.

So we don't actually need to posit a literal reading of Romans 1:3. Paul already routinely applies allegorical readings to directly parallel statements elsewhere. Hence when I say the literal cosmic reading is more likely, I do so not because I need to, as if doubting the historicity of Jesus requires me to. I do so because I think the evidence establishes it's more likely. But even if it didn't, the next most likely reading is still the allegorical. *And both are the case even if Jesus historically existed.* As we just saw from Philippians: Paul cannot have meant Jesus descended from David, because he believed Jesus descended from outer space. So we still don't get any secure evidence for historicity here. Did Paul mean "seed" allegorically (as he does mean elsewhere when he speaks of seeds and births) or cosmically (as would require the fewest assumptions to fit all the evidence) or is he referring to a claim of biological descent—even though his vocabulary does not match such an assertion, but that of direct manufacture? At best it's equal odds. We can't tell. We just aren't given enough information to know.

Consequently, we can't use this verse to argue for historicity. We can't use it to argue for myth, either, since it can still be referring to a miraculous but actual birth—or even, if Paul was going against his own idiom and statements elsewhere, a mundane one. But that leaves us back where we started: not knowing which it is. And it's telling that even the Gospels are ambiguous on this point. As the angel in Luke 1:32 declares, David was indeed *the father* of Jesus—not merely his ancestor. So, how? Did the Gospels mean "Son of David" metaphorically, allegorically, or *literally*?

That's why using these verses, in Romans 1:3 and Galatians 4:4, to "prove" historicity is a fatally weak argument. It's not at all clear that they do evince historicity. They are strangely worded no matter which way you read them. And they can too easily have been meant allegorically or cosmically in the context of Paul's style of writing and speaking generally. We have no evidence it's more likely Paul meant these things the way historicists need him to, and there's even some evidence he didn't. So we can get no evidence out of this, either way.

Logic Dictates No Other Conclusion

Of course, that these verses are unclear is itself weird. Why should Paul speak so weirdly, evasively, and unclearly about the parentage of Jesus? One should sooner suspect something weird is thus *meant*, when Paul chooses to speak so weirdly as we find him doing here. But even if we put that clue aside, all we need know is one thing: *if* Jesus was only understood by Paul and the other apostles to have been a celestial and not a terrestrial being, *then* would they be teaching he had to have "come from the seed of David," in any sense, whether cosmic or allegorical? In other words, how expected is that outcome? The answer is that it's *exactly* what we should expect. We can reliably predict this to near one-hundred percent certainty. And that's why this passage in Romans cannot be used as evidence Jesus existed. Because the content of Romans 1:3 is just as expected on either theory, whether Jesus did exist or not.

Consider an analogy. If we knew a Young Earth Creationist was going to be posed with two beliefs she needs to maintain, that God made everything all at once roughly 6,000 years ago, *and* that the fossil record is stratified, what can we expect her to say? We can validly predict, with near one-hundred percent certainty, that this Creationist will start arguing that Noah's Flood must have done something to cause the stratification. We can fully anticipate such a teaching to arise. It's exactly what we expect a Creationist to write in a letter, for example. And we could fully predict it from a conjunction of other beliefs. And when we do this, in no way are we saying that their belief is true. We are just saying it's no surprise to us that that belief exists.

This is what's happening in our examination of Romans 1:3. In no way are we arguing Jesus *actually was* spawned by cosmically stored seed direct from David's belly. Rather, we are observing that, *if* Jesus didn't really exist, *then* the first Christians were posed with two beliefs they needed to maintain: that the celestial messiah received from God a body of flesh to be sacrificed in (Philippians 2, Hebrews 9), *and* that God promised through scripture that the messiah would come from the seed of David (2 Samuel 7:12–14). We can then validly predict from these two facts, with near one-hundred percent certainty, that such Christians will start teaching that God did that directly—that he manufactured the cosmic messiah's body directly out of the seed of David, just as he directly manufactured the body of Eve out of a rib from Adam's belly. We can fully anticipate such a teaching to arise. It's exactly what we expect an apostle to write in a letter, for example. And we could fully predict it from a conjunction of other beliefs. And when we do this, in no way are we saying that their belief is true. We are just saying it's no surprise to us that that belief exists. This is the effect of recovering our background knowledge of the time and place these people were writing in: they had different ideas about the world than we do, and thus what we think is improbable to imagine now, wasn't then.

This is why the cosmic seed hypothesis is not *ad hoc* and *not* improbable. To the contrary, we have correctly anticipated a belief any mythicist Christian would hold, from a conjunction of other beliefs we know for a fact they *did* hold. Only if the prophecy of the messiah "coming from" Davidic seed *didn't* exist—or it *wasn't* true that messianic Jews would not dare reject or contradict a Torah prophecy in any system of beliefs they constructed—would the content of Romans 1:3 be unexpected on mythicism, and thus only then would the cosmic seed hypothesis be "a gerrymander," an *ad hoc* excuse to explain away otherwise contrary evidence. Unlike a gerrymander, our background knowledge conjoined with the hypothesis, in this case mythicism, *entails* the observation. It effectively has a one-hundred percent chance of being observed; indeed, you could have reliably predicted it ahead of time with the same information. Which is because our background knowledge includes those two indisputable facts: that prophecy said this; and messianic Jews made their systems of beliefs conform to prophecy. Likewise, that ancient peoples readily conceived weird things like this. Those are not conjectures. Those are all established facts.

Which even makes this a stronger prediction than the Creationist's "the flood caused it" excuse, which *is* a gerrymander *for them*, albeit still a one-hundred percent predictable one. If the Old Testament actually said, even as written thousands of years ago, that the flood had stratified animal carcasses in the pattern matching what we actually now observe, only then would "the flood caused it" *not* be for *their* theory a gerrymander. Whereas in the cosmic seed case, scripture *really does literally say that*. And ancient Jews *really did* believe in miraculous and cosmic events of a like kind. And messianic Jews always *did* construct their belief systems to cohere with scripture. They *also* routinely accepted allegorical interpretations of scripture—so that other thesis, too, holds equally well. You can't object to any of these things that it was "improbable." None of it was.

How This Happened

We need merely think through how this would happen to get the point. We can start with what we know about the origin of the Christian religion from the only contemporary who discusses it: Paul. In 1 Corinthians 15, Paul reveals that the original apostle, the true "founder" of Christianity, was Peter—then better known as "Cephas," the Aramaic version of his Greek name, either of which means "The Rock." As no such name existed in Aramaic, it was likely a cultic title he assumed, which may have had some spiritual meaning within the Church at the time. This Peter had, by Paul's report, the first revelation of the Lord teaching the secret gospel and kerygma of the Christ (per Romans 16:25–26).

Peter was probably already a prominent if not leading figure of some fringe, countercultural sect of messianic Jews, something akin to the sect or sects represented in the Dead Sea Scrolls. Because scholars have long noted there are several ethical, doctrinal, and other similarities between the sect(s) at Qumran and earliest Christianity, including a particular organizational similarity: at least one Qumran sect already had a committee of "twelve" working under their organizational leader running the community (as Joseph Baumgarten shows in "The Duodecimal Courts of Qumran"). Which is to be expected, as that would emulate the twelve tribes of Israel, and messianic Jews did indeed hope for a resurrection and return to dominance of those twelve tribes, who would need leaders ready-set to govern them. So Peter probably already had at his command some council of "twelve" (Paul never says they are disciples, and he never says Peter was one of them), who soon after Peter likewise claimed revelations of the Christ appointing *them* to the Apostolate, too, alongside him—something so convenient as to be totally predictable before it even happened. Then under their inspiration more visions followed, adding more missionaries to the movement; last of all Paul, who was the first to start making entry to the movement easier for Gentiles, changing the religion forever. The original sect, which was strictly Jewish, dwindled and eventually died out. Paul's sect, overwhelmed with Gentiles, evolved into dozens of warring sects, one of which would come out on top politically and use its power to suppress all the others. Such was the fate of Christianity.

If what started all that was in fact what the leading mythicist thesis proposes, then what happened was this: Peter was running a fringe messianic sect of Jews, likely searching the scriptures for years or decades for hidden messages about how God planned to end the world and deliver his faithful, and then at last (possibly at a time he calculated from those scriptures) Peter had a revelation that opened up to him all the secrets he'd been looking for. Many ancient people had what were to them convincing revelations from their gods, bringing them new teachings and prophecies. And here likewise being "revealed" to Peter would have been the risen Christ Lord, now explaining to him that God's first created archangel (the very "image of God" himself) had just secretly undergone a cosmic incarnation, death, and resurrection among Satan and his minions above (the "archons of this eon") to atone for all sins once and for all, and thereby usher in the end of days.

Even if this were merely a dream Peter had, according to ancient beliefs and assumptions he would be certain it was a genuine visitation, a revelation from the Lord himself. Because most ancient peoples believed that dreamed encounters with gods were real encounters with gods and would just as readily call them "appearances" of that god. Convinced now that this cosmic event had happened, and the end was now indeed nigh as he'd long hoped, Peter would search the scriptures with a new eye, seeking to reinterpret everything he read there in light of this new revelation. The resulting ingenuity in his "opening" the scriptures this way, and his charismatic confidence in its truth, would no doubt move many others of Peter's sect to follow and have like experiences confirming the same things to them. And so the movement began—as all other messianic movements have, from Zoroastrianism of yore to the Cargo Cults of today. Even Islam and Mormonism follow the same model.

Now knowing he had to reinterpret the hidden meaning of every messianic scripture in light of his new divine knowledge, what do you think Peter would do with the scriptures declaring the messiah would arise "from the seed of David"? Would Peter now conclude all his revelations must be false, because what they told him could not be true, as the messiah could not but be a human man descended from David? That's literally the least likely thing Peter would do. In fact, its probability can confidently be said to be as near to zero as makes no odds. No.

What Peter would surely do is "reveal" to his sectarian followers a new meaning of those passages, one that explains Peter's revelation and makes God look even more ingenious, and Satan even more the fool for being tricked by His hidden plan.

There are, after all, only two ways other messianic Jews responded to verses of scripture that contradicted reality or each other: they either reread the offending verse allegorically so as to remove the difficulty; or they reread it in such a way as removed the difficulty while retaining its literal sense. This is what always happened. Therefore we can be certain it's what would have happened here. The result is therefore not unlikely. It is in fact one-hundred percent expected. And this is why Romans 1:3 cannot demonstrate Jesus existed; because it does not tell us whether Paul meant it allegorically, cosmically, or mundanely, and none of those readings is inherently more likely than the others. No matter what, the messiah had to come from David's seed. "How" was irrelevant. And we can be certain any propounder of a cosmic Jesus would come up with a clever answer to that question. We can be *equally* certain that the one thing they would *never* do is declare those prophecies false or impertinent. Therefore references to them in the writings of Paul are entirely expected. *Whether Jesus existed or not.*

The Literal Reading Is the Simplest Reading

The only way to argue against this conclusion is to argue it's *more likely* that someone like Peter who came so forcefully to believe in a celestial Christ narrative would *abandon* that belief as soon as they were confronted with the Davidic seed prophecy, than that such a person would simply *reinterpret* the Davidic seed prophecy to match their celestial Christ narrative. And there is no evidence whatever that any messianic Jew would ever have done the former. They would always have done the latter. So that argument fails to carry any weight against the conclusion: since we fully expect Paul to say what he does in Romans 1:3 regardless of whether Jesus really existed or not, what Paul actually says in Romans 1:3 can never be evidence Jesus existed—*even if he did*. It could well be Paul nevertheless means some form of ordinary biological descent—but we just can't tell from the data available.

It thus does not matter how "weird" the reinterpretation of the Davidic seed prophecy is that Paul may have had in mind. Christianity and Judaism are full of weird reinterpretations of prophecy when confronted with prophecies they can't otherwise make fit the facts or their most cherished beliefs. The Gospels' nativity narratives are evident examples: they don't even try to depict biological Davidic descent; they instead choose the far weirder solution of direct divine manufacture of the body of Jesus. Which nevertheless is therefore *still* declared to be Davidic. If that's not weird, then neither is a cosmic version of the very same thing.

But really, in context, this interpretation isn't even weird. In the Babylonian Talmud, *Niddah* folio 16, we are told "the name of the angel who is in charge of conception is Laylah" (the Hebrew word for "Night") and this angel named Laylah takes up every "drop" of semen to heaven "and places it in the presence of the Holy One" and asks, "Sovereign of the universe, what shall be the fate of this drop? Shall it produce a strong man or a weak man, a wise man or a fool, a rich man or a poor man?" If Jews could so readily come up with this bizarre idea, then the idea that God could *store* one of those drops from David that the angel Laylah would thus have delivered for inspection—all to effect His secret plan to defeat Satan in the lower reaches of outer space and also fulfill an otherwise failed prophecy—cannot even be called strange. It's no weirder than the "fact" that Paul relates without blush that God "stores" our future resurrection bodies for us up in heaven (2 Corinthians 5) or that we could visit the Garden of Eden there (2 Corinthians 12). There have likewise been many tales in Jewish lore of semen—even semen cast onto the ground or into one's bed—being grabbed by demons who could inseminate themselves with it, or others. And what demons could do for ill, any Jew could readily imagine God doing for good.

Christians readily gravitated to such weird ideas. The late second-century Christian critic Irenaeus complained repeatedly in the first book of his treatise *Against Heresies* of Christian sects who advanced even stranger cosmic seed scenarios for the birth of Jesus. That book starts right out of the gate with an example; we find another in its fifth chapter.

So such a thing can't have been unlikely, since it was commonly being contrived. The idea of a magical sperm bank producing a messiah was likely even already popular in Zoroastrian tradition at the time, which had already extensively influenced Judaism—the Jews having fully embraced from it the ideas of resurrection, apocalyptic history, a flaming hell, an elaborate angelology and demonology, and a Satanic war with God, among other things. So to also adopt the idea of a messianic sperm bank, too, is fully within precedent. And even if they didn't get that idea from there, the fact that ancient Zoroastrians also readily thought of it, means it's not unlikely ancient Jews would too, particularly to solve exactly the same theological problem.

Thus we find that a ninth-century Zoroastrian collection of legends preserves the ancient lore that "a virgin" will bathe in and drink from lake Kasaoya and thereby became pregnant with the "seed" of the ancient Zoroaster who deposited his semen there thousands of years prior. And thus she shall give birth to the messiah, Zoroaster's own son (*Denkard* 7.8.55-57), a notion confirmed in various pre-Christian Zoroastrian texts as well (*Yasht* 19.92; *Vendidad* 19.5). This idea of stored semen and similar notions appear elsewhere in ancient religions. According to the ancient mythographers Pausanias and Arnobius, semen of the god Attis was stored in a magical almond, that was then able to impregnate the virgin Nana merely by being placed on her belly. The *Fables* of Hyginus relate that Dionysus was miraculously *re*-conceived by his mother Semele by drinking a slushy of his corpse, not all that conceptually different from his "seed" being stored in a potion.

Once again this is no weirder than the tale of Eve coming from Adam's rib, or a deceased Adam being stored in the third heaven, or Paul's idea that God keeps a warehouse of empty bodies somewhere up in space, or a mass resurrection of all the world's dead, or even expecting an immortal superhero to fly down from outer space and snatch us up into the sky—as Paul outright says all Christians believed in 1 Thessalonians 4:16–17. If Jews had no qualms about adopting those absurd beliefs, they could hardly have scrupled against adopting notions of God storing David's semen to effect His future secret plans. There simply isn't any case to be made that that would be "too weird" to have happened. It's not even too weird to be probable. This sort of thing happened all the time. And it requires the fewest assumptions for us to suspect it. But once again, if you can't accept that they believed a thousand weird things like this back then, even though in fact they did, it's still the case that they also read a thousand different scriptures allegorically. So there is no way to get to any certainty Paul was speaking of ordinary human biology in either Romans 1 or Galatians 4. One way or another, you don't honestly know.

Accepting the Conclusion

So there is no way around this. The only way to read Romans 1:3 as *more likely* if Jesus really existed than if he didn't, is *to be sure* of Peter's abandoning his cosmic Christ belief when confronted with Nathan's prophecy. But that simply isn't at all plausible. He would surely have instead reinterpreted Nathan's prophecy. Because all Jews had to, just to rescue it from being falsified by history. Either way the result would be the very words Paul echoes in Romans 1:3, that the messiah came from David's seed just as Nathan predicted. Since this is the only likely thing Peter and the first apostles would have done, we therefore cannot discern from their doing that whether they did it for a real or an imaginary Jesus. And that is why Romans 1:3, and likewise Galatians 4:4, afford no evidence at all that Jesus really existed. We simply cannot tell what Paul means in these two verses, with any probability sufficient to prove any reading more likely than another.

Once someone "had a revelation" they believed came from God's most exalted angel, a revelation that this cosmic Jesus event had occurred, and has at last saved everyone, and now signals the end of days, and solves all their imminent political troubles, the probability of their giving that up in the face of Nathan's prophecy is effectively zero. And as the first Christians were devout, indeed fanatical, messianic Jews fond of reading scripture like a pesher, the probability of their declaring Nathan's prophecy a lie from God, or of no relevance to God's promise of an eternal throne for his chosen Son, is effectively zero. Therefore the probability that Paul and his Christian peers would *not* believe what he says in Romans 1:3—even if they believed Jesus's incarnation and death were exclusively celestial events—is effectively zero. Therefore the probability that, if Jesus didn't really exist, Paul would nevertheless still say what he does in Romans 1:3, is effectively one-hundred percent. The same, too, of Galatians 4:4, which is even more obviously an allegorical reference to God's manufacture of a body for Jesus in accordance with Philippians 2, and thus doesn't tell us at all whether Paul thought Jesus actually had an ordinary human mother or not.

This is just as true even if the first apostles made it all up. Because they would only do that if they fanatically believed a celestial messianic sacrifice was a necessary solution to their present political and social troubles, as every precedent in the history of religion establishes. One can easily conclude Islam and Mormonism were fabricated, yet they were never abandoned in the face of any difficulty, *even by their fabricators*. In the Christian case, Nathan's prophecy *had* to be true. No matter what. Whether they were genuinely feeling inspired by revelation, or sincerely committed to a noble lie, a religious fanatic convinced of a thing does not abandon it, ever, on any such technicality as that. I can't even think of a single example of that ever happening in the whole of human history. Which is as low a probability as you can get in mundane affairs.

The cosmic seed hypothesis is just the most parsimonious way a superstitious Jew of that era would react to Nathan's prophecy once already committed to their other beliefs, and thus it's simply the most probable way they'd harmonize that prophecy with those beliefs. The way scripture gets weirdly reinterpreted in the pesher texts at Qumran already shows how normal this would be. Likewise in later Christian treatises like *Hermas*, and other Christian texts weirder still. They all prove there is nothing unusual about this at all. "It's weird, therefore it's improbable" clearly has zero predictive success as a principle for understanding ancient history. "It's weird" was so normal as to be everywhere, in both Jewish and Christian apocalyptic thought. And that's the exact opposite of improbable. To the contrary, the cosmic seed hypothesis is the only reinterpretation of Nathan's prophecy that requires no *ad hoc* assumptions. It relies solely on a literal, plain reading of what he said, and nothing but what were then *widely* known to be the supernatural options for gods to effect their plans.

Even so, mythicism's probability would still be unaffected by it being the other way around. We've already seen that Nathan's prophecy could have been interpreted as fulfilled allegorically, for example. And Paul outright says he is speaking allegorically when speaking of being born of a "woman" in Galatians, and likewise of coming from "Abraham's" seed. All that we know *for certain* is that it would have been interpreted to fit *somehow*, and thus would *always* have been affirmed as true, on virtually every possible historical model of cosmic messianism. Essentially no Jew would declare that prophecy false, or abandon their inspired plan or belief in the face of it. Essentially every Jew would instead make that prophecy fit their beliefs, as every precedent establishes they always did. Even the Gospels imagined Nathan's seed prophecy was fulfilled in some bizarre, miraculous way that isn't substantially different from what mythicism already entails. Whether they thought God manufacturing a body for Jesus in Mary's womb fulfilled that seed prophecy literally or allegorically, it's still God manufacturing that body, not biological descent. And that's why seeing this same seed prophecy affirmed in the letters of Paul should have no effect on the probability of Jesus having ever been real. We can't tell *where* Paul thought this happened. Therefore that Paul said it did can't really be used as evidence Jesus existed.

9

The Peculiar Cult of the Brothers of the Lord

The Son of God, Jesus Christ Our Lord, Paul says, is "the firstborn of many brethren" (Romans 8:29), because all who are baptized into Christ "are the sons of God" (Romans 8:14). And they are so because they've been "adopted as sons" and thus cry out to God, "Abba! Father!" (Romans 8:15). And since, Paul tells his fellow Christians, "the Spirit now testifies" that we have become "the children of God" (Romans 8:16), that is the reason we are now "the heirs" to God's kingdom, "indeed, we are co-heirs with Christ" (Romans 8:17). Thus, Paul says of all who are "baptized" into Christ, "you are all the sons of God" and therefore they are all "heirs" to his kingdom (Galatians 3:26–29).

We're even told Christ chose to become incarnate and die precisely "so that we might receive adoption to sonship" in order to give us a share in the Kingdom of God. How? Paul answers:

Because you are also His sons. God sent the Spirit of His Son into our hearts, the Spirit who calls out, "Abba! Father!" So you are no longer a slave, but God's child. And since you are His child, God has made you also an heir. (Galatians 4:5–7)

And for this reason scripture even predicted, Paul says, that all his fellow Christians "shall be called Sons of the Living God" (Romans 9:26).

Note what this means: Paul repeatedly makes very clear that all baptized Christians are the brothers of Jesus, coequal heirs to God's Kingdom, because Jesus is *the* Son of God and thus *the* Heir. It is thus by being the Lord's brother that we get to claim eternal life and power with him. It's very clear that this was a fundamental and pervasive understanding in the Christian sect. It is what they believed made them special, what singled them out as following the right path, what made them a distinct sect among the Jews. They were the Sons of the Living God. And so they share in the inheritance of the *firstborn* Son of God, the Lord Jesus—being *also*, like him, the adopted sons of God, and thus the brethren of Christ their Lord. Which means Paul's Christians all understood themselves to be Brothers of the Lord. Paul says this so explicitly, so often, that it's quite beyond dispute.

Which is why it isn't a very good argument to say, as many scholars still attempt to do, that "Jesus had a brother named James and Paul actually knew him, and that proves Jesus existed, because if Jesus didn't exist, then he wouldn't have had a brother." Because Paul never, ever says Jesus had a *biological* brother. When he ever specifies at all, Paul only ever says Jesus had *cultic* brothers: baptized Christians. In fact, the only reason Christians kept assuming they are the brothers *of each other* (as Paul reveals repeatedly in his letters they did) is that they are all brothers *of Jesus*. So we actually have no reason to assume that when Paul mentions "Brothers of the Lord" that he meant anything else. The only Brothers of the Lord Paul appears to know about are those baptized into Christ. Even at best, we cannot tell *whether* Paul means by Brothers of the Lord what he elsewhere means, his fellow Christians—the Sons of the Living God—or some special other different kind of Brother of the Lord: Jesus' actual kin, a member of his earthly family. Paul never mentions there being an earthly family of Jesus, or any family of Jesus, distinct from the spiritual family of the Christians themselves. So why would we ever assume he meant otherwise?

The Only Real Argument for Historicity

That seems pretty clear to me. So this is a very weak argument for the existence of Jesus. Nevertheless, I've long noted it's the best evidence there is. Indeed, really, it's the *only* evidence there is.

All other evidence for a real Jesus falls apart on inspection. Everything outside the Gospels just derives from them and thus can't corroborate them; in the Gospels we can't tell whether anything is true about Jesus, or just a story being told for its instructional or symbolic meaning; and in the Epistles we get nothing clear enough to hang a hat on. Epistles forged in the second century, like 2 Peter or 1 Timothy, being fake, can't evince anything; and every other Epistle appears only to know of Jesus as a being one would only have met in dreams or visions. We've already seen attempts to argue that references to his "coming from" the "semen of David" and "coming from" some generic "woman" don't work, because they're either allegorical or cosmically obscure. At best it's 50/50 what they mean. So we can't get any evidence from those passages either. And any other passage one might adduce also, weirdly, doesn't say anything specific enough—like Jesus being "crucified" by "the archons of this eon" (who are those people? where did this happen?) or Paul's vision of Christ secretly inaugurating the Eucharist ritual at some past time (with whom? where?).

I've already addressed all that. And yet in *Historicity* I still counted some of this as evidence *for* historicity, particularly those mystically obscure passages that a committed interpreter today might think reference his father and mother, *and* the only passages where Paul might likewise be thought to be mentioning a real family for Jesus: his brothers. The latter consists of just two passages where Paul uses the full phrase "Brother of the Lord," which we're examining now, last of all, because it's the best historicity has. But that's not saying much. Because as we just saw, there's no reason to believe Paul or his intended readers would have understood anything else by Brother of the Lord than baptized Christians. No evidence *in Paul* suggests otherwise. So why cling to this hope? It falls apart on inspection as surely as the rest.

Because We Must Attend to What the Original Greek Says

The problem is not the validity of the historicist's argument, but its soundness. *If* Paul said he met a biological brother of Jesus, *then* Jesus assuredly existed. The reasoning is correct. But not only must a sound argument be valid, but its premises *also* have to be well-established as true—or at least not much in doubt. Otherwise any doubt we have in the premises transfers to the conclusion, and we then have to doubt the conclusion—as much or even more. And ample doubt should exist as to the central premise of the historicist's argument at this point: that Paul ever says he knew an actual biological brother of Jesus.

We'll start with Galatians 1:19, where Paul says he met "James the Brother of the Lord." The context is this (and here I am carefully translating Paul's Greek myself, to avoid the hidden presumptions as to the meaning found in modern Bibles):

> I make known to you, Brothers, regarding the gospel I preached, that it did not come from a man. For I neither received it from a man nor was I taught it, except by a revelation of Jesus Christ. You've heard of my former conduct within Judaism, that beyond exaggeration I used to hunt down the church community and was destroying it. And because I was extremely zealous for the traditions of my forefathers, I was advancing within Judaism beyond many peers among my countrymen. But when, by His grace, it pleased Him who had selected me from my mother's womb to call and reveal His Son within me, so I could preach him among the Gentiles, I did not consult with flesh and blood right away. Nor did I go to Jerusalem to those who were Apostles before me. Instead I went to Arabia, and returned again to Damascus. Then after three years I went to Jerusalem to get acquainted with Cephas [i.e., Peter, the first Apostle], and stayed with him for fifteen days. But I saw no other Apostle, only James the Brother of the Lord. (Galatians 1:11–19)

The key line here is, of course, "But I saw no other Apostle, only James the Brother of the Lord." Experts in the peer-reviewed literature have long established that the usual translation of this verse found in most Bibles has the grammar wrong. The New King James translation reads, "I saw none of the other apostles except James, the Lord's brother." But that's not what the Greek says. The New International Version has corrected that erroneous translation to match the actual Greek, and thus now reads, "I saw none of the other apostles—only James, the Lord's brother." A similarly corrected reading appears in the modern Berean Literal Bible.

A strictly literal translation of the key phrase here would be "I did not see another of the apostles, but only James." A cleaner equivalent in English is, "I saw none of the other apostles, only James." In other words, "I saw no other apostle, only James," meaning this James was not an apostle. This is not only clear from the actual grammar Paul chose to use but also from the even more obvious fact that had Paul meant to say he met two apostles, Cephas and James, he would simply say, "I met only two apostles, Cephas and James" or "I met only the apostles Cephas and James." But he didn't say that. *So we know that's not what he was telling the Galatians.* He chose a far more convoluted structure peculiar to ancient Greek, and the only reason for him to do that would be to tell the Galatians that he met only *one* apostle, Cephas, plus another *member of the church*, a certain James—meaning someone of lower rank, a *mere* brother, someone "just" a Christian.

To fully understand what's going on here, consider a common armchair reaction to being told this. "No one can think Peter was not *also* a Brother of the Lord," someone will say, "so why is only James being called that?" The answer is the same reason as it would be now, when for example we distinguish pastors and priests and bishops from just "Christians." If we say, "the only pastor I met was Pete, but I also met a Christian named Jacob," we are not saying Pastor Pete is not also a Christian; we are saying Jacob is not a pastor—but still a Christian. This is why Paul's grammar is so convoluted in this passage. Rather than simply say, "I met two apostles, Cephas and James the Brother of the Lord," a way of saying this that *would definitely mean* Cephas was not whatever a "Brother of the Lord" was, Paul chose instead to say he met *no* other apostle, but just a Brother of the Lord named James. So just as with Pastor Pete, Paul is not saying an apostle is not *also* a Brother of the Lord; he is saying this James he happened to meet then was not an apostle, that he was *merely* a Brother of the Lord. Just as Jacob is merely a Christian.

Even though this is actually quite clearly what the Greek says and why Paul chose this peculiar construction, Christian dogma so regularly distorts how scholars translate or read a passage that most have simply overlooked how distorted this verse becomes in English, and thus missed what Paul was *actually saying*. Only careful experts who actually pay attention get it right. And so these days Bible translations will range from the grammatically accurate, "I saw none of the other apostles—only James, the Lord's brother" (NIV) to the completely inaccurate, "The only other apostle I met at that time was James, the Lord's brother" (NLT). The latter is definitely not what the Greek says. It's an interpretation of what the translator *thinks* the Greek text *is supposed* to mean; but it's not. The former is.

Now, whether Paul is actually lying about who he did or did not meet, or how he actually came by his knowledge of the Christian mysteries, is not relevant to what Paul wants the Galatians to think, and thus what Paul means to say. And what Paul wants the Galatians to believe is that almost no one in Judea ever met him. He swears to this most emphatically (see Galatians 1:20). But Paul knows the Galatians also communicate with Peter and the Jerusalem Apostles. So he has to admit there *were* some exceptions, but *only* two, Peter and James—and only for a brief time, and only years after he saw the Lord personally. These are all points Paul goes out of his way to emphasize. But in so doing, why wouldn't he just say, "Of them that were apostles before me, I met none except Peter and James"? Why does he construct the convoluted sentence, "I consulted with Peter, but another of the apostles I did not see, except James"?

As L. Paul Trudinger put it in his own peer-reviewed study of this passage, "this would certainly be an odd way for Paul to say that he saw only two apostles, Peter and James." To say that, a far simpler sentence would do. So why the complex sentence instead? Paul could perhaps mean that he *consulted* with Peter (in Paul's Greek, *historeô*) but only *saw* James (in Paul's Greek, *eidô*)—that is, he didn't *discuss* anything with James. But if that were his point, he would make sure to emphasize it, since that would be essential to his argument. Yet he doesn't. In fact, if he is saying that he *saw* none of the other apostles, that would entail he was claiming he did not *consult* with any, either. So Paul definitely means he *met* only the Apostle Peter and only one other Judean Christian, a certain "brother James."

Paul is therefore saying that this James was not an apostle. Trudinger cites several other peer-reviewed experts who concur, as does Hans Dieter Betz, who actually wrote the Fortress Press commentary on the Epistle to the Galatians. There were of course men named James who *were* apostles. So Paul chose this grammatical construction to make clear he didn't mean one of those men (much less a biological brother of Peter, which could be implied by Paul's Greek without his specifying whose brother he was). And when we combine this observation with the previous one—that Paul only ever mentions knowing about cultic Brothers of the Lord, never biological ones—we should conclude he meant the same here, a regular "Brother of the Lord," an ordinary non-Apostolic Christian, but a Christian all the same. Which was important for Paul to mention, since he had to list every Christian he met on that visit, lest he be accused of concealing his contacts with anyone who knew the gospel at that time.

Ironically, in his attempt to answer Trudinger, George Howard, the only person to challenge Trudinger's conclusion in the peer-reviewed literature, argued that the grammatical examples Trudinger referenced as proving his point still involve "a comparison between persons or objects of the same class of things," such as new friends and old friends belonging to the general class of friends, and indestructible elements and destructible elements belonging to the general class of elements. Illogically, Howard thought this fact argued against Trudinger. In fact, it corroborates Trudinger. Because it means Paul meant Peter and James do indeed belong to the same class—Brothers of the Lord—since Jesus is "the firstborn of many brethren." Which *entails* Paul intended a distinction here between Apostolic and non-Apostolic Brothers of the Lord, just as Trudinger's examples show a contrast being made between destructible and indestructible elements and old and new friends. Howard's objection thus actually confirms the very thing I'm arguing here. It thus does not argue against Trudinger at all. He would agree both Peter and this James *did* belong to the same class of things: Christians.

Similarly, Howard's only other objection was to suggest that Paul could have said James was not an apostle by an even more convoluted sentence. Which is illogical. It is never "more" likely that an author will use a "more" convoluted way to say the same thing. In fact, that's vanishingly less likely when the structure that was chosen is already fairly convoluted, as here. Occam's Razor entails Paul would have used any of several obvious grammatical ways to say, "I met two apostles" in Greek, had that been what he meant, all of which are much simpler. Exactly as Trudinger observes. At least two modern translation committees now agree. Howard thus has no argument left to make. So it's time to acknowledge that this verse has always been mistranslated, by scholars importing their own assumptions into the text, instead of actually reading the text and thinking about what Paul can only have meant by it, given the peculiar choices he made in saying it.

We Also Must Attend to the Actual Context

So the grammar is clear: Paul is saying this James he met was not an apostle, and therefore just an "ordinary" Brother of the Lord, like every other baptized Christian was. Could Paul have "also" meant that he was a biological brother of Jesus? Well, odds are Paul would have to *say* that, if that's what he meant. Because he would be creating confusion otherwise. Which kind of Brother of the Lord is this James? A baptized Christian? Or Jesus' family? If Paul knew there were both kinds, he would have to specify here, if he meant the latter.

Paul would have to say something like "brother of the Lord according to the flesh" or some such expression, to clarify he was *not* talking about the only kind of Brother of the Lord Paul elsewhere ever specifies knowing, making clear that he meant a very *specific* James who was not merely a Brother of the Lord but *also* someone who actually shared natural parentage with the Lord. Because there were tons of men who would be known as James the Brother of the Lord—as Paul makes clear throughout his letters, every baptized Christian named James would be so known. There was already more than one apostle of that then-common name (the name is actually Jacob, by the way, traditionally still miswritten in English as "James"). There would have been many more mere brethren of that name. So it's pretty clear that Paul chose to dismissively tack on a nod to having met a mere rank-and-file James, a nobody; he choose *not* to specify a specific, renowned James. Thus he cannot have meant the biological brother of Jesus, just as he cannot have meant an apostle. Any such intent would have required being more specific. And Paul wasn't. So that can't have been his intent.

Of course, to maintain Paul nevertheless did mean a biological brother of Jesus, without being at all clear about it, requires you to also accept that this brother of Jesus was not an apostle—a move most Christians would not be willing to take, given their dogmatic commitments. But assuming you can choke that down, and destroy the village to save it as it were, you still are nowhere near to demonstrating that Paul meant anything more specific, when he chose not to be more specific. At best it's 50/50 which he meant, just another Brother of the Lord or Jesus' actual brother. We can't tell. *Because Paul doesn't say.* So we can't use this as evidence for historicity. It is, alas, too vague—even if Paul *did* mean a biological brother of Jesus.

So defenders of historicity, stymied at this point, will retreat to the only trench left to defend: the only other passage where Paul uses the full phrase "Brothers of the Lord," this time of no named person in particular. This appears in 1 Corinthians 9:4–6, where Paul makes the following argument:

> Don't we have the right to food and drink? Don't we have the right to take a sister-wife along, like the other Apostles and Brothers of the Lord and Cephas do? Or do only I and Barnabas lack the right of not working for a living?

Here the preceding text is missing the argument Paul is responding to—something has been removed between the end of chapter eight and the beginning of chapter nine. But it's clear from how the argument of chapter nine proceeds that Paul and his companion Barnabas were being criticized for expecting the churches they visited to pay for their keep— as well as that of any wives they brought along ("sister-wife" meaning a Sister of the Lord who was also someone's female companion, which typically would mean someone's wife who was also a believer). Paul appears elsewhere to say he was unmarried, so in this context he might mean Barnabas's wife. But what exactly the criticism was that he was answering is unknown; in the surviving text, Paul says they hadn't even taken advantage of this right (9:12). He argues only that he *has* this right.

Once again, whether Paul here means by Brothers of the Lord biological or cultic brothers is unclear. He doesn't specify. We again know for sure only that he knew of the cultic kind. And again, surely he'd need to clarify if he meant a more specific kind of brother. But even discounting that obvious point, it's 50/50 which he meant. So we can't use this passage as evidence for historicity either. That would be a circular argument, assuming what the text meant, in order to argue that's what the text meant. Worried by this realization, defenders of historicity will attempt to restore their preferred understanding of this passage with, once again, weak arguments that ignore the Greek, the context, and even ancient methods of composing arguments.

For instance, someone will argue that if "Brothers of the Lord" meant mere Christian, then Paul would not have placed it in between "Apostles" and "Cephas," on the anachronistic assumption that ancient Greek rhetoric would always follow modern English style by listing examples in ascending or descending order of strength. That's incorrect. Ancient Greek rhetoric was fond of what's called "chiastic" argument structure, whereby the strongest example—or whichever the arguer wanted to call the most attention to—would be placed *in the middle* of a list. In ancient Greek that was a common means of calling attention to a point. This isn't a practice in modern English, hence why only someone not versed in ancient rhetoric would mistakenly think otherwise. When we restore the correct background knowledge, of how ancient Greeks often composed arguments, the historicist's argument dissolves. In actual fact, by centering it in the list, Paul is calling attention to the Brothers of the Lord as his *strongest point*. That's why it's the centerpiece, forming the chiasmus (or "cross") of Apostles : Mere Christians : Apostle.

And that is precisely why Paul cannot likely mean the family of Jesus here. His argument depends on his being the equal or superior to the persons he lists, because his argument is, "If they get this right, then so should I." But how could Paul claim equality with the family of Jesus?

Why would he even attempt such a claim here? It could only backfire against his entire pose of humility and equality of honor. Paul would sooner not even mention them as an example—much less *emphasize* them as his *strongest* example supporting his argument, by placing them in the center position of his list. So how could "the Brothers of the Lord get this right, therefore so should I" be Paul's strongest argument? There is only one logical way that can be: that whoever these "Brothers of the Lord" were, Paul outranked them. This is another rhetorical device, called arguing *a fortiori*, or arguing "from a stronger premise" than necessary. Paul is saying, "If *even* rank-and-file Christians get this right, then surely I, *an actual apostle*, should as well." The argument Paul is making thus requires "Brothers of the Lord" here to mean a rank below apostle; it therefore requires Paul to mean mere Christians, ordinary brethren traveling on church business—not the surviving kin of the Lord Jesus Christ. Further on the side of this point: even though we know for a certainty that Paul believed all baptized Christians were Brothers of the Lord, the only two occasions in which he uses the full phrase, rather than its ready abbreviation of simply "Brother," are precisely the only two occasions in his letters when Paul needs to distinguish Apostolic from non-Apostolic Christians, a coincidence that again seems unlikely.

And once again, even if you aren't sure, you can't really tell. There is no way to discern whether Paul is saying ordinary Christians get this privilege, therefore so should he, or that even the surviving family of Jesus get this privilege, therefore so should he (though that seems quite the more unlikely). So even at best it's 50/50. We therefore cannot use this passage to argue for historicity, *no matter what Paul actually meant*. The matter is simply an unknown.

Late Legends Cannot Replace Early Facts

The first time we ever hear any clear assertion that Jesus even had biological brothers is the Gospel of Mark, written a lifetime after the religion began, and a decade or more after Paul was dead. "Mark" appears to have invented them, just as previous mythologers invented brothers and sisters for the mythical Moses, and many another mythical hero. Subsequent Gospels then borrowed Mark's invention. But there is no other evidence these brothers existed. Since mythical heroes *typically* had mythical families (pagan school children even had to memorize them!), this simply isn't enough to connect back with, so as to "reinterpret" anything Paul said decades before. To the contrary, Mark introduces the "brothers and sisters" of Jesus simply to have Jesus renounce them, specifically to illustrate that *Christians* would instead be his brothers and sisters (Mark 3:31–35). Mark has no idea of any of them ever being apostles or ranking church members or ever even Christians.

Even the earliest purported history ever written of Christianity, the book of Acts, written by "Luke" many decades after Mark, which alone ever mentions Jesus' "brothers" being believers in the church (1:14), has no knowledge of any brother of Jesus ever holding any significant role in the church thereafter. The entirety of Acts, which covers the history of the Christian mission through a whole generation, from the 30s to the early 60s A.D., never mentions any "James" the brother of Jesus—at all, much less as a leader or prominent figure, or anyone Paul met. After a single mention of Jesus' "brothers" in the first chapter, they entirely disappear from Christian history—as do both of Jesus' parents; in fact, the entirety of his family relations, as if he never had any. That's certainly strange. Unless there *was* no family of Jesus.

No brothers of Jesus are found anywhere else in the New Testament, either; not even the Epistles with their names on them, James and Jude, claim to be written by his brothers. The evidence for Paul having thus known any is actually worse than dismal: it argues more to the contrary conclusion, that only much later contrivers of legend invented brothers for Jesus, perhaps even by misinterpreting or reinterpreting Paul. And I do mean *later*: we hear no undisputed mention of there being actual brothers of Jesus from any source outside the Gospels for over a hundred and fifty years after the religion began. And that first mention, in an absurd apocryphal legend quoted by Hegesippus around 180 A.D. about a certain "James the Just," might be a misinterpretation of a lost Acts of James that never actually said he was a biological brother of Jesus. By contrast, for example, the author of 1 Clement, writing a century or so earlier and who would have been an actual or near contemporary to any such family, has no knowledge of there being any brothers of Jesus, much less a so-called James the Just.

There is a supposed mention of Jesus' brother James near the end of the first century in the *Antiquities* of Josephus. But as I already mentioned in chapter four, that is almost certainly a textual corruption, accidentally transposing a scribal note into the text (you can find my peer-reviewed academic study demonstrating that in my book *Hitler Homer Bible Christ*). And even if this passage *were* fully authentic, it does not assure us of anything more than a faulty assumption made by Josephus as to the meaning of "Brother of the Lord," the very point at issue here. What evidence do we have that Josephus understood the difference between a cultic and a biological brother in the Christian ranks? None. So that doesn't get us anywhere. For all we know, he simply heard a story of a Brother of the Lord being killed, and just repeated it, oblivious to the actual meaning of that phrase.

We are left with no credible evidence whatever that Jesus ever had brothers, much less such as Paul ever knew.

Conclusion

To judge from Paul's repeated emphasis on Christians being the Sons of God, "Brothers of the Lord" appears to be the original name the Christians knew themselves by, well before the alternative name "Christian" was even coined. And what have we seen was the history of this sect? Apart from doubtful fabrications in the Gospels, and derivative tales inspired therefrom, we don't find a history with any real Jesus in it.

Outside the Bible, there's no evidence of there ever really being a Jesus, except repetitions of claims published in the Gospels, which so far as we can honestly tell are all just legendary embellishments of one single Gospel, the Gospel According to Mark. Which just appeared out of nowhere, citing no sources for anything it relates, in a language and land foreign to the very events it purports to relate, a lifetime after the fact. It's also chock-full of mythic themes and structure, and nothing in it specifically relating to Jesus is corroborated anywhere else. Of all other comparably woven mythographies of religious heroes, few can be claimed to have been about real persons, yet all purport to place their heroes in human history. The same even happened to the mythical patriarchs, from Abraham to Moses. Accordingly, that the same thing happened to Jesus should leave us in reasonable doubt whether he was any more likely to exist than any of them. We only trust in the historicity of any such people when we have good evidence establishing it. But we have none of that for Jesus. So why do we act differently when suddenly it's Jesus we're talking about, and not Aesop or Romulus or Moses?

Our earliest source, Paul, repeatedly says the gospel and teachings of Jesus were known only by revelation and scripture—meaning the ancient Jewish scriptures. There is actually no clear evidence anywhere in Paul that anyone had ever seen Jesus during his incarnation or death. The first Christians definitely believed Jesus was a real eternal angelic being who descended from outer space to assume a mortal human body to die in, to effect the requisite blood magic to cancel the powers of death and atone for all the world's sins—to reverse the failures of Adam and the Israelites, and the rebellion of Satan. But there is no clear evidence in Paul that they imagined this as having happened anywhere they could have been witness to it, any more than to the rebellion of Satan, the counterpart myth to Christ's. No other Epistles of Paul's time evince anything else either. Then, decades after Paul, suddenly the Gospel of Mark appears, fully mythologizing a tale for Jesus, as had once been done for Moses and other heroes of both Jewish and Gentile society. In ensuing decades, Mark's story gets rewritten and expanded by subsequent authors, leaving a trail of some forty known Gospels, all substantially bogus, none naming any sources, nor plausibly having any. Eventually, decades after many of these Gospels had circulated, we find mentions outside the Bible of the claims or tales contained in them. But not a single source ever endeavored to corroborate those claims or tales. They simply repeat them.

So where is this amazing evidence we're supposed to have, that Jesus was any different from any other mythologized hero? Why are we to be so confident there ever really was a Jesus? I cannot discern any good reason. Can you? The best anyone can come up with are a handful of hopelessly vague passages about Jesus maybe possibly having a mother, father, and brothers, but as we've seen, in actual context, none of those passages is at all so clear about that.

We know for a fact that this cult of the Brothers of the Lord had dreams or visions of a celestial savior named "Savior," and never clearly set him on Earth, that only a much later mythographer did, emulating what was done for every other mythical savior in the ancient world; and we know for a fact that everything else we have only derives from or builds on that single book. Doubt is the only reasonable response to this dismal condition of evidence. And if this book of mine hasn't convinced you, or you are confronted with scholarly objections or argumentative minutiae not already exposed as feeble or bogus herein, my book *On the Historicity of Jesus* covers nearly every further question you may have; and if it doesn't, somewhere on my blog at richardcarrier.info is likely to be an article that does. Consider all the evidence, all the rhetoric of those defending Jesus' historicity, all their false statements and fallacies and exaggerations—and the peculiar fact that they even need them. Then ask yourself, honestly, why should you be so sure there was a real Jesus?

Bibliography

Principal Works of Scholarship

Richard Carrier, *On the Historicity of Jesus* (Sheffield-Phoenix 2014)

———, *Proving History* (Rowman & Littlefield 2012)

Raphael Lataster, *Questioning the Historicity of Jesus* (Brill 2019)

Gerd Theissen and Dagmar Winter, *The Quest for the Plausible Jesus* (John Knox 2002)

Robert Van Voorst, *Jesus Outside the New Testament* (Eerdmans 2000)

Additional Works Cited

James P. Allen, *The Ancient Egyptian Pyramid Texts*, 2nd ed. (SBL Press 2015)

Reza Aslan, *Zealot* (Random House 2013)

Anthony Barrett's *Caligula: The Corruption of Power* (Yale University Press 1990)

Joseph Baumgarten, "The Duodecimal Courts of Qumran, Revelation, and the Sanhedrin," *Journal of Biblical Literature* (March 1976)

Fernando Bermejo-Rubio, "Why is the Hypothesis That Jesus Was an Anti-Roman Rebel Alive and Well?" *The Bible & Interpretation* (April 2013)

Darrell Bock, "Sources for Caesar and Jesus Compared," *Bible & Theology* (June 11, 2015)

Thomas Brodie, *The Birthing of the New Testament* (Sheffield Phoenix 2004)

F. F. Bruce, *The New Testament Documents: Are They Reliable?* 5th rev. ed. (InterVarsity 1960)

Richard Carrier, "McGrath on the Amazing Infallible Ehrman," RichardCarrier.info (March 25, 2012)

———, "Ehrman on Historicity Recap," RichardCarrier.info (first edition published on July 24, 2012)

———, *Hitler Homer Bible Christ* (Philosophy 2014)

———, "Okay, So What about the Historicity of Spartacus?" RichardCarrier.info (July 5, 2015)

———, "Virgin Birth: It's Pagan, Guys. Get Over It," RichardCarrier. info (September 19, 2016)

———, "Josephus on Jesus? Why You Can't Cite Opinions Before 2014," RichardCarrier.info (February 15, 2017)

———, *The Scientist in the Early Roman Empire* (Pitchstone 2017)

———, "Dying-and-Rising Gods: It's Pagan, Guys. Get Over It," RichardCarrier.info (March 29, 2018)

———, "Mark's Use of Paul's Epistles," RichardCarrier.info (October 25, 2019)

Ava Chitwood, *Death by Philosophy* (University of Michigan Press 2004)

John Crossan, *The Power of Parable* (HarperOne 2012)

Gregory Daly, "Even If He Wasn't God, He Was Certainly a Man," *The Thirsty Gargoyle* (January 2006)

Bart Ehrman, *The Lost Gospel of Judas Iscariot* (Oxford University 2006)

———, *The Orthodox Corruption of Scripture* (Oxford University 2011)

———, "Did Jesus Exist," *Huffington Post* (March 20, 2012)

———, *Did Jesus Exist?* (HarperOne 2012)

———, *How Jesus Became God* (HarperOne 2014)

Matthew Ferguson, "Ten Reasons to Reject the Apologetic 10/42 Source Slogan," Archive.org (tinyurl.com/ycgd7ykr; first edition published on October 14, 2012)

Benjamin Foster, *Before the Muses: An Anthology of Akkadian Literature*, 3rd ed. (CDL Press 2005)

Robin Lane Fox, *Pagans and Christians* (Penguin 1986)

Gabriele Giannantoni, *Socratis et Socraticorum Reliquiae* (Bibliopolis 1990)

James Hannam, "Is Jesus Christ a Myth? Part 4," Patheos.com (December 26, 2010)

Randel Helms, *Gospel Fictions* (Prometheus 1989)

Dexter Hoyos, *Hannibal's Dynasty* (Routledge 2005)

George Howard, "Was James an Apostle? A Reflection on a New Proposal for Gal. I 19," *Novum Testamentum* 19 (January 1977)

Serge Lancel, *Hannibal* (Blackwell 1999)

J. F. Lazenby, *Hannibal's War* (University of Oklahoma Press 1998)

Naphtali Lewis and Meyer Reinhold, eds., *Roman Civilization*, 2 vols., 3rd ed. (Columbia University Press 1990)

M. David Litwa, *How the Gospels Became History* (Yale University 2019)

Dennis MacDonald, *Two Shipwrecked Gospels* (Brill 2013)

———, *Mythologizing Jesus* (Rowman & Littlefield 2015)

M. McMenamin, "Depiction of the Alps on Punic Coins from Campania, Italy," *Numismatics International Bulletin* 41.1–2 (2012)

Tryggve Mettinger, *The Riddle of Resurrection: "Dying and Rising Gods" in the Ancient Near East* (Almqvist & Wiksell 2001)

Richard Miller, *Resurrection and Reception in Early Christianity* (Routledge 2015)

Candida Moss, *The Myth of Persecution* (HarperOne 2013)

George Nickelsburg, "The Genre and Function of the Markan Passion Narrative," *Harvard Theological Review* 73 (January–April 1980)

A. J. Pfiffig, "Eine Nennung Hannibals," *Studi Etruschi* 35 (1967)

John Prevas, *Hannibal Crosses the Alps* (Da Capo 2001)

Kenneth Sacks, *Polybius on the Writing of History* (University of California Press 1981)

E. P. Sanders, *The Historical Figure of Jesus* (Penguin 1993)

Aldo Schiavone, *Spartacus* (Harvard University Press 2013)

Albert Schweitzer, *The Quest of the Historical Jesus* (A. & C. Black 2010)

Brent Shaw, *Spartacus and the Slave Wars: A Brief History with Documents* (Bedford 2001)

A. N. Sherwin-White, "The *Tabula* of Banasa and the *Constitutio Antoniniana*," *Journal of Roman Studies* 63 (1973)

L. Paul Trudinger, "[*Heteron de tŏn apostolŏn ouk eidon, ei mē iakōbon*]: A Note on Galatians I 19," *Novum Testamentum* 17 (July 1975)

Sam Wilkinson's *Caligula* (Routledge 2003)

Aloys Winterling, *Caligula: A Biography* (University of California Press 2015)

N. T. Wright, *Jesus and the Victory of God* (Fortress 1996)

Ancient Works Cited

Appian, *Civil War* (~150 A.D.)

Aristophanes, *The Clouds* (~423 B.C.)

Arrian, *The Anabasis of Alexander* (~125 A.D.)

Athenaeus, *The Dinnersages* (~225 A.D.)

Cicero, *Against Verres* (~70 B.C.)

————, *Response to the Haruspices* (~57 B.C.)

Diodorus of Sicily, *Library of History* (~30 B.C.)

Eusebius, *History of the Church* (~320 A.D.)

Hippolytus, *Refutation of All Heresies* (~225 A.D.)

Idomeneus, *On the Followers of Socrates* (~300 B.C.)

Irenaeus, *Against Heresies* (~180 A.D.)

Jerome, *Commentary on Ezekiel* (~410 A.D.)

Flavius Josephus, *The Jewish War* (~75 A.D.)

———, *Antiquities of the Jews* (~93 A.D.)

Livy, *From the Founding of the City* (~20 B.C.)

Lucian, *Hermotimus* (~160 A.D.)

Lucian (?), *On the Syrian Goddess* (~150 A.D.)

Origen, *Comments on Ezekiel* (~225 A.D.)

———, *Against Celsus* (~248 A.D.)

Ovid, *Metamorphoses* (~8 A.D.)

———, *Fasti* (~8 A.D.)

Philo of Alexandria, *On the Confusion of Tongues* (~25 A.D.)

———, *Embassy to Gaius* (~40 A.D.)

———, *Flaccus* (~40 A.D.)

Pliny the Younger, *Letters* (~110 A.D.)

Plutarch. *On Isis and Osiris* (~100 A.D.)

———, *Life of Crassus* (~100 A.D.)

———, *Life of Romulus* (~100 A.D.)

Polybius, *Histories* (~140 B.C.)

Sallust, *Catiline War* (~40 B.C.)

———, *Histories* (~40 B.C.)

Seneca, *On Consolation to My Mother Helvia* (~40 A.D.)

———, *On Rage* (~45 A.D.)

———, *On the Constancy of the Wise* (~55 A.D.)

Sosipater Charisius, *Grammatical Arts* (~360 A.D.)

Suetonius, *Life of Caligula* (~120 A.D.)

Tacitus, *Life of Agricola* (~98 A.D.)

———, *Annals* (~116 A.D.)

Theocritus, *Idylls* (~250 B.C.)

Only works cited by title are listed above. Also cited were: *Inscriptiones Graecae* (eadh.org/projects/inscriptiones-graecae); *L'Année Epigraphique* (http://www.anneeepigraphique.msh-paris.fr); the books of the New and Old Testament and the writings of 1 Clement and Ignatius; the *Gospel of Thomas*; the *Ascension of Isaiah*; the *Life of Adam and Eve*; the *Second Treatise of the Great Seth*; the *Revelation of Gabriel*; the Zoroastrian scriptures (including the *Denkard*, *Yasht*, and *Vendida*); the Babylonian Talmud (including tractate *Niddah*); and the Mishnah (including tractates *Yoma* and *Sanhedrin*).

Concordance

Except when another book or article is cited in any given paragraph, the statements made on nearly every page of this book are backed with evidence, argument, and cited scholarship in Richard Carrier's books *On the Historicity of Jesus* (Sheffield-Phoenix 2014) and *Proving History* (Rowman and Littlefield 2012). Here you can look up every page number in *Jesus from Outer Space* (JFOS), and listed to the right are the associated pages in *On the Historicity of Jesus* supporting the claims made there. If instead the corresponding pages are in *Proving History* they are preceded by PH. Note that pages are consistently listed in this concordance only the first time a claim is made that is backed up in either book; not always for subsequent repetitions. But regardless, anything missed here you can find using the indexes of either book.

7	11–14, 48–52; PH 7–15	*14–15*	8–10, 52–55, 235–238
8	63, 178–197	*15*	519, 524–525, 528–531
9	36–55, 349–356		
10	14–17	*15–16*	37–40, 184–185; 63, 178–197
11–13	281–289		
12	400–401	*16*	66–73; 92–96; 124–141
13	61–62		
13–14	239–242	*16–17*	544–545; 87–88, 137–143
14	31–35		

55	405, 456, 506–509; 57–58, 86–87, 93–94, 159, 414, 480, 482, 518; 511–514; PH 169–172, 175–177, 187
56	PH 169–172, 175–177, 187; PH 121–205
56–57	427, 555
58	445–446; 399, 408–409, 425–426; 87–88, 137–141; PH 131–133, 139–141, 179–180
59	313, 443; 339–340, 442, 445–446; 153–159; 541–545; PH 132, 141, 157
60	389–395; 153–159; 541–545; 565–566
61	332–337
62	114–124, 443; PH 11–15, 156
63	428–430, 465; 532–537; 311, 557; 582–592; 235–253
64	222–234; 254–256; 332–346; 444–451
65	28, 308, 335, 374, 391, 515–516; PH 80–81, 104–105, 277–80; PH 30–31
66	387–509; 141–146, 153–163, 541–545; 400–401; PH 139–141, 179–180; 142–145
66–67	312, 314, 400, 438, 443, 453, 560–561; PH 151–154
67–68	4–7; PH 156; 121–205
69–70	428–430
70–72	332–337
70	67–73, 245–246
72	337–342
73	254–280; 510–528
74	293–305, 332–349; 18–27, 354–356, 555–556
74–77	306–331; 254–280; 332–349
76	257
77–78	148–152; 281–289; 214–222
79	510–595; 254–280; 308–315
80–81	67–73, 245–246
81	306–308
82	21–27
82–85	289–293
85–88	*see* JFOS 82
88–91	21–24
92–104	*see* JFOS 82
105	306–308
105–109	*see* JFOS 107
110	21–27
111	168–173; 96–108; 114–116
112	214–234
113	58, 214–222, 387–402; 235–238; PH 114–118, 121–205
113–116	56–58, 100–103, 168–173, 615; 389–395
113–127	*see* JFOS 117

Index

About the Author

Richard Carrier, PhD, is a philosopher and historian of antiquity, specializing in contemporary philosophy of naturalism and Greco-Roman philosophy, science, and religion, including the origins of Christianity. He is the author of numerous books, including *Sense and Goodness without God*, *Not the Impossible Faith*, *Hitler Homer Bible Christ*, *Proving History*, *On the Historicity of Jesus*, *Science Education in the Early Roman Empire*, and *The Scientist in the Early Roman Empire*. They are all also available as audiobooks, read by Dr. Carrier. For more about Dr. Carrier and his work see www.richardcarrier.info.